The Exclusion
of Black Soldiers
from the Medal of Honor
in World War II

# The Exclusion of Black Soldiers from the Medal of Honor in World War II

## The Study Commissioned by the United States Army to Investigate Racial Bias in the Awarding of the Nation's Highest Military Decoration

Elliott V. Converse III, Daniel K. Gibran, John A. Cash, Robert K. Griffith, Jr., *and* Richard H. Kohn

*with a foreword by*
Julius W. Becton, Jr.

McFarland & Company, Inc., Publishers
*Jefferson, North Carolina, and London*

*The present work is a reprint of the library bound edition of* The Exclusion of Black Soldiers from the Medal of Honor in World War II: The Study Commissioned by the United States Army to Investigate Racial Bias in the Awarding of the Nation's Highest Military Decoration, *first published in 1997 by McFarland.*

LIBRARY OF CONGRESS CATALOGUING-IN-PUBLICATION DATA

The exclusion of black soldiers from the Medal of Honor in World War II : the study commissioned by the United States Army to investigate racial bias in the awarding of the nation's highest military decoration / Elliott V. Converse III ... [et al.] ; with a foreword by Julius W. Becton, Jr.
   p.   cm.
Includes bibliographical references and index.

**ISBN 978-0-7864-4044-3**
softcover : 50# alkaline paper ∞

1. World War, 1939–1945—Medals—United States.   2. Medal of Honor.   3. World War, 1939–1945—Afro-Americans.
4. United States—Armed Forces—Medals, badges, decorations, etc.
I. Converse, Elliott Vanveltner.

D796.5.U6E93   2008         940.54'6—dc21         96-50355

British Library cataloguing data are available

©1997 Elliott V. Converse III, Daniel K. Gibran, John A. Cash, Robert K. Griffith, Jr., and Richard K. Kohn. All rights reserved

*No part of this book may be reproduced or transmitted in any form or by any means, electronic or mechanical, including photocopying or recording, or by any information storage and retrieval system, without permission in writing from the publisher.*

On the cover: Field of Stars at the National World War II Memorial, Washington, D.C. (Shutterstock)

Manufactured in the United States of America

*McFarland & Company, Inc., Publishers*
  *Box 611, Jefferson, North Carolina 28640*
    *www.mcfarlandpub.com*

# Contents

| | |
|---|---|
| *Acknowledgments* | vii |
| *Foreword by Julius W. Becton, Jr.* | 1 |
| *Preface* | 3 |
| *Executive Summary* | 7 |
| 1 Introduction | 15 |
| 2 Blacks in the U.S. Army in World War II: An Overview | 21 |
| 3 Medal of Honor Award Policies and Practices, 1941-48 | 37 |
| 4 Valor Awards to Black Soldiers in the European Theater of Operations | 69 |
| 5 Valor Awards to Black Soldiers and Airmen in the Mediterranean Theater of Operations | 93 |
| 6 Valor Awards to Black Soldiers in the Pacific and in the China-Burma-India Theater | 139 |
| 7 Black Recipients of the Distinguished Service Cross in World War II | 167 |
| 8 Conclusions and Recommendations | 179 |
| *Bibliography* | 185 |
| *Index* | 191 |

# Acknowledgments

In a research study of this nature, the assistance of many people is critical to success. The authors are grateful to those individuals who have helped with this study, whose contributions we happily acknowledge here.

Our research took us to several archives and other document repositories across the country. At the Washington National Records Center, where most of the archival research took place, we are indebted particularly to Mr. Richard Boylan, assistant chief of the Military Reference Branch; Ms. Becky Collier and Mr. David Giordano, archivists; Mr. Morris Izlar, supervisory archives technician, and his staff; and Mrs. Victoria Washington, research room supervisor. At the National Archives, Dr. Timothy Nenninger, chief of the Modern Military Records Branch, and Mr. Richard Peuser, archivist, were equally supportive. Our appreciation goes also to archivists at three Presidential repositories, including Mr. Tom Branigar at the Dwight D. Eisenhower Library, Director Verne Newton and his staff at the Franklin D. Roosevelt Library, and Mr. Dennis Bilger at the Harry S Truman Library. At the United States Army's Military History Institute, we were ably assisted, in spite of snowstorms and reduced working hours, by Dr. Richard Sommers, chief archivist; Mr. David Keogh, assistant archivist; and Ms. Pamela Cheney, technician. Mr. Thomas Camden, director for library and archives, and his assistant, Mrs. Marti Gansz, at the George C. Marshall Research Library were extremely helpful, as were Mr. William G. Seibert, branch chief, and Mr. Paul Cooper, archivist, at the National Personnel Records Center; Mr. Edward J. Boone, Jr., archivist, at the Douglas MacArthur Memorial Library and Archives; and Ms. Carol Leadenham, archivist, at the Hoover Institution Archives.

Others not associated with a document repository to whom we owe thanks are Dr. Thomas Keaney (Colonel, USAF, retired) at the National War College; Colonel Carl Reddel, USAF, at the USAF Academy; and Colonel Albert F. Gleim (USA, retired). Each read portions of the manuscript in draft. Colonel Gleim also generously shared his expert knowledge of military awards records. Mr. Paul Martin, reference librarian at the Pawtucket, Rhode Island, Public Library, identified and provided microfilm copies of newspapers for our research, and Ms. Avant Deishinni of the Rhode Island Black Heritage Society provided rare copies of a newspaper for similar purposes. Lieutenant Colonel

Major Clark, USA, retired; Dr. Hondon B. Hargrove; and Mr. Jehu C. Hunter—all veterans of the 92nd Infantry Division and historians of its experience in World War II—provided the kind of assistance only first-hand participants can give. Lieutenant Colonel Patricia Single, USA; Major Peter Danes, USA; Major Michael Wawrzyniak, USA; and Ms. Arlette White, all of the Military Awards Branch, Total Army Personnel Command, served as contracting officers and frequently assisted our work in numerous ways. Mr. Harry Shatto, contract specialist, Defense Supply Service in Washington, assisted similarly, particularly on contractual matters.

Several people loaned photographs, provided leads to good illustrations, or aided us by giving permission to use materials in their possession or care: Colonel William A. De Shields, USA, retired, president of the Black Military Institute of America; Lieutenant Colonel Major Clark, USA, retired; Mr. Spencer C. Moore of Magnolia, New Jersey; Mr. Joseph Galloway and Mr. Jim Fiedler, Jr. of *U.S. News and World Report*; Ms. Arlene Fox of Houston, Texas; Mrs. Allene Carter of Cerritos, California; Mr. David Poremba of the Burton Historical Collection, Detroit Public Library; Mr. Charlie Archambault; and Mr. David J. Williams. Ms. Laura Riley of Durham, North Carolina, restored two of the photographs to publishable quality with uncommon skill. Ms. Gloria Long of the Department of Veterans Affairs was extremely helpful by providing information, as the book went to press, about events following the filing of the report. Retired Army Lieutenant General Julius W. Becton, Jr., not only graciously agreed to write a foreword for the volume, but helped us in a number of ways in bringing the volume to early publication, and the overall project to a timely conclusion. To all, the authors express their gratitude.

Finally, we thank Dr. Talbert O. Shaw, president of Shaw University, for his interest, his generous support, and his unfailing cooperation. Dr. McLouis Clayton, former vice president for academic affairs, was also very supportive. Mr. Sama Mondeh and other members of his staff, Mr. Dallas Joseph, Mr. Edwin Okoye, and Ms. Tracie Williams, kept our checks coming on time. To Ms. Carol Bunch, we owe a special debt of gratitude. And to Mrs. Brenda Cool, who typed the entire manuscript of this study with patience and skill, we are especially grateful.

# Foreword

When I began my 40 years of military service at the age of 17 in the middle of World War II, the United States Army, like all of our other armed services and most of American society, was segregated by race. Black Americans knew they were fighting on two fronts: the first, against the very dangerous enemies of our country and of all human values, in Germany, Italy, and Japan; and the second, against an insidious, and personally demoralizing, enemy called Jim Crow, at home in the United States.

We black soldiers hungered for action. We wanted our chance to fight directly against that enemy abroad in order to help defeat the enemy at home. We knew that men who risked their lives for their country, some of whom would pay the ultimate price, would help establish the claim to equal citizenship for ourselves, our families, our community, and untold generations of black Americans to come. And despite the barriers of segregation, of being assigned mostly to service and support units, we went into combat and by our deeds helped to battle the racial discrimination that so crippled our country.

I was a platoon leader in the first major combat unit to embark from the continental United States in 1950 for Korea, and the Army was still segregated. But very soon thereafter the barriers began to fall, and those of us in various branches were allowed to advance and to contribute, more and more, according to our talents and our efforts instead of the color of our skin. Over the course of my career the United States Army, like its sister services, grew stronger with, and because of, integration. We began to reflect the best of American ideals and even to lead our nation in progress toward equality before the law and equal opportunity for all. By the time I served once again in combat, in Vietnam, this time as a cavalry squadron commander and deputy brigade commander, the Army leadership, as well as most soldiers, knew that Americans bled the same color blood and that members of an army, like a society, had to live together, work together, sacrifice together, and succeed together—or fail.

In 1983, when I retired from the Army, I felt great satisfaction in having served my country in three wars and, along with other black soldiers, demonstrating by our actions that we were a significant part of the civil rights revolution so long delayed in the country we love. I knew that I, like scores of black leaders, had stood on the shoulders of black soldiers going back three centuries and that black soldiers and all Americans, black and white, for generations to come would benefit from our efforts.

Part of treating individuals equally, and in the military using them effectively according to their ability, involves recognizing accomplishment, especially heroism in battle, on a just and equitable basis. We knew back in World War II that black soldiers, because they were not permitted the same chance to serve in combat as whites, would not have the same chance to gain that renown. But as this fascinating history demonstrates, blacks did courageously serve in combat, did selflessly share in the dangers of taking the war to the enemy, and did bravely perform many notable acts of valor. Yet no blacks were awarded the nation's highest decoration for valor, the Medal of Honor. In every other American conflict since the Civil War, one or more black soldiers had earned and won this honor; in World War II, however, even though more blacks served than in any of our previous wars, none received this honor.

Commendably, our Army in 1993 undertook to explain this inconsistency, by commissioning the pages you are about to read. An independent team of scholars went back to the sources and documents to discover whether the old enemy, racism, had been responsible for the absence of any bestowal of the Medal of Honor upon a black soldier. The answer, thoroughly researched and persuasively argued, lies in this book. The Army and our government took notice and, honoring a promise by the secretary of war in 1946 to rectify injustices in the award of medals and decorations, acted in a positive way to remedy the problem. The Army and the government grasped this essential truth: that rendering justice requires righting past wrongs just as much as acting impartially in the present, not only to keep the faith with those who came before but also to strengthen the bonds of trust between today's citizenry and its army and between the people and the nation, now and in the future.

*Julius W. Becton, Jr.*
Lieutenant General, United States Army (Retired)
Former President, Prairie View A & M University

# Preface

For over half a century, the African-American community has resented the fact that no black soldier received the Medal of Honor for heroism during World War II. From the creation of the Medal in the Civil War to today, black Americans have shared in this distinction—in every war except World War II. Yet nearly a million served in the Army during that conflict, more than in any other American war. Despite the official policy of racial segregation and the assignment of black soldiers overwhelmingly to service and support roles, tens of thousands of African-American soldiers did serve in combat units. Thousands experienced battle of various kinds, in the air as well as on the ground, in the Pacific as well as in Europe, as infantrymen and artillerymen, as quartermasters and as engineers—in all sorts of roles under all sorts of conditions. From early 1942 until the war ended in 1945, black soldiers fought bravely, performing many acts of heroism and gaining numerous medals for valor under fire. But none received the highest award, that symbol of selflessness and sacrifice, that special mark of loyalty to the nation and of individual courage under fire: the Medal of Honor.

Many in the black community, at the time and after, blamed the absence of a Medal of Honor on the same racism that led to segregation in the Army and to numerous acts of discrimination experienced at the time. Some even suspected an unwritten understanding among the white military leadership that no black soldier would be recommended for, or be awarded, the Medal, no matter how meritorious or significant the action. Over the years, many individuals and groups pressed the Army to review the records and correct what seemed to them a very clear injustice.

To respond to this pressure and to forestall action from Congress, Acting Secretary of the Army John Shannon decided in 1992 to commission an independent study examining why no black soldier had been awarded the Medal. To gain the confidence of the black community and assure neutrality of judgment, while at the same time maintaining the highest standards of scholarship and historical analysis, Shannon ordered the study done outside the government, by a historically black college or university. When the Army advertised in 1993 for a contractor to investigate the awarding of the Medal of Honor during the War, discover any nominations of black soldiers or Army airmen for the award, and analyze why no one nominated was subsequently awarded the Medal, Professor Daniel Gibran of Shaw University in Raleigh, North Carolina, assembled a team of scholars and won the contract. For fifteen months, we five authors reviewed the historical literature on World War II black service, combed government and private archives, interviewed veterans, and produced a document that examined the problem in depth. That report, titled "The Medal of Honor and African Americans in the United States Army During World War II," went to the Military Awards and Decorations Branch of the United States Army Total Personnel Command in January 1995. The pages that follow are the exact text of that report, modified only slightly to correct a handful of minor errors of fact or language.

The report showed that the Medal of Honor was administered differently in the various theaters during the War. Blacks were denied, by segregation and the general policy of exclusion from combat, the same opportunities to earn the Medal as whites. Further, the racism that pervaded the Army during the War not only hurt the effectiveness of some black units in combat, but undermined the fighting efficiency of the black combat units most in action, and may have prevented any black soldier in those units from being nominated for the Medal. Yet despite these obstacles, black soldiers served with distinction. The report suggested that the Army might consider for the Medal of Honor the nine black awardees of the Distinguished Service Cross, the second highest decoration for valor in combat, and also a tenth soldier whose company commander insisted that a nomination for the Medal of Honor had been filed immediately after the action in which the soldier had lost his life.

Upon receiving our report, the Army's Military Awards and Decorations Branch sent it for review to the Army Center of Military History, the Adjutant General's Department, various offices in the Army personnel system, and up the chain of command. Secretary of the Army Togo West read the study and, along with the Army's senior uniformed leadership, concluded that the report's recommendations deserved action. A Senior Army Decorations Board met in formal session on October 19 to consider the award of the Medal. Three Army lieutenant generals, one major general, and one command sergeant major reviewed the records. Two board members were African-American, one of the five was a Medal of Honor recipient, and all were veterans of combat on the ground in Vietnam or in other battle actions. As a result of the board action and Joint Chiefs of Staff approval, seven of the black World War II soldiers discussed in this book were recommended for the Medal of Honor: Vernon J. Baker (the only one still living), Edward A. Carter, Jr., John R. Fox, Willy F. James, Jr., Ruben Rivers, Charles L. Thomas, and George Watson. Secretary West approved and sent the recommendation to the Secretary of Defense, who forwarded it to the President, who by law is the final approval authority.

Before the President could award the Medal, however, Congress had to waive the 1952 statutory time limitation to grant the Medal of Honor for deeds of heroism in World War II. On orders from the Secretary of Defense, the Army proposed language to Congress and, as a rider to the 1997 defense authorization law, Congress ruled that "the President may award the Medal of Honor to the [seven] persons ... each of whom has been found by the Secretary of the Army to have distinguished himself conspicuously by gallantry and intrepidity at the risk of his life above and beyond the call of duty while serving ... during World War II." When President Bill Clinton signed the defense authorization into law on September 23, 1996, the Medal of Honor went into effect for seven of the ten black heroes named in this study. "The President believes this is an honor that is long overdue and rights a wrong," stated Clinton's spokeswoman some months earlier. "These are medals that should have been bestowed during their service."

And so at a moving ceremony in the East Room of the White House on January 13, 1997, the President presented the Medal of Honor to First Lieutenant Vernon J. Baker, Company C, 370th Infantry Regiment, 92nd Infantry Division, "for conspicuous gallantry and intrepidity at the risk of his life above and beyond the call of duty" in battle in Italy, April 5 and 6, 1945, and to the representatives or relatives of the other six black heroes from World War II, all now deceased. In attendance were the Joint Chiefs of Staff, members of the Cabinet and Congress, and numerous dignitaries, veterans, citizens, and soldiers of many ages and races. "In no small way, this is an act of healing at a time when it may very well mean more than it might have 50 years ago," Secretary Jesse Brown, himself a veteran of the Vietnam War and the first African American to head the Department of Veterans Affairs, had written earlier. "We will all be better for it."

# Executive Summary

*Chapter 1. Introduction*

1. This study investigates the nomination of African-American soldiers for the Medal of Honor in the U.S. Army during World War II. The purpose of the study is to discover why no black soldier received the Medal for service during the War. The Army, under contract MDA903-93-C-0260, directed Shaw University to document the process by which the Medal of Honor was awarded during and immediately after the War (from 7 December 1941 through 1 September 1948, the end of the period for processing awards after the fighting), from the level of the War Department down to the battalion level in those commands in which blacks served; to identify all units up through theater in which African Americans served; to identify by name all black soldiers who were submitted for the Medal and to document any errors in the processing of their nominations; and to compile a list of all black Distinguished Service Cross recipients, with descriptions of the actions that produced the decoration.

2. The team assembled by Shaw University to accomplish the work consisted of Shaw University professor Daniel K. Gibran (Ph.D., International Relations/Strategic Studies, University of Aberdeen, Scotland), Colonel John A. Cash, USA, Retired (M.A., History, Rutgers University; M.A., Latin American Studies, University of Wisconsin-Madison), Colonel Elliott V. Converse III, USAF, Retired (Ph.D., History, Princeton University), Lieutenant Colonel Robert K. Griffith, Jr., USA, Retired (Ph.D., History, Brown University), and University of North Carolina at Chapel Hill professor Richard H. Kohn (Ph.D., History, University of Wisconsin-Madison). Most of the research involved searching thousands of wartime Army records, from War Department through company level, with special attention devoted to awards policy and practice. Over a dozen archives and manuscript repositories were used. Research was also conducted in a wide variety of newspapers, government documents, private papers collections, books, and articles. Over 30 people involved with black service in World War II were interviewed. Midway through the research, when the team could find no official evidence documenting a black nominee for the Medal, attention turned (at the request of

the Army) to finding black recipients of the Distinguished Service Cross, the next-highest Army award for valor in World War II.

## Chapter 2. Blacks in the U.S. Army in World War II: An Overview

3. In colonial times in 17th-century America, blacks participated in military duty but invariably under the burdens of racial discrimination and their status as slaves. Inevitably they served under exceptions to laws or official policies that usually prohibited black service, and they were used only because of some crisis need for manpower. During the War for Independence, African Americans served in the Continental Army and in state units. During the Civil War, they began regular service on a continuing basis in the U.S. Army.

4. The Army entered World War II with racial assumptions about the inferiority of black soldiers as combat troops based in part on a misreading of the experience in World War I; these assumptions dominated Army thinking, supported the policy of segregating African Americans in separate units, and underlay the policy that relegated blacks overwhelmingly to service in noncombatant units. Denied their own officers (particularly at field grades), segregated in separate units and often relegated to secondary roles, their morale undermined by racial policies and by a pattern of conflict between white officers and black enlisted men, black units lagged behind in training and effectiveness. Under pressure from the black community, black combat units were formed, and as their number increased, policy changed to allow the creation of separate black divisions. Midway through the war, pressure mounted to use the units in combat, and in early 1944, the 93rd Infantry Division was deployed to the Pacific. In the summer of 1944, the 92nd was committed to battle in Italy. During the War, soldiers in these and many other black units, such as artillery, amphibian truck, and engineer units, came under fire and performed many feats of heroism, receiving awards for valor.

## Chapter 3. Medal of Honor Award Policies and Practices, 1941–1948

5. In an effort to reserve the Medal of Honor for truly extraordinary acts, and to award the Medal uniformly across several theaters of operations in a worldwide conflict, the War Department reserved for itself final authority to award the Medal of Honor and to disapprove a nomination; neither approval or disapproval was delegated to theater or other subordinate commanders. Recommendations for the Medal had to be forwarded even if field commanders recommended disapproval, although the original instructions on this point

required clarification. A War Department Decorations Board evaluated each Medal of Honor submission and then recommended approval or disapproval to the chief of staff and secretary of war for final action. Approval for a Medal of Honor often took several months and could involve as many as eight command echelons and several elements within each echelon.

6. In theory, the Board protected the uniqueness of this highest award by applying a common standard of merit, but documents reveal a lack of clarity in policy-determining procedures for processing Medal recommendations; combined with the decisions of a few commanders, this prevented some cases from reaching the War Department. Another problem was the difficulty in distinguishing among the degrees of heroism each of the three top awards (the Medal of Honor, the Distinguished Service Cross, and the Silver Star) was intended to recognize. Language describing each of the three was quite general, imprecise in defining acts of bravery, and often overlapping. "Gallantry," for example, characterized both the Medal and the Silver Star; all three required "heroism" setting the individual apart from comrades. For the Medal, heroism had to be "above and beyond the call of duty," whereas for the Distinguished Service Cross it was to be "extraordinary." As one officer on the War Department Decorations Board put it in 1946, "The personal equation enters." Furthermore the Medal required "incontestable proof" in which eyewitness testimony was essential. The officer initiating the recommendation had to have "personal knowledge" of the act or be an eyewitness; "personal knowledge" was not defined or differentiated from eyewitness testimony, and the phrase "when practicable" undermined this requirement. The number of eyewitnesses was never clarified. As the War progressed, the War Department found that some statements by eyewitnesses lacked the kind of detail constituting incontestable proof and asked the field commands to provide better evidence.

7. At the theater level, awards policies contained an inherent conflict. On the one hand, War Department policy stipulated an equal standard for all candidates for awards, including the Medal, across all theaters and all organizations and in all kinds of combat. On the other hand, the War Department delegated authority to commanders to award medals below the Medal of Honor, to permit commanders to use decorations in a timely way to improve morale and inspire the troops. Furthermore, an analysis of the process clearly shows that War Department regulations contained inherent ambiguities of language that unintentionally permitted variations among the different theaters and commands. At first it was not clear that commanders had to forward all nominations for the Medal of Honor, even if they disagreed with the recommendation; when the War Department clarified the policy late in the War, commanders fell into line. An analysis of the process reveals that not all theaters and commands pursued the same policies and that the implementation of policy contained inherent inconsistencies and differences. The line between the valor meriting a Medal of Honor and that deserving a Distinguished Service

Cross, the next-higher valor award, was indistinct and very much open to interpretation. Sometimes the several echelons disagreed on Medal of Honor recommendations. In the European Theater, for example, some Medals that were eventually awarded by the War Department did not receive favorable endorsements at lower echelons; conversely, endorsement all along the line did not guarantee a favorable ruling by the War Department. Pacific commander Douglas MacArthur did not establish a decorations board at his headquarters until January 1945, even retaining sole responsibility for judging the Distinguished Service Cross nominations in his command and delegating it only under very limited circumstances. Moreover, MacArthur withheld from the War Department those Medal of Honor recommendations that he disapproved and released them only after the fighting ended, after two formal requests from Washington and a visit to his headquarters by a General Staff officer. It is nearly certain, on the basis of Fifth Army and Mediterranean Theater awards records, that Medal of Honor processing irregularities occurred in that Theater, preventing some Medal of Honor recommendations from ever reaching Washington.

8. This study found no explicit, written evidence in official documents proving that African Americans were discriminated against in the awarding of medals in general or the Medal of Honor in particular. However, in a 1994 interview for this study, Truman K. Gibson, the World War II Civilian Aide to the Secretary of War for Negro Affairs, maintained that the climate of racism and segregation prevailing in the Army explains the lack of a black Medal of Honor winner. The African-American press at the time complained about the problem, and many African-American soldiers insisted then and still now insist that there was discrimination in the awarding of medals and that there were, at the unit level, informal, unwritten policies that no black should win the Medal of Honor. Whether these claims are true or not, the Army's postwar statement that medals were not given with knowledge of race was not true, since senior Army officers knew that all of the enlisted men in the 92nd and 93rd Infantry Divisions were black and since each individual's personnel file, included among the documents assembled for each decoration case considered by the War Department Decorations Board, clearly identified service members by race.

*Chapter 4. Valor Awards to Black Soldiers in the European Theater of Operations*

*Chapter 5. Valor Awards to Black Soldiers and Airmen in the Mediterranean Theater of Operations*

*Chapter 6. Valor Awards to Black Soldiers in the Pacific and in the China-Burma-India Theater*

9. This study found no official documentation for a Medal of Honor nomination for a black soldier during the War. Other evidence, such as statements by individuals who were interviewed for this study or whose contemporary letters or writings were reviewed, reveals that four black soldiers may have been recommended for the Medal. In one case, circumstantial evidence indicates that the nomination may have been stopped by the acting battalion commander for reasons of racial prejudice. These four cases—those of Staff Sergeant Ruben Rivers, First Lieutenant Vernon J. Baker, Corporal Waverly B. Woodson, and Staff Sergeant Edward A. Carter, Jr.—and the documentation referring to the possibility that they were recommended or considered for the Medal of Honor—are reviewed in detail.

10. Although there is no explicit, official documentation for racial prejudice in the award process for the Medal of Honor, and although the study found no official documentation for a black nominee, this report concludes that the failure of an African-American soldier to win a Medal of Honor most definitely lay in the racial climate and practice within the Army in World War II.

11. To begin with, blacks served in their own units segregated by race and led, especially above the company level, overwhelmingly by white officers, who often shared the racial assumptions prevalent in white America at the time. Segregating units by race complicated and slowed training, exacerbated relations between officers and enlisted men and between commanders and their units, and undermined the morale of these units in both obvious and subtle ways. As a result, black units were seen to be less effective and efficient. They were less desired by higher commanders for use in the field. Most were used reluctantly or in secondary roles by Army leaders.

12. Second, because the Army assumed, partly on the basis of a misreading of black combat performance in World War I, that African Americans were inherently inferior as combat soldiers, they were at first relegated primarily to service or combat-support units. Under pressure from the black community, however, numerous black combat units were activated and eventually deployed into combat. But by the end of the War, despite serving in the Army in approximately the same proportion as their percentage in the American population, African Americans had a much more limited chance to experience combat and thus to win awards for valor.

13. Third, the attitude of key commanders of the 92nd Infantry Division, the largest black unit and the one to compile the most manhours in combat, was most definitely characterized by racial prejudice. That prejudice had to affect their judgment in awards and quite likely explains why no black officer or soldier in that Division was recommended for a Medal of Honor.

14. An analysis of the experience of African Americans in the three major areas of the world where Americans fought—the European Theater, the Mediterranean Theater, and the Pacific area—illustrates all three of the above points.

15. In the European Theater, less than 10 percent of the black soldiers served in combat units, a much lower percentage than that for all soldiers in the Army.

16. In the Mediterranean Theater, a higher percentage of African-American soldiers served in combat because of the presence of the 92nd Infantry Division (eventually including the attached 366th Infantry Regiment), which deployed to Italy and served in the Allied front lines from August 1944 to May 1945. To understand the awards process for blacks in this Theater, however, one must understand that a pattern of racial prejudice on the part of the white leadership pervaded the 92nd Division, contributed to the very low morale of that unit, and poisoned the relationships between the senior officers and African-American junior officers and enlisted men. The context of racial policies and practices produced a heavy burden of distrust, which carried over into battle. Over the course of the Division's participation in combat, white leaders came to believe that black soldiers of all ranks lacked the personal attributes necessary to perform effectively as infantry in battle and that this alone explained the poor performance of the Division. Exceptions proved the rule. Consistently, senior commanders characterized African-American infantry officers and noncommissioned officers in combat as lacking in initiative, aggressiveness, dependability, and responsibility. The enlisted men reportedly lacked pride, were careless, feared combat, and were prone to panic. Senior white officers concluded that black troops were not suitable for use as infantry and that the deficiencies were so great that African Americans could not be made into effective combat infantry for generations to come. In a special report assessing the Division in the summer of 1945, after the fighting ended, the leadership of the Division attributed its poor performance entirely to the racial characteristics of African Americans, advancing no other explanations for the problems the Division experienced in combat, reasons such as the leaders' own policies or actions as commanders. These views about the abilities of African Americans to fight as infantrymen undoubtedly prejudiced judgment and objectivity about the heroism of black soldiers in specific situations. Black veterans who served in the 92nd in Italy certainly believed that black soldiers were not recognized for their heroism and that in fact there was an unwritten policy, or at least a general understanding among the Division's white leaders, to limit both the number and the level of the highest awards for African-American officers and enlisted men. This view was held by most African Americans in the Division then and is still held today; it is supported by evidence. In granting the highest awards to African Americans, General Edward Almond, commander of the Division, clearly linked successful unit performance to the recognition of individual heroism. It is likely that the Division leaders' racial views precluded the nomination of blacks for the Medal of Honor, for they recommended only one man: a white company commander whose black platoon leader performed, in the same action, demonstrably more

courageous acts that did far more damage to the enemy (both won Distinguished Service Crosses).

17. African Americans also served with distinction in the Pacific and in the China-Burma-India Theater, but mostly in support roles. The 93rd Infantry Division, the largest black unit in the Pacific, and the 24th Infantry Regiment, though both combat units, were used largely for garrison duty and for mopping-up operations on islands seized earlier by American forces. The Division and the Regiment thus experienced relatively little combat. Some of the service and combat support units, such as some of the DUKW companies, performed extraordinarily dangerous duty. These amphibian four-wheel-drive utility vehicles functioned as both a truck and a boat to transport troops and equipment from ship to shore during amphibious invasions. At Iwo Jima, the three Army amphibian truck companies attached to the Marines won 19 Silver Stars, 14 by black enlisted men, in four days under intense fire (19–22 February 1945).

## Chapter 7. Black Recipients of the Distinguished Service Cross in World War II

18. Chapter 7 lists each of the African-American winners of the Distinguished Service Cross and describes the heroic acts that merited the award. Heretofore only six Distinguished Service Crosses were publicly known to have been won by black soldiers in the Army during World War II. Research for this study uncovered another three awards, for a total of nine: First Lieutenant Vernon J. Baker, Staff Sergeant Edward A. Carter, Jr., Staff Sergeant Leonard E. Dowden, First Lieutenant John R. Fox, Private First Class Willy F. James, Jr., First Lieutenant Robert J. Peagler, First Lieutenant Charles L. Thomas, Private First Class Jack Thomas, and Private George Watson.

## Chapter 8. Conclusions and Recommendations

19. The final chapter recounts the racial context of black service in the Army in World War II and reviews the reasons why no African American won the Medal of Honor in spite of many individual acts of heroism by blacks in battle. In internal studies after the War the Army admitted that differentiating the acts meriting the Medal of Honor from those deserving the next two highest valor awards was extremely difficult. In mid–1946 Secretary of War Robert P. Patterson, in defending awards policies and procedures, conceded: "There are cases that are reported inadequately. There are cases where human errors are made." A few months later, Patterson wrote to a U.S. senator and denied the charge that there had been discrimination in awards against

National Guard and Reserve troops but promised reevaluation of awards if appropriate. "Because of the large numbers of decorations already awarded, I am convinced that little can be done by retroactive action to correct any errors of the past without inducing greater errors and dissatisfaction," he argued. "However, where corrective action is found possible and meritorious, you may be sure that it will be taken."

20. Such corrective action has precedent. At the end of World War I, General John J. Pershing ordered a review of Distinguished Service Cross winners for consideration for upgrade because only 4 Medals of Honor had been awarded by the time of the Armistice; the result was 78 additional Medals of Honor. In 1943, General Dwight D. Eisenhower, the North African Theater Commander, asked his Fifth Army commander to do the same because Eisenhower wanted to increase the number of Medals of Honor in the Theater. "The number of Medals of Honor awarded to date to individuals of this theater seems unreasonably low in proportion to the total number of such awards," wrote Eisenhower. The War Department approved 4 more Medals of Honor out of the 6 Distinguished Service Crosses that the Theater sent forward.

21. On the basis of these findings and conclusions, this study recommends that the Army evaluate, for elevation to the Medal of Honor, the Distinguished Service Crosses earned by black soldiers during the War II; in addition, the study recommends that the Army evaluate whether Sergeant Ruben Rivers, who may have been nominated for the Medal for heroic acts in battle in 1944 and who in any case died unrecognized for the acts of valor that resulted in his death, also merits the award.

*Chapter 1*

# Introduction

## The Background and Purpose of the Study

This study is the product of a 1993 contract awarded by the Department of the Army to Shaw University to research the awarding of the Medal of Honor to black soldiers during World War II. The end of the War marked the beginning of a long quest for the nation's highest military recognition for valor to black Americans who fought in a segregated U.S. Army. Concerns were soon raised about the conspicuous absence of black recipients of the Medal of Honor.[1] They were kept alive throughout the years in sections of the media but even more so in the annual reunions of black veterans across the country.

During the War and after, knowledgeable people in the services and outside, and in the black community, charged that racism in the Army—either as a matter of policy or by the actions of individuals in the chain of command or both—had prevented black soldiers from being recognized for valor by the award of the Medal of Honor. But charges of racism aside, many of the concerns raised were also based on the more substantive issue of "black" combat performance before, during, and after this particular war. Historians today agree that blacks who served from the earliest times in American history in various branches of the Armed Forces did so with pride and distinction. Although many served as individuals during the colonial wars, the War for Independence, and subsequent conflicts, not until the Civil War did large numbers experience combat in units segregated by race. After the Civil War, the U.S. Army contained four separate regiments of black soldiers who served honorably and effectively during the Indian wars, in the Spanish-American War, and in the Philippines at the end of the 19th century. In World War I, blacks again served in combat in the 92nd Infantry Division and in units attached to allied armies. World War II found tens of thousands of blacks serving individually and in segregated units in the Army Ground Forces, Army Air Forces, and the Navy. Overwhelmingly, their service was within a rigid framework of segregation. In September 1944, black strength stood at 701,678, approximately 8.7 percent of the whole Army.[2]

At the end of February 1944, the War Department's Advisory Committee on Negro Troop Policies, which was established in August 1942 to answer questions and provide direction for the training and assignment of black soldiers, "met to consider a formal recommendation to the Secretary of War ... to commit Negro combat troops to action against the enemy."[3] As a result, black units were introduced into combat, a move that certainly helped to alleviate some of the political pressure on the Army and the War Department. Morris MacGregor rightly concluded, "After elements of the 93rd Division were committed on Bougainville in March 1944 and an advanced group of the 92nd landed in Italy in July, the Army staff found it easier to ship smaller supporting units to combat theaters, either as separate units or as support for larger units, a course that reduced the glut of black soldiers stationed in the United States."[4]

Of the more than 50,000 blacks who were actually engaged in combat against the enemy, many distinguished themselves by committing conspicuous acts of heroism, for which they were awarded numerous medals ranging in ascending order of merit from the Bronze Star to the Distinguished Service Cross. None, however, received the nation's highest and most prestigious award for gallantry in combat: the Medal of Honor. Of the 294 Medals of Honor awarded by the end of World War II, none were bestowed upon a black American.[5]

At the time and after, black servicemen and the black community believed strongly that this was not an oversight: that black soldiers performed acts of heroism that qualified for the Medal; that racism pervaded the Army and affected the awarding of medals; and that the Army ought to make restitution and review the awarding of the Medal of Honor during the War. In 1993, partly as a result of these concerns and the overhanging charges of racism in the Army either as a matter of policy or by the actions of individuals in the chain of command, the Army asked Shaw University to study the process by which the Medal of Honor had been awarded to soldiers during World War II. Moreover, the Army asked the team to identify black servicemen who had been recommended for the Medal and to determine whether the processing of those recommendations had been proper under public law and War Department regulations.

## The Research Tasks

Shaw's first task was to document thoroughly the laws, regulations, and methods by which the Medal of Honor had been awarded by the War Department during the period from the onset of hostilities on 7 December 1941 through 1 September 1948, the end of the postwar period of processing awards in the aftermath of the fighting. Research on procedures was to extend down every level of command to the battalion level in those commands and units in which blacks served, and the study was to include copies of the awards-processing instructions for each level of command.

Second, the study was to identify all headquarters, theaters of operations, major commands, and units in which African Americans served. Research was to focus on those agencies and organizations first to establish the procedures by which the Medal had been awarded and second to identify every black soldier or airman who had been nominated for the award.

The third task was to identify by name all black soldiers submitted for the Medal of Honor, to verify that the procedures used to process the recommendations met public law and War Department requirements, to identify any recommendations that were not properly processed, and to document the errors or mistakes involved in handling the nomination. The Army asked for a separate record or dossier on each of these individuals, to include the unit of assignment, the headquarters making the recommendation, the date or dates of the action, and all documentation relating to the act of heroism, such as the recommendations for the Medal, witness statements, forwarding or processing documents, and any unit operational logs or histories or reports confirming the person's actions.

The fourth and final task, added midway through research for the study, was to compile a list of all black Distinguished Service Cross recipients and to investigate each case in order to allow the Army, if it so chose, to reconsider some or all for the Medal of Honor.

## The Research Team

To head the project and produce this study, Shaw University assigned Daniel K. Gibran (Ph.D., International Relations/Strategic Studies, University of Aberdeen, Scotland), Assistant Professor of International Relations, as Principal Investigator. Dr. Gibran wrote the proposal for the Army contract, recruited the research team, assigned tasks, managed the research and writing, researched in the archives and participated in oral interviews, co-authored chapters 1 and 8, wrote the introduction to chapter 7; and edited the report. He also managed the fiscal aspects of the contract.

Colonel John A. Cash, U.S. Army (Retired) (M.A., History, Rutgers University; M.A., Latin American Studies, University of Wisconsin-Madison), researched in archives, interviewed over 30 veterans and participants in World War II, and provided valuable assistance to the entire study.

Colonel Elliott V. Converse III, U.S. Air Force (Retired) (Ph.D., History, Princeton University), researched in the archives, participated in interviews, authored chapters 3, 4, 5, and 6, and wrote the Individual Summaries section of chapter 7.

Lieutenant Colonel Robert K. Griffith, Jr., U.S. Army (Retired) (Ph.D., History, Brown University), researched in archives, newspapers, and secondary sources and wrote chapter 2.

Richard H. Kohn (Ph.D., History, University of Wisconsin-Madison), Professor of History at the University of North Carolina at Chapel Hill and Executive Secretary of the Triangle Institute for Security Studies, served as a consultant to the project, advising on sources, research design, method, and interpretation; he edited the report, co-authored chapters 1 and 8, and wrote the Executive Summary.

## The Research Methodology

From the beginning, the research team decided to interview every veteran or participant in World War II, visit every archive and manuscript repository, and search every collection of records or personal or official papers that might, within the one year allotted, produce information or provide leads to the two problems: in general, the policies, methods, and procedures by which the Medal of Honor was awarded and, in particular, each instance in which the nominee was black; and the discovery of black servicemen in the Army and Army Air Forces who had been, or might have been, nominated for the award.

Working with the Military Awards Branch of the Army, government history and personnel offices, veterans groups, black organizations, and interested individuals, the team attempted to find individual black nominations for the Medal. The relevant histories and monographs were searched, and a review of the African-American press, especially newspapers, was undertaken.

The major part of the research effort was devoted to searching the official records of the War Department, the Army, and its overseas commands during and immediately after the War and the papers of government officials and private individuals involved in administering the Army or commanding at the various levels that would have ruled on nominations for the Medal of Honor. In the National Archives, the team reviewed the records of the Secretary of Defense, Secretary of War, Secretary of the Army, War Department General and Special Staffs, Army Staff, Army Ground Forces, and Allied Operational and Occupation Headquarters. Below that level, the team looked at records from headquarters at the Army theater, Army command, Army group, army, corps, division, regiment, battalion, and company levels. At the division level and below, the entire records of black units were searched. At such manuscript repositories as the Roosevelt, Truman, and Eisenhower Libraries, the U.S. Army Military History Institute, the MacArthur Memorial Archives, the Library of Congress, the George C. Marshall Research Library, and elsewhere, every relevant file of records and every collection of personal papers and oral histories was reviewed to find evidence of the process of awarding the Medal of Honor and possible black nominees. The team devoted special attention to all records and files pertaining to awards, decorations, and medals; at the unit level, commanders' papers and operational logs and reports were carefully investigated. Individual case files were searched, and over 160 individual personnel records were reviewed at the National Personnel Records Center at St. Louis, Missouri. Colonels Cash and Converse and Dr. Gibran interviewed, separately or together, more than 30 people involved in directing policy and command in the War Department and the Army, in commanding black units, and in serving in or with those units. A complete listing of all the sources used for this study can be found in the bibliography.

When, midway through the research, the team could find no documentary evidence of any black nominees for the Medal of Honor in the Army, special efforts were devoted to finding black recipients and nominees for the Distinguished Service Cross, the next-highest award for valor in World War II.

This secondary objective is well grounded in precedents set by Generals John J. Pershing and Dwight D. Eisenhower in World Wars I and II respectively. By the Armistice at the end of World War I, only four Medals of Honor had been approved. To ensure fairness to all, and under specific instructions from General Pershing, various commanding officers of the American Expeditionary Forces were asked to submit recommendations for the Medal of Honor, the Distinguished Service Cross, and the Distinguished Service Medal. Five days after the Armistice, General Pershing not only directed that a careful and thorough review be made of each case that had been previously submitted for the award of the Distinguished Service Cross but also sent to the headquarters of each division an officer thoroughly familiar with the forms necessary to substantiate awards of the Medal of Honor. Between November 1918 and July 1919, several recommendations for the Medal of Honor and for other decorations were processed at General Pershing's headquarters at Chaumont, France, and at the War Department. During this period, 78 Medal of Honor awards were made.[6]

In late December 1943, General Eisenhower, then North African Theater Commander, requested that General Mark W. Clark, the Fifth Army Commander, review Distinguished Service Cross recommendations in order to determine whether any might merit the Medal of Honor. General Eisenhower believed that the theater had received too low a proportion of the total Medals of Honor awarded. General Clark submitted six Distinguished Service Cross cases to theater headquarters, including some for which an award had already been made. The War Department eventually approved four for the Medal of Honor.[7]

These precedents, combined with the constraining effects that segregation imposed on black combat participation and indications of racial discrimination with respect to awards in the 92nd Infantry Division, provide a firm basis for reexamining the records of black Distinguished Service Cross recipients in World War II for consideration for the nation's highest military award: the Medal of Honor.

Throughout the research, the team kept meticulous records of the collections and files searched, the individuals interviewed, and the books, articles, and other materials reviewed.

## Notes

1. See, for example, letter of Dr. C. F. Hopson to the President of the United States, 13 March 1946, folder "291.2, 1 Jan 46–31 Mar 46," Box 799, Decimal 291.2, G-1 Decimal File, June 1946–48, Record Group (RG) 165, Washington National Records Center, Suitland, Md.

2. Strength of the Army, 1 Jan 1946, STM—30, p. 61, cited in Ulysses Lee, *The Employment of Negro Troops [United States Army in World War II]* (Washington, D.C.: U.S. Government Printing Office, 1966), p. 415.

3. Lee, *Employment of Negro Troops*, pp. 481–82.

4. Morris J. MacGregor, Jr., *Integration of the Armed Forces, 1940–1965 [Defense Studies Series]* (Washington, D.C.: U.S. Government Printing Office, 1981), p. 43.

5. In this study, Americans of color and of African ethnic origin will be called "blacks" or "African Americans" interchangeably. The term used by the War Department at the time was "Negro" or "colored."

6. See U.S. Department of the Army, Public Information Division, *The Medal of Honor of the U.S. Army* (Washington, D.C.: U.S. Government Printing Office, 1948), p. 22.

7. See chapter 3 for details.

*Chapter 2*

# Blacks in the U.S. Army in World War II: An Overview

## The History to 1939

Black Americans have borne arms in virtually every American war from the colonial era to the present, though not always with official sanction and, until the post–World War II period, not always with the approval of white America. Indeed, the legacy of slavery continued to hold back blacks in their struggle for equality in the ranks of the armed forces well toward the present. If whites accepted blacks in the military at all, it was an acceptance born of expediency and one clearly limited by segregation and discrimination.[1]

The earliest colonial militia accepted all able-bodied males. But by the mid–17th century, all the colonies excluded blacks out of fear that arming and training them might lead to unrest and even revolt among slave populations. The exceptions to this policy tested the rule. In the mid–18th century, in the colonial wars that lasted beyond one campaign season, the New England colonies, in particular, tolerated blacks—freedmen and slaves—in their militia. Such exceptions occurred only when the lengthening conflict strained white manpower resources to the limit.

On the eve of the Revolution, blacks—both free and slave—were common in the Massachusetts militia, and several served with distinction in the initial actions around Boston in 1775. But as the rebellion spread to include colonies farther south and as the Continental Congress took up the challenge of establishing policy for the emerging nation, blacks quickly found themselves unwelcome. Southern delegates demanded and won the total exclusion of blacks from the Continental Line, the national army created early in the war. In very short order, General George Washington obtained an exception to the policy in the form of permission from Congress to reenlist blacks already serving. The colonies followed suit but barred blacks from their militia.

As has so often been the case in the nation's experience, the exigencies of the moment forced exceptions to policy. As the Revolution dragged on and the states found it increasingly difficult to fill their manpower quotas for the Continental Line, or even to maintain the ranks of state forces and local militia, recruiters turned to blacks while government officials turned a blind eye to the violation. One state, Rhode Island, recruited and maintained a battalion of blacks at an average strength of 150 men for three years, from 1777 to 1780. In all, approximately 5,000 identifiable blacks served the American cause in the War for Independence.[2]

The Militia Act of 1792, which, with occasional modifications, formed the foundation of American military manpower policy into the 20th century, implicitly excluded blacks from military service by declaring that all able-bodied white male citizens constituted the militia of the United States. What the Militia Act implied the states and the small regular army made formal by refusing to recruit or accept blacks for enlistment. Between the Revolution and the Civil War, blacks served under arms in the regular army only once. The exception again tested the policy. During the War of 1812, Louisiana established a militia unit recruited from its free black population. In late 1814, faced with a British advance on New Orleans, General Andrew Jackson, in open disregard for regulations and convention, called for the formation of another all-black volunteer unit. The two units served with distinction in the subsequent battle of New Orleans but were quickly disbanded and forgotten after the crisis passed.

At the outbreak of the Civil War, President Abraham Lincoln, wanting to avoid any course of action that might inflame secessionist sentiment in the border states, continued the policy and explicitly forbade the enlistment of blacks. Further, as in earlier conflicts, initial enthusiasm combined with the widespread belief that the war would be short to stimulate sufficient numbers of white volunteers to make unnecessary the service of blacks. Three factors coalesced to overturn the policy by 1863: abolitionist pressure; a large and growing population of freedmen and "contraband" (escaped slave) blacks in the North; and as the war dragged on, necessity, caused by the waning of volunteering among whites and the gargantuan manpower needs of an expanded war. As early as mid–1862, some Union generals raised black units in open disregard for policy. Following Lincoln's promulgation of the Emancipation Proclamation in 1862 and the passage of the first national conscription law in 1863, several states began raising black volunteer units to meet their manpower quotas. Altogether, over 390,000 blacks served in the Union Army and in state units in the Civil War. By the end of the war, the Union Army included 185,000 black soldiers organized in 166 black regiments of U.S. Colored Troops, in various independent and state units, and in labor units. Losses totaled more than 68,000. Of these, 2,751 were killed in action; the rest died of wounds or disease or were counted as missing.[3]

After the Civil War the United States reduced the size of its army, as it did after every war. At the end of Reconstruction, the Regular Army numbered 25 regiments with an authorized strength of approximately 27,500. Radical Republicans, who controlled Congress after the Civil War, insisted that the Regular Army contain six black regiments. Reductions later eliminated two. The four remaining units—the Ninth and Tenth Cavalry and the 24th and 25th Infantry—survived until the desegregation of the Armed Forces following World War II. Negro state militia units did not survive. These quickly became casualties of peace and of a desire by white society in the North and the South to put the Civil War to rest. With the rise of Jim Crow and the institutionalization of racial segregation in the last third of the 19th century, there was no place for black militia.

The black regiments, along with most of the rest of the Regular Army, went to the West, where they were disbursed among hundreds of "hitching post" forts to fight Indians, to escort settlers, and generally to police the West during the nation's longest period between major conflicts. In 1898, all four black regiments participated in the Spanish-American War. The Ninth and Tenth Cavalry joined the famous volunteer unit the Rough Riders in its (dismounted) charge up San Juan Hill. During the Spanish-American War, several states raised black militia units, and two black U.S. volunteer regiments, the 48th and 49th Infantry, were also organized. In these organizations, several blacks received commissions to lead some of the company-sized units.

The 48th and 49th Infantry, along with the black regiments of the Regular Army, later saw service in the Philippines in 1899–1902. The 10th Cavalry joined Brigadier General John Pershing (who had served in the 10th in Cuba) on the Punitive Expedition in Mexico against Pancho Villa in 1916–17. But these exploits were overshadowed in the minds of white society by two incidents that, during the era of segregation, confirmed whites' worst fears about armed blacks. In 1906, soldiers in the 24th Infantry stationed in Brownsville, Texas, rioted over disputes arising from their treatment by local authorities. Eleven years later, in Houston, men from the same regiment mutinied over similar issues, seized weapons, and went on a shooting spree, killing several civilians. In both cases, "justice" came swiftly. When the leaders of the Brownsville affair could not be identified, President Theodore Roosevelt ordered three companies of black troops summarily disbanded. The War Department tried nearly 120 men for involvement or complicity in the Houston riot; almost all were convicted and a score quickly hanged. The legacy of the Houston riot affected policy toward black military service for years to come.

The enactment of the first truly national selective service legislation, which followed the U.S. entry into World War I, ensured blacks the opportunity to serve in the wartime army on an unprecedented scale, but it did not ensure either equality of opportunity or equality of treatment. Over 400,000 blacks served in the U.S. Armed Forces in World War I. Black draftees accounted for 13 percent of the total men called (the total black population at the time was slightly over 10 percent of a U.S. population of about 104 million). The vast majority of these men served in service and support units.

None of the four black Regular Army regiments fought in France but instead served out the war on the border with Mexico or garrisoned at American island territories in the Caribbean or Pacific. They also provided cadre for the black units raised from draftees and, significantly, candidates for the all-black officer-training program that the War Department had established in 1917 at Fort Des Moines, Iowa.

The American Expeditionary Force (AEF) in France included two black divisions: the 92nd and 93rd. The 92nd Division was composed largely of draftees, and the 93rd contained units created from black state National Guard units. Black lieutenants and captains led most of the small units in these divisions, and a few black field-grade officers performed staff functions. Most field-grade positions and all command positions above company level were filled by whites.[4] In no case were black officers placed in a position where they might command whites.

The experience of one black Regular Army officer, Lieutenant Colonel Charles Young, demonstrated the extent to which the War Department was prepared to go to maintain this policy. Young had served with distinction in the Spanish-American War and the Punitive Expedition. By seniority and experience, he could have attained a colonelcy and command of one of the black cavalry regiments and, given the wartime expansion of the army, even attained the rank of brigadier general. White southern officers in the Tenth Cavalry, alarmed at this prospect, complained to members of Congress, who took the message to President Woodrow Wilson. The War Department quietly placed Young on the "disabled retired" list, where he served out the war.[5]

Of the two black divisions, only the 92nd was a "true" division containing its own combat support and service formations; the 93rd consisted only of four black regiments and a nominal headquarters. Both divisions experienced combat. The 92nd, commanded by Major General Charles Ballou, spent most of its time in France in a "quiet" sector. In September 1918 the division entered combat, initially alongside the French at the beginning of the great Meuse-Argonne Offensive. It performed "sluggishly," according to one historian, was withdrawn and reorganized, and returned to the offensive early in November as part of the Second U.S. Army commanded by Lieutenant General Robert L. Bullard, who had served with black National Guard troops in the Spanish-American War. In the final days of the war, one brigade of the 92nd performed well; the other continued to have problems, which Bullard interpreted as lack of aggressiveness. He withdrew the division from the final offensive and relieved Ballou.[6]

The separate regiments of the 93rd Division had a significantly different experience. Arriving in France late in 1917 and early in 1918 when the French were desperate for replacements, the regiments composing the 93rd were reorganized, issued French uniforms, and sent into combat through the summer and fall of 1918 as part of the French Army. The 369th Infantry, the best known of the four, was in combat for 91 consecutive days and, according to historian Bernard Nalty, "fought itself to exhaustion."[7] The other three regiments—the 370th, 371st, and 372nd—distinguished themselves equally as well. The very different experiences of these units and the postwar assessment of their performance figured prominently in War Department plans for the future use of blacks in combat.

Following the Armistice, the Army quickly shrank to peacetime levels. By the mid–1920s it numbered fewer than 125,000 officers and enlisted men; the combined strength of the four black Regular Army regiments averaged 4,000. During the 1920s and early 1930s, with no demonstrable enemy or seeming threat to national security, the Army's physical plant deteriorated and training lagged as the War Department suffered successive budget cuts. Regular Army units returned to numerous small posts, camps, and stations in the South, the West, and the Southwest, where the only organized division, the First Cavalry, continued to patrol the Mexican border. In many ways the Army of the interwar years resembled the Indian-fighting constabulary of the late 19th century more than the conventional force of 1917–18. But the General Staff of the Army never stopped planning for future contingencies, and when it considered manpower requirements for war, it developed fixed opinions regarding blacks, opinions based on the prevailing social attitudes toward blacks and on the performance of the 92nd Division in France. General Bullard set the tone. Writing in his memoirs in 1925, he declared the black man "hopelessly inferior" and added: "If you need combat soldiers, and especially if you need them in a hurry, don't put your time upon Negroes. The task of making soldiers of them and fighting with them, especially if there are any white people near, will be swamped in the race question. If racial uplift or racial equality is your purpose, that is another matter."[8]

In a series of studies performed by the Army War College, which in the interwar period served as a think tank for the General Staff, officers examining the issue of blacks in combat concluded that blacks were better suited for noncombat duties but that in future wars, political considerations would demand that blacks share the burdens of war proportionately with their numbers in society. Notwithstanding politics, the World War I experience showed that only 30 percent of blacks were suitable for combat units, and military efficiency demanded that they be organized and trained in units no larger than regiments in the initial stages of a mobilization. Furthermore, black divisions were to be formed only if the conflict lasted long enough to require the creation of more divisions than could be supported by the white manpower pool, and then only after receiving extensive training. Black artillery units, according to the view of the War College analysts, should be limited to those necessary to support black infantry: "They should never be employed in close support of white infantry. Any negro batteries in the vicinity would be blamed for all 'short' rounds and the physical damage to the infantry, however slight, would be magnified by rumors, and the consequent loss of infantry morale would be entirely disproportionate to the advantages gained by the addition of a few additional artillery units."[9] On the subject of black officers, the analysts concluded: "That the negro as an officer presents a difficult problem, but that he should nevertheless be given the same opportunities to qualify for commission as the white man and under the same standards.... That the negroes who advance to higher grades be utilized on the staffs of white commanders of negro units as racial advisors and morale officers. That negro officers should be absorbed as far as possible in negro noncombatant units requiring minimum of technical training and leadership ability."[10] The lingering memories of the Brownsville affair and the Houston riot led to one other unofficial policy regarding blacks: as late as 1936, it was understood in the War Department that in the event of war, no black units would be mobilized in Texas.[11]

The prevailing attitude of American society provided the overarching context for military policy regarding blacks during this era. The military attitude toward blacks and their "place" in uniformed service was eloquently expressed in a report prepared by students at the Army War College in 1940: "The negro's physical, mental, moral, and other psychological characteristics have made it impossible for him to associate socially with any except the lowest class of whites. The only exceptions to this are the negro concubines who have sometimes attracted men who, except for this association, were considered high class. This social inequality makes the close association of whites and blacks in military organization inimicable to harmony and efficiency."[12]

## Segregation Policy in the Army on the Eve of World War II

White America's attitude toward blacks can be neatly synthesized by considering the extent to which segregation had become institutionalized in the U.S. Army between the world wars. Segregation by unit had prevailed in the Army since the Civil War, and despite voices raised in protest both inside and outside the Army, a beginning toward the integration characteristic of today's services would not be made until the Korean War. Faced with global conflict a decade earlier, neither the Roosevelt administration nor the War Department felt that the armed forces should or could lead the rest of the nation in breaking down racist barriers or in promoting desegregation.

The need to actively recruit blacks was not pressing during the 1920s and 1930s. Every black unit had waiting lists, even in the economically prosperous 1920s when most white units had difficulty maintaining authorized strength. Throughout the interwar period, the Regular Army maintained a recruiting force, but it ignored blacks. Because the black units enjoyed extremely high reenlistment rates, few vacancies existed for new volunteers. To enlist, the prospective soldier had to travel at his own expense to the unit and convince the unit commander that he was worthy. Training between the wars was accomplished at the unit level, so blacks trained blacks. Since the Army housed enlisted men by unit, segregation was virtually complete. Mobilization for World War II modified, but never eliminated, segregation.[13]

The antidiscrimination features of the 1940 Selective Service Act guaranteed that Army enlisted strength would be essentially 10 percent black. In response to public and political pressures, including the intervention of President Roosevelt, the Army adopted the principle of proportionate representation of blacks in all arms and services. The quota system that resulted led to the creation of certain units designed more to absorb the prescribed black troop allotments than to fill a military need. Blacks could enlist only in one of the four Regular Army "colored" regiments or in the quartermaster and medical units established in direct support of those regiments. Prestige arms like the Air Corps excluded blacks altogether, and the Air Corps became a prime target as early as the late 1930s as black organizations began actively questioning the army's segregationist policies. The Army refused to accept black pilots on the grounds that "there were no [aviation] units composed of colored men," while the Air Corps refused to create black squadrons because there were no black pilots.[14]

The beginning of World War II in Europe in September 1939, followed by the rapid successes of the Nazi blitzkrieg culminating with the fall of France by June 1940, prompted a partial mobilization by the United States. While the nation debated the larger issue of whether or not to intervene in the growing world conflict, the Army expanded again and again in an effort to prepare for whatever contingency the future might bring. Leaders of the black community, such as Walter White, Executive Director of the NAACP, and A. Philip Randolph, head of the Brotherhood of Sleeping Car Porters, aided by a loose coalition of black newspapers in northern and upper midwestern urban centers, found supporters in Congress and the Roosevelt administration who were willing to consider a larger role for blacks in the military. Their goal, expressed in the "Double V" slogan, was victory against the enemy abroad and against discrimination at home. Although the complete desegregation of the armed forces became an ultimate objective, achieving a black presence in all arms and services proportionate to black numbers in society (approximately 10 percent) represented the key intermediate goal. Black civilian leaders especially sought proportionate representation in combat units.

The passage of the Selective Training and Service Act of 1940, the first peacetime draft in U.S. history, provided black leaders with their first real opportunity for change. During final debate on the bill in the House of Representatives, Congressman Hamilton Fish of New York, who had commanded a company of the 369th Infantry in World War I, successfully amended the measure to prohibit discrimination by race or color in the selection and training of men for the armed forces.

Civilian and uniformed leaders in the Armed Forces, on the other hand, resisted and resented these efforts, which they saw as counterproductive to the war mobilization effort. General George C. Marshall, who became Chief of Staff of the Army on 1 September 1939, clearly stated the Army's position. In a letter to Senator Henry Cabot Lodge, Marshall wrote: "It is the policy of the War Department not to intermingle colored and white enlisted personnel in the same regimental organization. The condition which has made this policy necessary is not the responsibility of the Department, but to ignore it would produce situations destructive of morale and therefore definitely detrimental to the preparations for national defense in this emergency."[15]

Secretary of War Henry L. Stimson shared General Marshall's views. Although he believed in "full freedom, political and economic, for all men of color," Stimson did not support integration, particularly during an emergency. Indeed, Stimson resented the tactics of black leaders "to stir unrest and force new policies for which the Negroes themselves were unprepared," and he considered the opinions espoused by the black press "shockingly biased and unreliable."[16]

President Franklin D. Roosevelt gave great credence to the War Department's views, but he was a master politician. Embarked in 1940 on a race for an unprecedented third term in the White House, Roosevelt sought to fashion a politically acceptable compromise. He directed the Army to accept blacks into all arms of the service, including the Air Corps, but he continued to support the military leaders' position that units should remain segregated by race. Later, Roosevelt made token appointments of blacks to advisory positions in the Selective Service System and the War Department and approved the promotion of Benjamin O. Davis, Sr., as the first black Regular Army brigadier general. These decisions by Roosevelt, all made in the fall of 1940, essentially fixed the policy regarding blacks in the Army for the duration of the War. Whites, advised by a few blacks, determined the policy. Blacks gained a larger presence in the military, and by their larger numbers contributed more to the war effort, but with very few exceptions their contribution remained circumscribed by segregation. On 16 October 1940 these considerations were embodied in the Army's official statement of policy toward black service personnel:

> It is the policy of the War Department that the services of Negroes will be utilized on a fair and equitable basis. In line with this policy provision will be made as follows:
> 
> a. The strength of Negro personnel in the AUS [Army of the United States—the combined forces of regular army, volunteers, national guard, and reserves] will be maintained on the general basis of proportion of the Negro population of the country.
> 
> b. Negro organizations will be established in each major branch of the service, combatant as well as non-combatant.

c. Negro Reserve officers eligible for active duty will be assigned to Negro units officered by colored personnel.

d. When officer candidate schools are established, opportunity will be given to Negroes to qualify for Reserve commissions.

e. Negroes are being given aviation training as pilots, mechanics, and technical specialists. Negro aviation units will be formed as soon as the necessary personnel has been trained.

f. At arsenals and Army posts Negro civilians are accorded equal opportunity for employment at work for which they are qualified by ability, education and experience.

g. The policy of the War Department is not to intermingle colored and white enlisted personnel in the same regimental organizations. This policy has proven satisfactory over a long period of years and to make changes would produce situations destructive to morale and detrimental to the preparations for national defense. For similar reasons the Department does not contemplate assigning colored Reserve officers other than those of the Medical Corps and Chaplains to existing Negro combat units of the Regular Army.[17]

## Mobilization and Training

The mobilization of African Americans during World War II was thus on a completely segregated basis, primarily into noncombat units. They were accepted into the armed forces in accordance with their proportion to the total population.

Expansion of the Army after 1939, and especially after the passage of the 1940 Selective Service Act, created more openings for blacks. Initial numerical increases in late 1939 and early 1940 allowed the Army to recruit existing units up to full strength. The call-up of the National Guard in August 1940 and the activation of new units in September 1940 and thereafter, to receive draftees as well as volunteers, brought the total black strength of the Army to 100,000 (out of 1.6 million) by November 1941.

Although blacks were now represented in every branch of the Army, the training as well as the effectiveness of black units lagged well behind that of comparable white units. Both the 92nd and the 93rd Divisions required extended training before they were considered ready for division maneuver exercises—a prerequisite to deployment overseas. The 827th Tank Destroyer Battalion provides an extreme example. This unit spent two and a half years training in the United States, and failed five battalion tests, before being deployed to Europe in November 1944.[18] Situations like these led to a "self-fulfilling prophecy" regarding the ability of blacks to train for higher skilled positions and regarding their potential value as combatants. Several factors, well established in Army policy, contributed to this situation.

First, in housing black units separately from white units, the Army generally located cantonments for black units some distance from the main sections of the posts. The rapid expansion of the Army also created a housing

Black selectees arriving at the reception center, Fort Benning, Georgia, August 1941, to begin their Army training. U.S. Army Photograph, National Archives and Records Administration, courtesy Col. William A. DeShields, U.S. Army (Retired).

shortage. Since the Army constructed new housing in divisional-size units, and since black units could not, by policy, exceed regimental size at the beginning of the buildup, quarters for black units were frequently built last at new or expanding posts, leaving black soldiers to live in tents or other substandard facilities. Indeed, housing policies affected training. Locating black housing away from the major post facilities increased movement time to and from training. Since training guidelines dictated that troops receive instruction together in groups, and since black units awaiting housing filled up slowly, they took longer to train, thereby contributing to the notion that black units were "slow."

The second policy that delayed the effective development of black units was the Army's use of a cadre system to provide experienced troops to leaven new units. Adhering to "separate but equal," the Army sought black noncommissioned officers from Regular Army regiments to act as cadre for the new black formations. But there were not enough black Regulars to provide an effective training nucleus. Moreover, black noncommissioned officers (NCOs) were mostly infantrymen and cavalry troopers whose lack of other technical experience mitigated against the development of troops in other branches. The net result was delayed or inferior training in larger units or in specialties other than the areas in which blacks had traditionally served.

Soldiers of the 92nd Infantry Division practicing on the machine gun range at Camp Breckinridge, Kentucky, 12 February 1943. U.S. Army Photograph, National Archives and Records Administration, courtesy Lt. Col. Major Clark, U.S. Army (Retired).

The Army, including the Army Air Forces (AAF), expanded rapidly after Pearl Harbor. By the end of 1942 it had grown to over 4.5 million, with blacks constituting 10.3 percent of the total.[19] True to President Roosevelt's commitment, blacks served in all arms and services of the Army, but even more than previously, they were underrepresented in the combat arms.

Creating additional black infantry and artillery units was not difficult. In addition to the 24th and 25th Regular Army infantry regiments, the Army created the 366th, 367th and 368th Regular regiments and the 372nd National Guard regiment. The creation of additional black artillery units also moved ahead without incident. To accommodate the requirement to have black representation in all branches of the Armed Forces, the National Guard redesignated some black infantry units, including the 369th Infantry, as artillery regiments. Later, when the Army began creating tank-destroyer battalions, several black artillery units were redesignated as "T. D. battalions" (not to be confused with tank battalions).

Creating black combat units in those arms in which African Americans had never served proved more challenging. The most celebrated case involved black units in the Army Air Forces. The AAF had long resisted all efforts to break its color line.[20] When President Roosevelt and the War Department decreed that all arms and services would be open to blacks, the AAF established special units specifically for the purpose of meeting this requirement. These included base security detachments, aviation "training" squadrons, aviation quartermaster truck companies, and air-base transportation platoons.

The establishment of black aviation units proved most difficult and came about because of the convergence of pressure from the black community and from the other arms of the service that did not want the AAF to avoid taking its share of African Americans. In January 1942, the AAF bowed to the inevitable and announced that a black fighter squadron, the 99th Pursuit Squadron, would be formed. But Jim Crow prevailed. The 99th Pursuit, three additional fighter squadrons, and a bomber group were trained, at greatly added expense, at a separate aviation training complex established at Tuskegee, Alabama, for that exclusive purpose. The fighter units served with distinction in the Mediterranean; the black bombardment group never made it to operational status because Tuskegee could not meet the demands of training replacements for the fighter units and for bomber crews simultaneously. Training individual replacements for units already in combat took priority over training entire crews for units not yet deployed.

In contrast, the establishment of independent tank units in the Armored Force went smoothly. Armored Force leaders initially resisted the creation of black units on grounds that theirs was an experimental organization that should not be disrupted by the additional requirement of having to train blacks and create separate segregated units. Such protests failed, however; the first black tank battalion, the 78th, a Light Tank Battalion, was activated in June 1941. Initially, 32 white enlisted instructors were attached to the 78th because no black cadre existed. Two additional tank battalions were also activated—the 761st and the 784th. These three tank battalions, with the 78th redesignated as the 758th, formed the 5th Armored Group, activated on 23 May 1942.[21]

## The Creation and Deployment of Black Divisions

As the number of black combat units increased, the War Department reconsidered its policy of opposing separate black divisions. The decision to create black divisions was based more on expediency than on any intention to employ such formations in combat. Divisions provided administrative entities that could absorb the growing number of independent black regiments, battalions, and batteries. Thus, despite continuing misgivings about the ability of blacks to perform in combat in units larger than regiments, General Marshall agreed to the creation of three black divisions: the 2nd Cavalry and the 92nd and the 93rd Infantry.[22]

Carrying mortar shells to the front lines some 500 yards distant, 2nd Battalion, 93rd Infantry Division soldiers fording a river on Bougainville Island, 3 April 1944. U.S. Army Photograph, National Archives and Records Administration, courtesy Col. William A. DeShields, U.S. Army (Retired).

The existence of large numbers of black units training throughout the United States caused friction with local white populations. Anti-black racial incidents mounted and were reported in the black press. Black leaders demanded redress, which, when it came, was rarely satisfactory. By 1943, with U.S. units engaged in offensive operations in the Pacific and North Africa, black leaders added a new demand—the use of black combat units in combat.

The recommendation to commit large black units to combat in World War II came from the War Department's Advisory Committee on Negro Troop Policies and was framed by Truman Gibson, the black civilian aide to the secretary of war. Secretary Stimson trusted Gibson for "his honesty and courage."[23] Gibson worked closely with Assistant Secretary of War John J. McCloy, who was Stimson's close adviser in the War Department and to whom all "Colored matters" were referred. McCloy supported the Advisory Committee's recommendation on the grounds that it was better to make use of black units than to have them train endlessly at home, where they suffered discrimination and drew the attention of the black press.[24] Stimson and Marshall reluctantly agreed in March 1944, and the Army Staff began to develop detailed plans to deploy advanced units of the 92nd and 93rd Divisions to Italy and the Pacific respectively. Even then, the War Department treated the action as an experiment. To determine how well black units performed in combat, the Advisory Committee decided to commit a regimental combat team of the 93rd Division, already in the Solomon Islands, to combat without special preparation. On the other side of the world, a handpicked regimental combat team made up of men selected from all units of the 92nd Division, still training at Fort Huachuca, Arizona, would be intensively trained for commitment to combat.[25]

Once the decision was made to commit the large black combat units to active theaters of the War, the ice was broken. Theater commanders requested, received, and used the smaller, independent tank-destroyer and tank battalions. Black divisional, corps, and army artillery units moved into the Pacific and the European theaters along with the black divisions in general support of the advancing armies. These units, like their white counterparts, performed with varying degrees of distinction, and the exploits of some of these soldiers are reported in subsequent chapters of this book. In virtually all cases, blacks fought as they had since the beginnings of the American nation: in separate units and in circumstances molded more by race issues than by military efficiency or necessity. It would take another generation to break that tradition.

## Notes

1. This chapter summarizing the black military experience in the U.S. Army draws on several sources: Richard M. Dalfiume, *Desegregation of the U.S. Armed Forces: Fighting on Two Fronts, 1939–1953* (Columbia: University of Missouri Press, 1969); Ulysses Lee, *The Employment of Negro Troops [United States Army in World War II]* (Washington, D.C.: U.S. Government Printing Office, 1966); Morris J. MacGregor, Jr., *Integration of the Armed Forces, 1940–1965 [Defense Studies Series]* (Washington, D.C.: U.S. Government Printing Office, 1981); Bernard C. Nalty, *Strength for the Fight: A History of Black Americans in the Military* (New York: Free Press, 1986). Only direct quotes or statistical data are footnoted hereafter.
2. Nalty, *Strength for the Fight*, pp. 15, 18.
3. Dudley Cornish, *The Sable Arm: Negro Troops in the Union Army, 1861–1865* (New York: Longmans, Green and Company, 1956), p. 288.
4. One regiment of the 93rd Division was commanded by a black National Guard officer, but he was replaced by a white officer by the end of the war. Lee, *Employment of Negro Troops*, p. 5.
5. Nalty, *Strength for the Fight*, pp. 15, 18.
6. *Ibid.*, pp. 115–16.
7. *Ibid.*, p. 118.
8. Maj. Gen. Robert L. Bullard, *Personalities and Reminiscences of the War* (New York: Doubleday, 1925), p. 298, as cited in Lee, *Employment of Negro Troops*, p. 15.
9. "Use of Negro Manpower in War," Supplement No. 3 to Report of Committee No. 3, Army War College, 12 November 1936, files of Robert K. Griffith, Jr.
10. *Ibid.*
11. *Ibid.*

12. Quoted in Richard J. Stillman, "The Role of the Negro in the U.S. Armed Forces, 1939–1968," *Irish Defense Journal*, March 1969, pp. 102–3.

13. This paragraph and others on the interwar army draw heavily on Robert K. Griffith, Jr., *Men Wanted for the U.S. Army: America's Experience with an All-Volunteer Army between the World Wars, 1919–1941* (New Haven, Conn.: Greenwood Press, 1982).

14. Lee, *Employment of Negro Troops*, pp. 55–64.

15. George C. Marshall letter to Henry Cabot Lodge, 27 September 1940, Adjutant General's File 341, Record Group 407, Washington National Records Center, Suitland, Md.

16. Henry L. Stimson and McGeorge Bundy, *On Active Service in Peace and War* (New York: Harper Brothers, 1947), p. 461.

17. "Negro Personnel Digest of Policies," 16 October 1940, Adjutant's General File 291.21, U.S. Army Military History Institute, Carlisle Barracks, Penn.

18. Lee, *Employment of Negro Troops*, pp. 489–96, 679–80.

19. *Ibid.*, p. 134.

20. See Nalty, *Strength for the Fight*, ch. 10, "The Army's Black Eagles," and Lee, *Employment of Negro Troops*, pp. 113–19.

21. Lee, *Employment of Negro Troops*, pp. 119–21.

22. The Second Cavalry, which included the two black cavalry regiments that dated to the Civil War (the Ninth and Tenth Regiments), was subsequently disbanded and converted to a support organization after its arrival in North Africa. This action also fueled demands for the commitment of the remaining black divisions to combat.

23. Stimson and Bundy, *Active Service*, p. 464.

24. Despite his obvious role in shaping policy regarding blacks in the Army during World War II, McCloy apparently placed little significance on it in later years. His personal papers, which he edited himself, contain no documents about the Advisory Committee. The only documents relating to "colored matters" are copies of letters sent to Eleanor Roosevelt and responding to her queries about racial incidents at Army bases.

25. Lee, *Employment of Negro Troops*, pp. 481–85; MacGregor, *Integration*, pp. 42–44.

*Chapter 3*

# Medal of Honor Award Policies and Practices, 1941–1948

## Introduction

As of the middle of 1947, Army and Army Air Forces personnel had received more than 1.8 million decorations for service during the course of World War II.[1] The three highest awards for valor in combat against an enemy of the United States—the Medal of Honor, the Distinguished Service Cross, and the Silver Star—accounted for approximately 5 percent of the total.[2] After the War, the War Department frankly admitted to problems with the decoration system. Secretary of War Robert P. Patterson conceded: "Many a soldier whose conduct merits recognition does not get formal recognition by way of a decoration. There are cases that are never reported. There are cases that are reported inadequately. There are cases where human errors are made." Nevertheless, Patterson believed that "deliberate favoritism or discrimination [had been] rare."[3]

The rapid growth in the Army's size—from just under 200,000 in September 1939 to nearly 8.3 million by May 1945—and the need to wage war on every continent, often under harsh and swiftly changing conditions, complicated the process. A postwar Joint Board to Study Decorations in 1948 concluded that the Army and Navy had failed "to plan for and provide a system that would meet the needs of war on a global basis."[4] Two valid considerations worked against each other. On the one hand, the authority to bestow certain decorations was delegated to field commanders in order to give awards more promptly and to stimulate morale. On the other hand, empowering hundreds of different individuals with award authority complicated the equally desirable objective of establishing uniform standards for each decoration.[5] Commanders held a variety of attitudes toward awards, and the Army's policy defining standards of merit for each award was very general.

The authority to award the Medal of Honor, the nation's highest decoration for heroism, was never delegated but was reserved to the War Department acting for the president in the name of Congress. Within the War Department, a special board of officers (the War Department Decorations Board) evaluated each Medal of Honor recommendation and proposed either approval or disapproval before submitting the case to the chief of staff and secretary of war for final action. In theory, the board protected the Medal's integrity by applying a common standard of merit. Despite this centralizing safeguard, a lack of clarity in policy that determined procedures for processing Medal of Honor recommendations, combined with the arbitrary action of individual commanders, prevented some cases from reaching the War Department.

## Definition and Policy

Only 256 soldiers and 38 airmen from among the millions who served in the Army and the Army Air Forces during World War II received the Medal of Honor. Slightly over half of this total were posthumous awards.[6] In 1918, Congress had established the basic criteria regulating the Medal, and this legislation became the source of the well-known stricture that its recipient must "distinguish himself conspicuously by gallantry and intrepidity at the risk of his life above and beyond the call of duty."[7] The Army repeated and elaborated on this policy in its regulation on decorations, Army Regulation (AR) 600-45.[8] Several War Department circulars, memoranda, letters, and messages to field commands supplemented the regulation.

The formal standard in AR 600-45 justifying the awarding of the Medal of Honor remained constant throughout the War. The circumstances had to involve "actual conflict" during which the individual had to "distinguish himself conspicuously" from his comrades by "gallantry and intrepidity at the risk of his life" or "the performance of more than ordinarily hazardous service." Since exposure to personal danger is an inherent part of military service in wartime, the quality of heroism recognized for the Medal of Honor had to be for a deed that, if not performed, "would not justly subject [the individual] to censure as for shortcoming or failure in the performance of his duty."[9]

The Medal of Honor ranked at the top of what the Army called a "Pyramid of Honor" of military decorations.[10] Other awards recognized lesser degrees of heroism. Among these, in descending order of importance, were the Distinguished Service Cross and the Silver Star. By 1947, over 4,500 Distinguished Service Crosses had been awarded to Army personnel in World War II.[11] "Extraordinary heroism" in operations against an enemy was its benchmark. Such valor called for "an act or acts of heroism so notable and involving a risk of life so extraordinary as to set [the individual] apart from his comrades."[12] The Silver Star was given for "gallantry in action" not meriting either of the other two decorations. "Gallantry" was further defined as "heroism at the risk of life and so exceptional as to set the individual apart from his comrades."[13] Approximately 75,000 soldiers and airmen received this award.[14]

Contemporary observers noted a vexing problem with the three top valor awards: the difficulty in distinguishing among the degrees of heroism each was intended to recognize. One member of the War Department Decorations Board commented, "There is no sharp cleavage between acts meriting Medal of Honor, Distinguished Service Cross, or Silver Star."[15] The regulations describing each of the three were quite general, were imprecise in defining acts or behavior, and were often strikingly similar. The word "gallantry" characterized both the Medal of Honor and the Silver Star. All three awards required "heroism" that set the individual apart from his comrades. For the Medal of Honor, that heroism was to be "above and beyond the call of duty," whereas for the Distinguished Service Cross, it was to be "extraordinary." Since heroism could not be quantified, descriptive words were never more than a rough measure. As one officer on the War Department Decorations Board put it, in the evaluation of acts of valor, "the personal equation enters."[16]

In addition to describing the heroism required for valor awards, AR 600-45 set other policies. For example, only an officer could initiate a decoration recommendation.[17] The recommendation for a Medal of Honor had to be supported by "incontestable proof," of which eyewitness testimony seemed an essential ingredient (as it was for all valor awards, although only the Medal of Honor required "incontestable proof").[18] Here again, the regulation obscured more than it clarified. In the version of AR 600-45 in effect at the War's beginning, the person initiating the recommendation had to have "personal knowledge" of the act or be an eyewitness. If he was neither, then the recommendation must be accompanied ("when practicable") by the testimony of two individuals who had "personal knowledge" or who were eyewitnesses.[19] "Personal knowledge" was not further defined, nor was it differentiated from eyewitness testimony. Furthermore, including the phrase "when practicable" undermined the requirement for eyewitness testimony.

Acknowledging the hopelessly confusing character of these instructions, a 1942 War Department Circular stated more simply, "Recommending officers will insure that all recommendations for awards for individual acts of heroism or gallantry are accompanied by affidavits of eyewitnesses."[20] Unable to let the issue alone, however, the War Department, while dropping the enigmatic "personal knowledge" in its late 1943 revision of AR 600-45, now required only the statement of one eyewitness, "preferably the recipient's immediate commander."[21] In fact, Army policy published during the War never clarified the number of eyewitness testimonies required.[22] Yet the number was not the real issue; "incontestable proof" was. As the War progressed, the War Department found that some eyewitness statements lacked the kind of detail constituting incontestable proof and asked the field commands to provide better evidence.[23]

Medal of Honor policy did not always make its way into regulations

The three highest awards for valor in the Army in World War II: the Medal of Honor (courtesy Charlie Archambault, all rights reserved); the Distinguished Service Cross; and the Silver Star (both from *Armed Forces Decorations and Awards*).

or other formal documents. By March 1943, 59 Medals of Honor had been awarded (15 Army and 44 Navy).[24] At a cabinet meeting late that month, President Franklin D. Roosevelt expressed concern that the Medal of Honor might be awarded for actions that were not beyond the call of duty. He recalled what he believed had been a mistake by Secretary of the Navy Josephus Daniels in awarding about 40 Medals of Honor for a minor engagement during the conflict with Mexico in 1914. Roosevelt also referred specifically to the Medal of Honor awards then being proposed for airmen who had shot down large numbers of enemy planes. Such exploits, he thought, constituted no more than a pilot's duty and would more appropriately merit the Distinguished Service Cross. The president's comments, as recorded by Secretary of War Henry L. Stimson, were quickly passed to the War Department Decorations Board.[25] What impact they had on subsequent Medal of Honor recommendations is not certain. Nonetheless, they were the commander-in-chief's views. Very likely they acted as a powerful damper on any tendency (certainly not demonstrated by the Army up to that point) of the armed services to be overgenerous with the Medal of Honor.[26] As late as April 1944—nearly two and a half years into the War—the number of Army and Army Air Forces recipients of the Medal totaled a mere 35.[27]

Were there other, more informal—even unwritten—policies or practices influencing the award of the Medal of Honor? A recent history of the Army in World War II has claimed that one unwritten rule "said an aid man couldn't qualify for anything higher than a Silver Star" but that this rule was "relaxed slightly" by Army Chief of Staff General George C. Marshall to allow a Medal of Honor for one combat medic in the Pacific and one in Europe.[28] Actually, 5 medics received the Medal of Honor and more than 100 the Distinguished Service Cross.[29]

More problematic, given the extent of racism in American society in the 1940s and the segregated Army it had produced, was numerous African-Americans' conviction that a policy of some kind—either written or unwritten—precluded black soldiers from receiving the Medal of Honor. Toward the end of the War, African-American newspapers began to point out how few of the highest awards for valor had been won by black soldiers.[30] Most noticeable was the failure of any African-American soldier to be awarded the Medal of Honor. The *Baltimore Afro-American*'s war correspondent alleged, "All awards for heroism are stepped down a notch wherever colored are concerned." Early in 1946, the *Cleveland Call and Post* asserted that it was the result of "another deliberate, unwritten policy based purely on prejudice and racial bias."[31] Indeed, the *Omaha Star* charged that one of the few black Distinguished Service Cross recipients, Staff Sergeant Edward A. Carter, Jr., had originally been recommended by his superior officers for a Medal of Honor but was denied it because of his race.[32]

Some support for the existence of an unwritten policy denying black soldiers the Medal comes from Truman K. Gibson, who served in the War Department from early 1943 to late 1945 as civilian aide on black affairs to the secretary of war. Interviewed in 1994, Gibson explained the failure in terms of the racial climate then prevailing in the Army: "It's not at all surprising. You had a feeling on the part of senior officers in the Army that blacks were just absolutely inferior and when that gets down it's not surprising that black soldiers weren't recommended. Nobody would be encouraged to put anything in writing [i.e., for a Medal of Honor]—in fact they would be discouraged."[33] When asked, however, whether he had ever encountered any protests or complaints regarding awards for black soldiers, Gibson responded that it "never came up."[34]

The Army's World War II records contain many protests about discrimination against African-American soldiers in the United States and overseas in promotion, assignment, housing, recreational facilities, social opportunities, and transportation.[35] Research for this study uncovered only a few protests concerning awards for heroism. In 1948, for example, Trezzvant W. Anderson, a veteran and a journalist in civilian life, expressed his deep disappointment to the Army's assistant chief of staff for personnel over the War Department's disapproval of a Distinguished Unit Citation for the largely African-American 761st Tank Battalion, which had seen extensive combat in the European Theater. Not only did the 761st deserve a Distinguished Unit Citation, Anderson wrote in a letter to Lieutenant General Willard S. Paul in 1948, but the heroism of several members of the unit had not been properly recognized. Citing the example of the valor demonstrated by First Sergeant Samuel J. Turley on 8 November 1944, Anderson, a former member of the 761st, exclaimed: "General Paul: In MY book that was a performance worthy of the Congressional Medal of Honor ... but Sam Turley received a posthumous Silver Star. Do you think that was fair?"[36]

Others who believed black servicemen had been short changed in awards went directly to the White House for an explanation. Soon after the War, President Harry Truman received several letters noting that no black serviceman had received the Medal of Honor.[37] Dr. C. F. Hopson, Director of West Virginia's Bureau of Negro Welfare and Statistics, told the president: "I am familiar with the fact that the basic recommendation for such an award does not rest with you. Could it be, then, that somewhere along the chain of command certain meritorious services have been overlooked or not properly evaluated?"[38]

The War Department responded to these letters, either by answering directly or by drafting a reply for the White House. Each Medal of Honor recommendation that came to the War Department, said the Army, was "given full consideration in light of the degree of gallantry displayed." Each was judged entirely on the facts presented "without knowledge of the race or creed of the individual concerned." It would not be "proper" to ask theater commanders for recommendations on behalf of "any particular class of individuals."³⁹ Although technically correct, the responses were disingenuous. The Army acted only on those Medal of Honor recommendations received by the War Department, and it knew that some (not necessarily those involving black soldiers) had never been forwarded by the theaters or commands to the War Department for final action. Furthermore, stating that Medal of Honor awards were made without knowledge of the individual's race was inaccurate. No senior Army officer could be unaware that the 92nd and 93rd Infantry Divisions were black divisions, with all of the enlisted men and most of the junior officers in those divisions being black. Moreover, individual personnel ("201") files clearly identified service members by race and were among the documents assembled for each decoration case considered by the War Department Decorations Board.⁴⁰ Yet such points are moot, for these is no evidence that a Medal of Honor recommendation for an African-American soldier ever went above battalion level, let alone reached the War Department. In fact, research for this report found no *written* Medal of Honor nomination for any black soldier at any time during World War II.

African Americans were not alone in suggesting inequity in Medal of Honor awards. In 1946, Senator Joseph F. Guffey of Pennsylvania wrote to Secretary of War Patterson voicing concerns expressed to him that a disproportionate share of the higher decorations had gone to Regular Army officers as opposed to National Guard and Reserve officers and enlisted men. Guffey thought it "ridiculous" that the Third Infantry Division had received "about ⅙ of all the Congressional Medals of Honor awarded in the Ground Forces" while about 25 other divisions had received none.⁴¹

The War Department steadfastly maintained that the very high standard of the Medal of Honor had been upheld during World War II. All those awarded met the test of "incontestable proof," replied Patterson, though there may "easily" have been "some cases which may have deserved the cherished award which did not come to light."⁴²

Yet to determine today whether recommendations for the Medal of Honor were properly administered, we need to carefully examine the course taken by these recommendations, from their initiation in the field through their consideration by various command echelons to their final approval by the War Department, in order to reveal the extent to which practice matched policy.

## Recommendation and Approval/Disapproval Process

Approval of a Medal of Honor recommendation often took several months and could involve as many as eight command echelons and several staff elements within each echelon. The process was governed, though neither clearly nor in much detail, by Army Regulation (AR) 600-45. All along the path from units in the field to the Pentagon, individual commanders played a dominant role.

Briefly, the process worked in the following way. In most situations, a company, battalion, or regimental commander initiated a Medal of Honor recommendation. Signed by him, the recommendation included a narrative describing the act of heroism, the affidavits of eyewitnesses, perhaps a map (usually a rough sketch but sometimes an elaborate colored drawing) showing where the action had taken place, and a proposed citation. These documents constituted the core of the "case file" that would pass through each headquarters—division, corps, army group, and theater—before being sent on to the War Department. Division, army, and theater were the most important field headquarters in the chain. At each, the adjutant general's section received the recommendation, checked that it met administrative requirements, and submitted it to a headquarters decorations board. These boards, usually made up of three to five officers (one a recorder), evaluated each recommendation on the basis of merit and passed it to Personnel (G-1), which had decorations policy responsibility. G-1 sometimes disagreed with the decorations board. In any event, the recommendation then went to the chief of staff or deputy commander (or both) before going to the commander, who made the final recommendation. The last stop was the adjutant general's section, which transmitted the case to the next-higher command level.[43]

No field headquarters possessed final authority over the Medal of Honor. Only the War Department could actually bestow the award. Until 1945, a recommendation followed a route in the War Department similar to that taken in a field headquarters. The functions performed by each War Department staff agency were similar as well. After receipt by the adjutant general, the recommendation went to the War Department Decorations Board, next to the assistant chief of staff for personnel (G-1), then through the deputy chief of staff and on to the chief of staff of the Army (and in rare instances to the secretary of war or the president). When a final decision was made, the adjutant general notified the individual's unit through the appropriate channels and published notice of the approved awards in War Department General Orders.[44]

Within the War Department, the Decorations Board, organizationally part of the Office of the Secretary of War but administered by the Army Staff, was the focal point of the review and evaluation process.[45] Formally established at G-1's initiative in March 1942, the Decorations Board for much of the War was composed of four retired generals and colonels, one representing the Army Air Forces and one serving as a recorder.[46] Its first president was Major General E. S. Adams, who had recently stepped down as the Army's adjutant general. In addition to awards for heroism (mostly Medals of Honor but sometimes lesser awards), the Board also reviewed proposed Distinguished Unit Citations, several types of decorations for meritorious service including the Distinguished Service Medal, U.S. awards to foreign military personnel, and military awards to civilians. By March 1945, the Board had processed nearly 10,000 decorations and would review another 8,000 in little more than a year afterward.[47] During Adams' tenure, the Board's usual procedure was to circulate individual decoration cases assembled by the adjutant general's office to each Board member for vote. According to Adams, when "a difference of opinion existed the Board engaged in roundtable discussion ... frequently resulting in unanimous decisions."[48] With respect to the Medal of Honor, the Board considered each case promptly and made sure that the presented facts supported the award.[49]

In March 1945, Major General John E. Sloan, who had commanded the 88th Infantry Division in North Africa and Italy, succeeded Adams as the Board's president.[50] Sloan was not happy with what he found. After discovering that the Board's policy files were incomplete, Sloan visited the adjutant general's office in order to bring the files up-to-date.[51] Sloan did not believe that the Board's current membership of three officers, all in their late 60s, was physically up to processing the flood of recommendations anticipated as the War ended.[52] One officer, he said, was mentally alert, but could not "perform a full day's work."[53] Sloan requested their relief and then doubled the Board's size, replacing them with younger officers with combat experience, including eventually both Reserve and National Guard members.[54] He also altered Board procedures by dividing its membership into two panels of three officers each to handle the increased workload.[55] Finally, Sloan expanded the Board's power by securing the right to take final action for the War Department on more types of decorations cases. By the end of 1945, this expanded authority also included the Medal of Honor, except in those cases where the Board disagreed with the recommendation of a theater commander, the chiefs of the Air, Ground, and Service Forces, or the heads of War Department General and Special Staff agencies (notably the G-1).[56] In such instances, final action would be the responsibility of the deputy chief of staff or the chief of staff.[57]

Just who within the War Department should be vested with the authority to take final action on Medal of Honor recommendations was a contentious issue and remained so even after the Board's authority expanded in 1945. "No one man, even the Chief of Staff," wrote one Board member, "should have authority to award. The Decorations Board ... should have final decision."[58] Sloan was more practical, recognizing that some decisions had to be left to higher authority.[59]

By the eve of Japan's formal surrender, the Board had considered 323 proposals for the Medal of Honor, recommending 203 for approval and 120 for disapproval.[60] At about the same time, the War Department began to suspect that some Medal of Honor recommendations were not reaching Washington. At the end of July 1945, the War Department cabled General Douglas MacArthur's headquarters and asked that all Medal of Honor recommendations, even those not approved, be sent forward for final action.[61] Less than a year later, the War Department made a similar request to all theaters.[62] A "Memorandum for Record" filed with this 1946 message noted that AR 600-45 *required* Medal of Honor recommendations to be submitted to the War Department and that failure to do so had "resulted at times in unfavorable publicity and inference that War Department had disapproved Medal of Honor cases because they do not know what goes on in combat."[63]

Because of its ambiguous language, what AR 600-45 required was a matter of interpretation; that was the principal, though not the only, reason that Medal of Honor recommendations were not reaching the War Department. With regard to who awarded the Medal of Honor, there was certainly no misunderstanding. War Department Circular 5, dated 8 January 1942, stated: "Awards of decorations are made by the War Department ... except that the commanding general of a separate army or of a higher unit in the field may award all decorations other than the Medal of Honor and the Distinguished Service Medal."[64] This policy was published as a formal change to AR 600-45 in October 1942.[65] The 1943 edition of the regulation was even more specific: "The Medal of Honor and the Distinguished Service Medal may be awarded by the War Department only."[66]

In the final analysis, the problem was not who could say "yes" but who could say "no." From the War Department's perspective, only the War Department could disapprove a Medal of Honor recommendation. The language in AR 600-45, however, was ambiguous and gave rise to misinterpretation. The 1932 edition of AR 600-45 had directed that any decoration case, including the Medal of Honor, should be forwarded through channels, indicating the favorable or unfavorable views of each commander through whom it passed.[67] An August 1942 change to the regulation distinguished between the Medal of Honor and other decorations by stating that each commander's "views or recommendations ... either favorable or unfavorable" should accompany any decoration case but that Medal of Honor "recommendations" should be forwarded to the War Department through channels.[68] In the 1942 change, the word "recommendation" was being used in two different ways. In the first, as applied to any decoration, "recommendation" meant either "yes" or "no"; in the second use, when linked directly to the Medal of Honor, "recommendation" could be interpreted to mean only "yes" or favorable recommendations. In other words, a commander might conclude that his "no" or unfavorable recommendation for a Medal of Honor need not be forwarded. The language used in the 1943 version deepened the ambiguity. This version dropped the distinction between the Medal of Honor and other decorations in outlining the transmittal process, but a new paragraph required that decoration "recommendations" should have enough detail so that "the appropriate commander or the War Department may determine whether the service was, in fact, sufficient to meet the requirements for the award."[69] The words "appropriate commander," when put on an equal plane with "War Department," might be interpreted to permit lower-echelon commanders to make final, unfavorable evaluations of Medal of Honor recommendations on their own. In May 1947, a change of language clarified the meaning of "recommendation": "Where disapproval is recommended, specific reasons will be shown."[70] By this time, theater headquarters knew, from the messages of July 1945 and May 1946, that the War Department wanted all Medal of Honor recommendations forwarded, regardless of what a lower-echelon commander's evaluation happened to be. Whether the War Department received every Medal of Honor recommendation cannot be established conclusively, but analysis of the process of transmittal in the various theaters strongly suggests that it did not.

## Medal of Honor Policy and Practice in the Mediterranean Theater of Operations

The Mediterranean Theater of Operations (MTO), a geographical area that encompassed fighting in North Africa, Sicily, and Italy, produced 60 Medals of Honor, about 750 Distinguished Service Crosses, and nearly 13,000 Silver Stars.[71] The War Department, through its regulations, circulars, letters, and messages, set overall decorations policy in the MTO. Theater headquarters supplemented those instructions with circulars relating decorations policy to specific theater circumstances, interpreting policy, and occasionally, breaking entirely new policy ground.[72] AR 600-45, for example, provided that the authority to award the Distinguished Service Cross could be delegated to a theater commander, who could, in turn, authorize certain subordinate commanders to make the award. At various times in the MTO, this authorization included the 15th Army Group, Fifth and Seventh Army commanders, and the theater's Army Air Forces and Services of Supply commanders.[73] At one point, the theater offered a lengthy interpretation of the War Department's policy with respect to the Legion of Merit (awarded for meritorious service).[74] The MTO, in its 1945 decorations circular, also came up with its own requirement, found nowhere in War Department policy, that half of all award recommendations (presumably including the Medal of Honor) would be for enlisted men.[75] Most subordinate commands issued their own decorations circulars or policy letters. The Fifth Army, for example, published two circulars in 1944 (shortly after the theater circulars came out).[76] These instructions fulfilled much the same function for the subordinate command that the theater circular had for War Department policy.

MTO circulars contained only a few direct references to the Medal of Honor. Among them was a statement that the theater commander did not have the authority to make the award and a brief description of the basis for the award.[77] Fifth Army circulars made no mention of the Medal of Honor. Both MTO and Fifth Army circulars, however, included general decorations policy bearing on the Medal of Honor. MTO Headquarters required that if an initiating officer lacked personal knowledge of a heroic act, then his recommendation had to be accompanied by "two affidavits from eyewitnesses or persons having knowledge."[78] Initial theater policy stipulated that recommendations were to be signed by "each commander concurring," leaving open the possibility that a commander who did not concur with a decoration recommendation did not have to forward it.[79] Beginning in March 1944, commanders were required to indicate their recommended approval or disapproval on proposed decorations.[80] Fifth Army policy, published the same month, was a model of clarity: "When a commander is not authorized to make an award, he will forward the recommendation through command channels stating his views, either favorable or unfavorable."[81] Though theater policy had not changed, in August 1944 the Fifth Army eliminated the provision from its decorations circular, perhaps because it was not practicing what it had been preaching five months earlier.[82] Suggestive, though not definitive, evidence indicates that several Medal of Honor recommendations not approved by certain commanders were never forwarded to the next-higher echelon. Before March 1944, the language in AR 600-45 was the likely reason; after that date, the reason for not forwarding disapproved recommendations is unclear.

Three examples illustrate different outcomes of the Medal of Honor recommendation process in the Mediterranean Theater of Operations in 1943. Technician Fourth Grade Martin Moritz, Second Medical Battalion, 30th Infantry Regiment, was recommended for the Medal of Honor for heroism in Sicily on 11 August 1943. An index card located in the records of the MTO adjutant general shows the path taken by Moritz's recommendation.[83] Received at the North African Theater of Operations Headquarters (MTO's predecessor organization, abbreviated NATO) on 23 October 1943, the recommendation was sent back to Moritz's unit for additional information and was returned to NATO Headquarters on 10 December. Three days later it was sent to the Army's adjutant general in Washington, who cabled disapproval back to the theater on 15 February 1944.[84] In the meantime, Lieutenant General George S. Patton, then Seventh Army Commander, had already awarded Moritz the Distinguished Service Cross.[85] This was the way the War Department expected the system to work.

In contrast, the Medal of Honor recommendation for Staff Sergeant Joe R. Harbeson of the 179th Infantry Regiment was initiated by his company commander on 22 July 1943 and approved by the regimental commander but was disapproved by the division and corps commanders. Patton, agreeing with the recommendation of the Seventh Army's decorations board, also disapproved and awarded Harbeson the Distinguished Service Cross on 11 September 1943.[86] There is no index card in the MTO records and no endorsement in Harbeson's awards case file located in the Seventh Army's records; thus there is no indication that the Medal of Honor recommendation was forwarded to theater headquarters or to the War Department.

MTO records do contain an index card for Captain John J. Kelly, Jr., of the 26th Infantry Regiment. He was originally recommended for a Distinguished Service Cross by his battalion and regimental commanders for valor in Sicily on 4 and 5 August 1943; both the division and the corps commanders recommended a Medal of Honor, and Patton concurred. But Eisenhower, then the NATO commander, disagreed, and Kelly received a Distinguished Service Cross.[87] The MTO index card documents receipt of the Medal of Honor recommendation at theater headquarters on 17 October 1943; the card also documents the dispatch of a letter on 23 October notifying Kelly's unit of the disapproval, but there is no entry indicating that the recommendation ever went to the War Department.[88] It is possible that Harbeson's and Kelly's recommendations were sent to Washington. Historical records, however extensive or meticulously kept, are rarely complete. The two recommendations may have been forwarded to the War Department in response to its 1946 request, but without the War Department's World War II Medal of Honor case files, that cannot be verified. (Unfortunately, with two or three exceptions, these case files have not been found and may have been destroyed.) Theater policy then in effect required only that concurring commanders sign the recommendations. Thus Patton, in Harbeson's case, and Eisenhower, in Kelly's case, may not have forwarded Medal of Honor recommendations that they did not approve or sign.

Fifth Army awards case files reveal compelling evidence that Medal of Honor processing irregularities occurred in the Mediterranean Theater even after clarification of the transmittal policy. On 26 March 1944, Captain Ralph C. Fisher, Sixth Armored Infantry Regiment, was recommended by his battalion commander for the Medal of Honor for heroic action in Italy. Though the award was approved by regiment and division, the corps commander, Major General Lucian K. Truscott, thought Fisher's exploits merited only a Distinguished Service Cross. Fifth Army Commander Lieutenant General Mark W. Clark's decorations board agreed.[89] On 20 April, the Fifth Army adjutant general's section sent a memorandum to Clark with the case file, the board results, and a proposed endorsement for Clark's signature transmitting the file to the theater commander and recommending a Distinguished Service Cross. Clark wrote a note to his deputy chief of staff on the memorandum: "No need go NATOUSA. Award DSC. Straighten G-1 out on this."[90] Clark's refusal to transmit Fisher's Medal of Honor recommendation directly violated policy stipulated in NATO Circular 26, dated 6 March 1944, and Fifth Army Circular 23, of 20 March 1944.

Fisher's was not an isolated case in the Fifth Army. Between August 1944 and February 1945, Private First Class William K. Nakamura (442nd Regimental Combat Team), Lieutenant Colonel Ray J. Ericksen (135th Infantry Regiment), Staff Sergeant Everett C. Knight (133rd Infantry Regiment), and Technician Fifth Grade James K. Okubo (a medic assigned to the 442nd) were all recommended for the Medal of Honor. Clark disapproved Nakamura's and Ericksen's recommendations; Truscott, who succeeded Clark as Fifth Army commander early in 1945, disapproved Knight's and Okubo's.[91] The first three received Distinguished Service Crosses while Okubo's award was downgraded to a Silver Star.[92] There is no index card for any of these four in MTO records. In contrast, cards do exist for First Lieutenant James M. Doyle, 337th Infantry Regiment, and Captain William W. Galt, 68th Infantry Regiment. Both officers had been recommended for the Medal of Honor, and the index cards show that both recommendations were favorably endorsed by the Fifth Army commander and the Theater commander and were then transmitted to the adjutant general in the War Department. The War Department disapproved the medal for Doyle in September 1944 but awarded it to Galt in January 1945.[93]

The Mediterranean Theater handled the Medal of Honor in another unusual way. Late in December 1943, Theater Commander Eisenhower wrote to Fifth Army Commander Clark, "The number of Medals of Honor awarded to date to individuals of this theater seems unreasonably low in proportion to the total number of such awards."[94] Eisenhower suggested that Clark screen Distinguished Service Cross recommendations and send the most outstanding ones to theater headquarters to be considered for the Medal of Honor.[95] Clark's staff reviewed not only recommendations but also the Distinguished Service Crosses that had already been awarded. The Staff selected nine for Clark to review but recommended only seven for forwarding to theater headquarters. In the end, Clark approved six.[96] Early in March 1944, General Jacob L. Devers, Eisenhower's replacement, approved the six that Clark had recommended and sent them to the War Department, which awarded Medals of Honor to four.[97] Obviously, the line between the valor meriting a Medal of Honor and that required for a Distinguished Service Cross was indistinct and very much open to interpretation. As described in chapter 1, a precedent existed for this unusual procedure. Less than a week after the armistice ending World War I, General John J. Pershing, Commander of the American Expeditionary Force, had ordered a review of all Distinguished Service Cross recommendations and awards to see if any merited a Medal of Honor.

Clark's special review was questionable in another respect, however. At least one of the Distinguished Service Cross recommendations that Clark considered but did not select—the award to Lieutenant Colonel Joseph B. Crawford of the 15th Infantry Regiment—had originally been a Medal of Honor recommendation that had not been forwarded to theater headquarters. The reason, apparently, was that Crawford's Distinguished Service Cross and one awarded to Second Lieutenant Edwin F. Gould had been personally presented by President Roosevelt, and in the words of one officer involved, it "may be desired to leave the cases as they are."[98] Whatever the reason, Clark vetoed sending the two up to theater headquarters.[99] Crawford's Medal of Honor recommendation and probably several others were never forwarded to the War Department.

## Medal of Honor Policy and Practice in the European Theater of Operations

More than half of the Army's total awards in World War II went to soldiers and airmen serving in the European Theater of Operations (ETO). They received 142 of the Army's 294 Medals of Honor, nearly 2,500 of the approximately 4,700 Distinguished Service Crosses, and about two-thirds of the 75,000 Silver Stars.[100]

As in other theaters and commands, War Department instructions governed the European Theater's overall decorations policy, and theater headquarters supplemented that guidance with circulars, letters, and messages for subordinate commands.[101] This policy directed them to establish decorations boards, delegated authority to award the Distinguished Service Cross to specified commanders in January 1944, and provided a sample form for submitting decoration recommendations.[102] Lower echelons, particularly army groups and armies, also issued their own decorations policy circulars and letters.[103]

In October 1944, the 12th Army Group, Commanded by General Omar N. Bradley, instituted a quota system for its subordinate units for the Distinguished Service Cross and the Silver and Bronze Stars.[104] Designed to ensure greater uniformity and fairness in recognizing acts of gallantry, the system was based on the authorized strength of about 13,000 of an infantry division for each week engaged in "offensive combat." For the Distinguished Service Cross, each division so engaged was entitled to three awards (2.5% of 1% of 13,000).[105] The system did not function well. There was an obvious difficulty determining the meaning of "offensive combat"; the defense of Bastogne, for example, might not qualify. Some commanders interpreted the policy as a mandate rather than the "guide" it was intended to be and consequently did not recommend deserving cases for awards because their unit's quota had been reached. Finally, the system was not adopted theater-wide; the Sixth Army Group did not adopt it.[106]

Because the army group lacked award authority, the 12th Army Group did not apply its quota system to the Medal of Honor. As in the MTO, there were only brief references to the Medal in the decorations policy published by European Theater Headquarters or its subordinate commands. Theater policy regarding eyewitness testimony for decorations mirrored the nearly impenetrable language of AR 600-45. If the officer who recommended an award did not have "personal knowledge" or was not an eyewitness, then the testimony of two persons having "personal knowledge" or who were eyewitnesses had to accompany the award.[107] The First Army's policy was more direct. If the initiating officer was not an eyewitness, then two eyewitness statements had to be obtained and submitted.[108] When the War Department returned several Medal of Honor recommendations for lack of adequate evidence, ETO Headquarters required that future recommendations "contain sufficient eyewitness

52     The Exclusion of Black Soldiers from the Medal of Honor

Lt. Gen. George S. Patton, Jr., Commander of the Third Army, pinning the Silver Star on PFC Ernest A. Jenkins, 176th Quartermaster Corps, 16 August 1944, for his heroism in the capture of Chateaudun, France. U.S. Army Photograph, National Archives and Records Administration, courtesy Col. William A. DeShields, U.S. Army (Retired).

accounts in detail to definitely establish" that the heroism met the Medal of Honor's high standard.[109] On the more significant question of the forwarding of Medal of Honor recommendations, European Theater policy was brief but indirect. Noting that the War Department awarded the Medal, it stated (cramming as many negatives into a single sentence as possible), "Recommendations for awards not requiring War Department action will not be forwarded to this headquarters if not approved by an army or air force commander, or higher commander."[110] Somehow avoiding the potential for confusion, nearly all European Theater commanders forwarded Medal of Honor recommendations up the chain of command regardless of their own personal evaluation of merit. In its postwar study of awards and decorations in the European Theater, the command's General Board, which produced analyses of every aspect of the War, noted that despite the difficulty in differentiating among degrees of heroism, the Medal of Honor was "very well handled by all echelons."[111] At least for the approval/disapproval process in the European Theater, that conclusion seems justified.

In the ETO, recommendations for Medals of Honor traveled a generally uniform route that involved favorable or unfavorable evaluations by commanders at as many as eight echelons prior to reaching the War Department for final action.[112] The Medal of Honor recommendation for Sergeant Jose M. Lopez, a Heavy Machine Gunner with Company K of the 23rd Infantry Regiment, illustrated the process. Lopez's heroism "above and beyond the call of duty" occurred on 17 December 1944 during the Battle of the Bulge. Repeatedly exposing himself to enemy fire over a seven-hour period, Lopez continued to operate his machine gun against oncoming tanks and infantry, killing more than 100 Germans and saving his company from being overrun. Initiated by his company commander, Lopez's Medal of Honor recommendation was favorably endorsed, in turn, by the commanders of the 23rd Infantry Regiment, the Second Infantry Division, the V Corps, the First Army, and the 12th Army Group as well as the European Theater's assistant chief of staff for Personnel (G-1). General Eisenhower, the Theater Commander, also approved it, as did the War Department.[113]

Besides those recommendations on which all commanders agreed, there were many on which they were divided. The Medal of Honor awarded on 24 March 1945 to Second Lieutenant Jimmie W. Monteith, Jr., for heroism on D-Day was not favorably endorsed by the V Corps and First Army commanders or by the 12th Army Group's decorations board. General Bradley, however, recommended a Medal of Honor, and so did Eisenhower, noting to his chief of staff, Lieutenant General Walter Bedell Smith: "I must say the thing looks like a M. H. to me. This man was good."[114] Though certainly important, Eisenhower's favorable endorsement did not always, in split-opinion cases, persuade the War Department. For example, the Medal recommended for First Lieutenant Shirley R. Landon of the 313th Infantry Regiment, disapproved in theater only by the Ninth Army commander, was also disapproved by the War Department.[115] There were also several instances of Distinguished Service Cross proposals that were elevated to Medal of Honor recommendations somewhere along the command chain. The Seventh Armored Division raised the Distinguished Service Cross originally recommended at battalion level for Captain Howard Ingling of the Medical Corps to a Medal of Honor. Succeeding echelon commanders, including Eisenhower, concurred, but the War Department did not.[116] The War Department did, however, approve Medals of Honor originating as Distinguished Service Crosses for Sergeant Day G. Turner of the 319th Infantry Regiment and Private First Class Ernest W. Prussman of the 13th Infantry Regiment.[117]

Whatever the command level approving or disapproving a Medal of Honor, or the balance of opinion among the echelons, standard procedure in the European Theater was to forward all Medal of Honor recommendations to the War Department.[118] In at least six cases, the only favorable recommendation in the theater chain of command came from the initiating unit.[119] In five of those, the War Department agreed that the heroic act did not merit the Medal of Honor. In the sixth, however, Washington reached a different conclusion, approving the Medal for Staff Sergeant Clyde L. Choate of the 601st Tank Destroyer Battalion, in spite of disapprovals by the Third Infantry Division and Seventh Army commanders and General Eisenhower.[120]

The record of overall integrity in the processing of recommendations for the Medal of Honor in the European Theater was nearly tarnished in the handling of the award initiated for Brigadier General Frederick W. Castle, Commander of the Fourth Bomb Wing (Provisional), for heroism over Germany on 24 December 1944. Approved by the Third Air Division commander, it was not favorably endorsed by either the Eighth Air Force or the U.S. Strategic Air Forces commanders. The recommendation did not reach Eisenhower's headquarters until late August 1945. As Eisenhower's assistant chief of staff for personnel explained: "The original recommendation for the Medal of Honor was not forwarded to this headquarters by Hqs, USSTAF after they had disapproved it, and awarded General Castle the Distinguished Service Cross (posthumously). It was withdrawn from USSTAF files after an inquiry as to its present whereabouts was received from the War Department." The G-1 recommended a Distinguished Service Cross, and Eisenhower agreed, but the War Department awarded Castle the Medal of Honor.[121] Given the general treatment of Medal of Honor recommendations in the European Theater, Castle's case seems likely to have been an isolated instance of irregularity. Once in the European Theater system, Medal of Honor recommendations were very likely to reach the War Department.

## Medal of Honor Policy and Practice in Pacific Commands

Soldiers and airmen fighting in the Pacific received 80 Medals of Honor, over 1,200 Distinguished Service Crosses, and nearly 14,000 Silver Stars—figures roughly comparable to the Mediterranean Theater's totals but well below those for the European Theater.[122] Since most African-American combat units, particularly the 93rd Infantry Division, belonged to forces under General Douglas MacArthur, this analysis focuses on decorations policy and practice in his command. Although a commander's attitudes and personality everywhere influenced awards, possibly in no case were these factors more pronounced than with Douglas MacArthur in the Pacific.

Probably recognizing that his forces would soon have their backs to the wall and knowing what the value of awards could mean in such circumstances, MacArthur issued his decorations policy less than a week after the Japanese attack.[123] A series of policy letters coalesced into regulation form in August 1943, and a new version was issued each year thereafter.[124] The late 1945 edition was longer and contained more details than even AR 600-45. These formal policy instruments were faithful to War Department guidelines; but what distinguished MacArthur's decorations policy was how tightly he controlled it and how jealously he guarded his own authority over Medal of Honor recommendations and Distinguished Service Cross awards. MacArthur did not establish a decorations board at his headquarters until after January 1945.[125] He retained sole authority to award the Distinguished Service Cross, delegating it under very limited circumstances only to the Tenth Army commander late in the war.[126] Finally, he withheld from the War Department those Medal of Honor recommendations that he had disapproved, releasing them on only two occasions, after formal requests from Washington.

In its initial decorations policy letters, MacArthur's headquarters spread the fuzzy language infecting AR 600-45 to subordinate commands. Almost immediately, MacArthur's command tried to deal with the lack of definition in the terms "extraordinary heroism" and "gallantry in action." Simply stating that an individual had been heroic or gallant was not sufficient, asserted the January 1942 policy letter. "The act or acts which constitute heroism or gallantry must be described in detail."[127] After almost a year's experience with award recommendations received from the field commands, MacArthur's headquarters staff had to confront the conundrum of "personal knowledge" and eyewitness testimony. The headquarters declared that proposed awards for heroism containing such statements as "I have personal knowledge of the mission of July 28, 1942," were inadequate; it told subordinate units that "the only 'personal knowledge' must of necessity be that of an actual eyewitness" and added that the testimony of one or more eyewitnesses had to be attached to each recommendation.[128]

Policy in MacArthur's commands regarding the transmission of award recommendations remained constant from 1941 through 1945. Each decoration case was to be submitted separately through command channels and was to state either the favorable or unfavorable views of the commanders through whom it passed.[129] In May 1942, lower echelons were told that only the War Department could award the Medal of Honor and that recommendations for it were to be "forwarded through this Headquarters."[130] That was the first and last time MacArthur's decorations policy instruments said anything about Medal of Honor recommendations passing through his headquarters on the way elsewhere. In fact, General MacArthur did not forward to the War Department those Medal of Honor recommendations that he disapproved.

Several incidents in 1942–43 involving the Medal of Honor in the Pacific may explain MacArthur's actions. In March 1942, MacArthur himself received the Medal of Honor. Proposed and largely written by General Marshall, the award was controversial for two reasons. First, MacArthur had abandoned his troops in the Philippines to avoid capture and to continue the war from Australia. Though MacArthur had been ordered to leave the Philippines by Washington, many thought his leaving was an act of personal cowardice. Second, others questioned whether MacArthur's "gallantry and intrepidity at the risk of his life" actually met the standards for the Medal of Honor.[131]

In 1942, MacArthur had left Lieutenant General Jonathan M. Wainwright in command of Army forces in the Philippines. Following their surrender that same year, the War Department proposed that Wainwright be awarded the Medal of Honor and asked for MacArthur's views. MacArthur, who had already awarded a Distinguished Service Cross to Wainwright, fiercely opposed a Medal of Honor, telling General Marshall that Wainwright's actions "fell far short of the requirements for the award" and stating that he, MacArthur, could not recommend it without revealing information about Wainwright that might later lead to "embarrassing repercussions."[132] Marshall and Stimson elected not to challenge MacArthur at that time, but in 1945, after Wainwright's release from confinement by the Japanese, President Truman presented the Medal to him at a ceremony in the White House.[133]

The controversy over a Medal of Honor for Major General Robert L. Eichelberger, who commanded I Corps in New Guinea late in 1942, also provoked MacArthur's undeniably territorial attitude toward the Medal. Originally submitted to MacArthur's headquarters by Eichelberger's chief of staff following the hard-fought victory at Buna, the recommendation was disapproved by MacArthur, who awarded the Distinguished Service Cross but did not forward the Medal of Honor recommendation to the War Department.[134] Not to be denied, Eichelberger had another officer on his staff personally deliver the recommendation to the War Department. When queried about it by the Army adjutant general in August 1943, MacArthur reacted furiously, urging that no Medal of Honor be approved, threatening that he might have to reveal damaging information about Eichelberger, and raging against officers who went out of channels to achieve their objectives.[135] The Distinguished Service Cross stood.

Less than a month later, MacArthur received a message from Marshall pointing out that the Distinguished Service Cross citations for Lieutenant Commander Charles Pearson and Captain Charles Mike Smith, both of whom served as liaisons with guerrilla forces in the Philippines, indicated that "these officers might be entitled to Medal of Honor. Request your views."[136] Here was a direct affront to MacArthur's judgment, and he responded with characteristic forcefulness: "The service performed by them falls far below the standard maintained in this command for the award of the Medal of Honor."[137] The Distinguished Service Crosses that MacArthur had awarded to Pearson and Smith were not elevated.

Whatever the merits of these cases, the fact was that MacArthur did not forward to Washington those Medal of Honor recommendations that he disapproved. General Marshall was not inclined to force the issue until the war was nearly over. On 28 July 1945, the Army chief of staff cabled MacArthur requesting that any Medal of Honor recommendations being retained by his headquarters, including those for which a Distinguished Service Cross had been awarded, be forwarded to the War Department.[138] Ordered to do so, MacArthur complied and sent seven cases to Washington.[139] The Medal of Honor recommendation for Sergeant Leonard C. DeWitt had been in MacArthur's headquarters since the summer of 1943 and First Lieutenant Leland Walker's since the summer of 1942.[140] The War Department disapproved all seven, validating MacArthur's award of the Distinguished Service Cross in each case.[141]

At this point, MacArthur's cooperation with the War Department stopped. No more disapproved Medal of Honor recommendations left MacArthur's headquarters for another year and a half despite a War Department message of May 1946 requesting them and despite a visit by a staff officer from the Pentagon seeking them out.[142] In December 1946, the Army's G-1, Major General W. S. Paul, wrote Brigadier General W. A. Beiderlinden, his counterpart on MacArthur's staff:

> The War Department on several occasions has directed [your headquarters] to send to the War Department all disapproved ... MH cases which you have on file.... Again, when Col. Hyzer of my office visited your headquarters he discussed the matter with Colonel Hackett and one of your Adjutant General officers explaining why it was necessary that the War Department have these cases.... We still have not yet received this information although I believe The Adjutant General has written on several occasions since. Our lack of this information in the War Department is embarrassing. We receive many inquiries from outside the War Department, particularly from Congress, concerning recommended awards and some of the correspondence refers to these cases which we have never seen.[143]

In January 1947, Beiderlinden responded that the recommendations would be forthcoming but would be incomplete because there was no way of knowing how many Medal of Honor recommendations might have been disapproved by subordinate units and because many records in MacArthur's own headquarters had been lost or destroyed in the course of its movements throughout the Pacific.[144] Finally, in March 1947, the War Department received information on 11 disapproved Medal of Honor recommendations.[145] In June, it sent letters disapproving 9 of the recommendations and upholding the Distinguished Service Crosses previously awarded.[146] (The Army's files do not show formal action on the other 2 recommendations, although neither received a Medal of Honor.) The War Department's formal disapproval of the Pacific Medal of Honor cases in 1945, and again in 1947, demonstrated that the issue went beyond the War Department's need to be informed about actions taken in the field to avoid possible public embarrassment. Rather, the issue was who in the Army had the authority to make final decisions on the Medal of Honor.

## Conclusion

War Department officials admitted that there were inequities in awards distribution during World War II but always asserted that instances of injustice were rare. The Medal of Honor, the Army consistently maintained, was awarded solely on the basis of merit and without regard to rank, Army status, race, creed, or any other factor. Although no written policy was found that contradicts the official position, the question of what was practiced remained contentious. Many African Americans were convinced that racial discrimination occurred in valor awards in spite of the written policy, just as discrimination pervaded so many other aspects of Army life.

Decorations policy, beginning with AR 600-45, was often vague, resulting in differing interpretations of its meaning. With respect to the Medal of Honor, policy ambiguity had its greatest impact on the process for submitting award recommendations. Some commanders believed that they had the authority to disapprove a proposed Medal of Honor and were not required to transmit it to higher headquarters unless their recommendation was favorable. Other commanders were probably well aware of the correct submission procedures but, for reasons of their own, elected not to follow them. Differing interpretations of this process by field commanders may have prevented a significant, though undetermined, number of recommendations from being considered by the War Department Decorations Board, where a uniform standard of merit could be applied.

As succeeding chapters will show, there is some indication that Medals of Honor were proposed for at least four African-American soldiers, but no written recommendations or other concrete evidence beyond statements by individuals many decades later have been discovered.

# Notes

1. "War Department Decorations and Awards, 7 December 1941 through 30 June 1947," Dept. of the Army, 30 June 1947, folder "200.6, 1 April 47–31 July 47," Box 693, Decimal 200.6, G-1 Decimal File, June 1946–48, Record Group (RG) 165, Washington National Records Center (WNRC), Suitland, Md. Purple Heart and Army Commendation awards were not included in the total.
2. *Ibid.*, p. 5.
3. "Statement of the Honorable Robert P. Patterson, Reviewing the Report of the Doolittle Board," War Department Press Release, 25 June 1946, folder "RPP/Off. Enl. Men (Doolittle Board) SAFE," Box 5, Secretary of War Subject File (Safe File), 27 September 1945–24 July 1947, RG 107, National Archives (NA), Washington, D.C.
4. Minutes of Meeting No. 15, Joint Board to Study Decorations, Report of the Heroism Committee, Section III (Miscellaneous Subjects), 8 March 1948, folder "Minutes of Joint Board to Study Decorations and Medals," Box 1515, Joint Board Decorations and Medals Studies, 1945–51, Personnel Policy Board, Assistant Secretary of Defense (Manpower, Personnel and Reserve), RG 330, NA.
5. Patterson Statement, 25 June 1946.
6. "Appendix: World War II Medal of Honor Recipients," in Edward F. Murphy, *Heroes of WWII* (New York: Ballantine Books, 1991), pp. 375–95.
7. U.S. Department of the Army, Public Information Division, *The Medal of Honor of the U.S. Army* (Washington, D.C.: U.S. Government Printing Office, 1948), p. 21.
8. Three editions of Army Regulation (AR) 600-45 spanned the war years: AR 600-45, "Award and Supply of Decorations for Individuals," 8 August 1932; AR 600-45, "Decorations," 22 September 1943; and AR 600-45, "Decorations," 27 June 1950. The Army published formal changes to the regulation at irregular intervals in the interim between editions. A collection of World War II War Department regulations and circulars is in the Modern Military Records Branch of the National Archives.
9. AR 600-45, 8 August 1932, paragraph (para) 7; AR 600-45, 22 September 1943, para 9.
10. *Medal of Honor of the United States Army*, p. 21.
11. "War Department Decorations and Awards," 30 June 1947, p. 5.
12. AR 600-45, 22 September 1943, para 10.
13. *Ibid.*, para 13.
14. "War Department Decorations and Awards," 30 June 1947, p. 5.
15. Colonel Guy M. Talcott letter to Major General J. E. Sloan, 17 May 1946, attached to Major General J. E. Sloan memorandum for the deputy chief of staff, "War Department Decorations," 1 July 1946, folder "200.6, 1 Jul 46–15 July 46," Box 694, Decimal 200.6, G-1 Decimal File, June 1946–48, RG 165, WNRC.
16. *Ibid.*
17. AR 600-45, 22 September 1943, para 16. The Army gradually modified the "officer only" policy. In a late 1946 letter to Pennsylvania Senator Joseph F. Guffey, Patterson wrote: "I agree with you ... that any officer or enlisted man should be allowed to initiate recommendations for any decoration. Actually this can be done and frequently has been done in the past. It appears in some instances that regulations which authorize 'any officer' to initiate a recommendation have been misinterpreted to mean that no one else can submit the facts for proper consideration." (Robert P. Patterson letter to Senator Joseph F. Guffey, 29 November 1946, folder "200.6, Rewards, Badges, Decorations and Citations," Box 203, Decimal 200.6, Office, Administrative Assistant to the Secretary of War, Coordination and Records, Decimal File, Feb 1946–Jun 1947,

RG 107, NA.) Change 11 (19 May 1947) to the 1943 edition of AR 600-45 provided that "any individual having knowledge of heroism" could submit a recommendation.

18. AR 600-45, 8 August 1932, paras 7 and 16; AR 600-45, 22 September 1943, paras 9 and 20.

19. AR 600-45, 8 August 1932, para 16.

20. War Department Circular 391, 3 December 1942.

21. AR 600-45, 22 September 1943, para 20.

22. Change 11 (19 May 1947) to the 1943 edition of AR 600-45 called for "eyewitness statements."

23. Interview of G. D. Gardner by Mr. Huntington, 20 May 1947, folder 12, Box 293, Medal of Honor U.S. Army, 1946–48, News Branch, Public Information Division, U.S. Army Chief of Information, RG 319, NA. Colonel Gardner was assigned to the Awards and Decorations Branch, Office of the Army Adjutant General, during the war and served as principal liaison between the Adjutant General's Office and the War Department Decorations Board.

24. Murphy, *Heroes of WWII*, pp. 375–95.

25. Brigadier General M. G. White memorandum for the president, War Department Decorations Board, 27 March 1943, "Decorations," with excerpt from notes made by the secretary of war after the 26 March 1943 cabinet meeting, folder "200.6, 1943–44," Box 344, Decimal 200.6, G-1 Decimal File, 1942–June 1946, RG 165, WNRC.

26. Stimson defended the Medals of Honor awarded by the Army in a letter to the President, 17 April 1943, folder "Medal of Honor," Box 351, *Ibid*.

27. Major General M. G. White, memorandum for the chief of staff, 7 April 1944, "Award of Decorations," folder "200.6," Box 341, *Ibid*.

28. Geoffrey Perret, *There's a War to Be Won: The United States Army in World War II* (New York: Ballantine Books, 1991), pp. 462–63.

29. Albert F. Gleim and George B. Harris III, *Distinguished Service Cross Awards for World War II*, rev. 2d ed. (Fort Myer, Va.: Planchet Press, 1991). The following Army medical personnel received the Medal of Honor: Private First Class Desmond T. Doss, Private Harold A. Garman, Corporal Thomas J. Kelly, Technician Fourth Grade Laverne Parrish, and Technician Fifth Grade Alfred L. Wilson.

30. Report of Trends in the Negro Press, 11 June 1945 and 14 August 1945, Analysis Branch, News Division, U.S. Army Bureau of Public Relations, folder "Negro Press," Box 223, Subject File, 1940–1947, Civilian Aide to the Secretary, Office, Assistant Secretary of War, RG 107, NA.

31. Report of Trends, 23 August 1945, folder "Negro Press," Box 223, and Report of Trends, 15 April 1946, folder "Press Analysis," Box 238, both in *Ibid*.

32. Report of Trends, 7 November 1945, folder "Negro Press," Box 233, *Ibid*. Research for this report uncovered no corroborating evidence that Carter was nominated for the Medal of Honor. See chapter 4.

33. Interview of Truman K. Gibson by John A. Cash and Daniel K. Gibran, 12 March 1994, Chicago, "Men like Marshall and others—Eisenhower—absolutely believed in the inferiority of blacks," said Gibson.

34. *Ibid*.

35. See, especially, the more than 30 linear feet of records of the Civilian Aide to the Secretary of War in RG 107, NA.

36. Trezzvant W. Anderson letter to Lieutenant General Willard S. Paul, 5 February 1948, folder "200.6, Rewards, Badges, Medals, etc., 11/21/45-11/23/45," Box 423, Decimal 200.6, Army Adjutant General Decimal File, 1940–45, RG 407, NA.

37. Richard A. Woods letter to President Truman, 2 October 1945, and Olyus

Hood letter to President Truman, 9 October 1945, folder "357F (Sep 45–Dec 45)," Box 1048, Official File, Papers of Harry S Truman, Truman Library, Independence, Mo.; and C. F. Hopson letter to President Truman, 13 March 1946, folder "291.2, 1 Jan 46–Mar 46," Box 799, Decimal 291.2, G-1 Decimal File, June 1946–48, RG 165, WNRC.

38. Hopson letter to President Truman, 13 March 1946.

39. Secretary to the president, William D. Hassett, letter to Richard A. Woods, 6 November 1945, folder "357F (Sep 45–Dec 45)," Box 1048, Official File, Papers of Harry S Truman, Truman Library; and Major General W. S. Paul letter to C. F. Hopson, 13 March 1946, folder "291.2, 1 Jan 46–31 Mar 46," Box 799, Decimal 291.2, G-1 Decimal File, June 1946–48, RG 165, WNRC.

40. Major General J. E. Sloan memorandum for G-1, War Department General Staff, 20 November 1945, folder "200.6, 16 Oct 45–31 Dec 45," Box 341, Decimal 200.6, G-1 Decimal File, 1942–June 1946, RG 165, WNRC; War Department Decorations Board Memorandum No. 1, 2 January 1946, folder 12, Box 293, Medal of Honor U.S. Army, 1946–48, News Branch, Public Information Division, U.S. Army Chief of Information, RG 319, NA.

41. Senator Joseph F. Guffey letter to Secretary of War Robert P. Patterson, 24 October 1946, folder "200.6, Rewards, Badges, Medals, etc., 10/21/46–10/25/46," Box 356, Decimal 200.6, Army Adjutant General Decimal File, 1946–1948, RG 407, NA.

42. Patterson letter to Guffey, 29 November 1946. The Third Infantry Division received 36 of the 226 Medals of Honor awarded to the 89 divisions the Army fielded. The next-highest totals belonged to the First Infantry Division with 16 and the 36th Infantry Division with 14.

43. This is a composite sketch drawn from a review of hundreds of the Army's World War II decorations case files. There are, of course, exceptions to the contents of particular case files, as there are to the routing of each through field headquarters. The most useful records collections containing Medal of Honor case files and illustrating their routing are the awards case files of the First, Third, Fifth, Sixth, and Seventh Armies; the records of the Awards and Decorations Branch, Adjutant General, Mediterranean Theater of Operations; the records of G-1, 12th Army Group; and those of the deputy theater commander and the secretary, General Staff, European Theater of Operations.

44. G. D. Gardner interview, 20 May 1947; Personnel Division G-1 to War Department Decorations Board, 15 December 1942, "Recommendations for the Award of the Medal of Honor and the Distinguished Service Medal," folder "200.6, 1943–1944," Box 344, Decimal 200.6, G-1 Decimal File, 1942–June 1946, RG 165, WNRC; and Major General S. G. Henry memorandum for the deputy chief of staff, 30 May 1945, "Operation of the War Department Decorations Board," Box 524, Decimal 334, G-1 Decimal File, 1942–June 1946, RG 165, WNRC. The president and the secretary of war (except in a few cases, such as the Medals of Honor bestowed on General Douglas MacArthur and Lieutenant General Jonathan M. Wainwright, and Roosevelt's intervention in March 1943, discussed above) appear to have played an essentially *pro forma* role in approving Medal of Honor recommendations.

45. Notes for conference with deputy chief of staff, 12 May 1945, "Operation of the War Department Decorations Board," Box 524, Decimal 334, G-1 Decimal File, 1942–June 1946, RG 165, WNRC.

46. Major General E. S. Adams letter to Mr. Huntington, 16 June 1947, folder 12, Box 293, Medal of Honor U.S. Army, 1946–48, News Branch, Public Information Division, U.S. Army Chief of Information, RG 319, NA; G. D. Gardner interview, 20 May 1947.

47. Major General J. E. Sloan memorandum for the deputy chief of staff, 30

March 1945, "Personnel for the War Department Decorations Board," folder "War Department Decorations Board," Box 524, Decimal 334, G-1 Decimal File, 1942–June 1946, RG 165, WNRC; Major General J. E. Sloan memorandum for the deputy chief of staff, 1 July 1946, "War Department Decorations," folder "200.6, 1 Jul 46–15 Jul 46," Box 694, Decimal 200.6, G-1 Decimal File, June 1946–48, RG 165, WNRC.

48. Adams letter to Huntington, 16 June 1947.

49. Notes for conference with deputy chief of staff, 12 May 1945; War Department Decorations Board Memorandum No. 1, 2 January 1946; and G. D. Gardner interview, 20 May 1947.

50. Sloan memorandum for the deputy chief of staff, 1 July 1946. General Sloan served until July 1946 and was replaced by Major General Harold R. Bull, who had held a number of high-level staff positions and commanded the Fourth Infantry Division in the European Theater of Operations during the War.

51. Major General J. E. Sloan memorandum for the assistant chief of staff, G-1, 9 April 1945, "Distribution of Information to War Department Decorations Board," folder "War Department Decorations Board," Box 524, Decimal 334, G-1 Decimal File, 1942–June 1946, RG 165, WNRC.

52. Major General J. E. Sloan Memorandum for the Deputy Chief of Staff, 30 March 1945.

53. *Ibid.*

54. Brigadier General K. S. Bradford memorandum for the chief of staff, 14 April 1945, "Personnel for the War Department Decorations Board," and Major General J. E. Sloan memorandum for the assistant chief of staff, G-1, 5 November 1945, "Recommendation for Reorganization of War Department Decorations Board," both in folder "War Department Decorations Board," Box 524, Decimal 334, G-1 Decimal File, 1942–June 1946, RG 165, WNRC.

55. War Department Decorations Board Memorandum No. 1, 2 January 1946. As they had under Adams, members voted on cases individually, in turn. If the vote of the panel members was not unanimous, then the three met to discuss the case. Sometimes the entire board membership considered particular cases.

56. Major General W. S. Paul memorandum for deputy chief of staff, 14 December 1945, "Processing of Decoration Cases," folder "200.6, 16 Oct 45–31 Dec 45," Box 341, Decimal 200.6, G-1 Decimal File, 1942–June 1946, RG 165, WNRC; Colonel W. E. Thurman memorandum for the assistant chief of staff, G-1, 19 December 1945, "Processing of Decoration Cases," folder "200.6, Sec IV, Cases 301–," Box 153, Decimal 200.6, 1944–45, Office of the Chief of Staff, Security Classified General Correspondence, 1942–47, RG 165, NA.

57. Colonel W. E. Thurman Memorandum for the Assistant Chief of Staff, G-1, 24 January 1946, "Processing of Decoration Cases," folder "200.6," Box 353, Decimal 200.6, 1947, Office of the Chief of Staff, Security Classified General Correspondence, 1942–47, RG 165, NA.

58. Talcott letter to Sloan, 17 May 1946.

59. Sloan memorandum for G-1, War Department General Staff, 20 November 1945.

60. Major General J. E. Sloan memorandum for the deputy chief of staff, 31 August 1945, "Operations Report of War Department Decorations Board for August 1945," folder "200.6, Sec III, Cases 221-300," Box 153, Decimal 200.6, 1944–45, Office of the Chief of Staff, Security Classified General Correspondence, 1942-47, RG 165, NA.

61. WARCOS Message to CINCAFPAC, 28 July 1945, folder "200.6, #5," Box 3328, GHQ SWPA/AFPAC, Adjutant General, General Correspondence, 1944–46, RG 338, WNRC. All theaters may have been similarly notified. See Lieutenant Colonel

P. C. Hyzer memorandum for General Paul, 28 December 1945, "Personnel on War Department Decorations Board," Box 524, Decimal 334, G-1 Decimal File, 1942–June 1946, RG 165, WNRC.

62. WARCOS Message for CG USFET Main, CINCAFPAC, CG MIDPAC, CG MTO, 17 May 1946, folder "200.6, 16 Jul 45–31 Jul 45," Box 342, Decimal 200.6, G-1 Decimal File, 1942–June 1946, RG 165, WNRC.

63. *Ibid.*

64. War Department Circular 5, 8 January 1942.

65. Change 6 (28 October 1942); AR 600-45, 8 August 1932.

66. AR 600-45, 22 September 1943, para 8b(1).

67. AR 600-45, 8 August 1932, para 16b.

68. Change 3 (18 August 1942); AR 600-45, 8 August 1932.

69. AR 600-45, 22 September 1943, para 20a(1).

70. Change 11 (19 May 1947); AR 600-45, 22 September 1943. Actually, the Army did not achieve perfect clarity until the 27 June 1950 edition of AR 600-45: "Whenever a recommendation for the award of a decoration is disapproved, the disapproving officer will indicate the specific reason or reasons for such action. The disapproval of a recommendation by an officer subordinate to the commander having authority to award the decoration will not alone constitute authority for the return of the recommendation to the initiator."

71. "War Department Decorations and Awards," 30 June 1947, p. 6. Before December 1944, the MTO's predecessor was the North African Theater of Operations (NATO), commanded by General Eisenhower through the end of 1943; until August 1944 by Lieutenant General Jacob L. Devers, who was senior American but Deputy Allied Theater Commander; and by General Joseph T. McNarney through the end of the war. MTO/NATO was the American component of Allied Force Headquarters (AFHQ).

72. The major MTO/NATO decorations circulars were NATO Circular 50, 5 April 1943; NATO Circular 126, 2 July 1943; NATO Circular 26, 6 March 1944; NATO Circular 89, 10 July 1944; MTO Circular 73, 12 May 1945; and MTO Circular 82, 24 May 1946, all in Boxes 1549–51, MTO Adjutant General, Headquarters Records, RG 492, WNRC.

73. NATO Circulars 50 and 26, MTO Circular 73.

74. NATO Circular 26, para 2.

75. MTO Circular 73, para 7j.

76. Fifth Army Circular 23, 20 March 1944, folder "200.6, Awards and Decorations (G-2 Section)," Box 65, Fifth Army Awards Case Files, RG 338, WNRC; Fifth Army Circular 44, 19 August 1944, folder "165-1.12, 5th Army, G-1 Circulars 5–49, 19 Feb–19 Sep 44," Box 2076, Fifth Army, RG 407, WNRC.

77. NATO Circulars 126, 26, and 89, and MTO Circulars 73 and 82 are all identical in this respect.

78. NATO Circular 126, para 9a(2).

79. *Ibid.*, para 9a(7).

80. NATO Circular 26, para 9d; NATO Circular 89, para 10d; MTO Circular 73, para 7e; MTO Circular 82, para 11f.

81. Fifth Army Circular 23, IV 2.

82. Fifth Army Circular 44, 19 August 1944, mentions transmittal of decoration recommendations only in the context of unit awards.

83. Index Card, Technician Fourth Grade Martin D Moritz, Box 1643, Index Cards for Awards and Decorations, Awards and Decorations Branch, MTO Adjutant General, RG 492, WNRC. These records contain 15,000 to 20,000 alphabetically arranged

index cards on individuals whose decoration recommendations were processed by MTO/NATO Headquarters during the War.

84. *Ibid.*

85. *Ibid.* Awarding a lesser decoration within a commander's award authority while awaiting approval of a higher decoration was a normal, though not universal, practice. If the higher award was approved, the General Order awarding the lesser decoration was revoked. This procedure had the advantage of speedily recognizing valor on the battlefield.

86. Staff Sergeant Joe R. Harbeson Decoration Case File, folder "200.6, 1943–1944," Box 79, Seventh Army Awards Case Files, RG 338, WNRC.

87. Captain John J. Kelly, Jr., Decoration Case File, *Ibid.*

88. Index Card, Captain John J. Kelly, Jr., Box 1641, Index Cards for Awards and Decorations, Awards and Decorations Branch, MTO Adjutant General, RG 492, WNRC.

89. Captain Ralph C. Fisher Decoration Case File, folder "AG 200.6, Spec. Binder 14, GO 73, 77," Box 315, Fifth Army Awards Case Files, RG 338, WNRC.

90. *Ibid.* NATOUSA was the acronym for North African Theater of Operations, U.S. Army. There is no index card in MTO records for Captain Fisher.

91. Private First Class William K. Nakamura Decoration Case File, Box 321; Lieutenant Colonel Ray J. Ericksen Decoration Case File, Box 318; Staff Sergeant Everett C. Knight Decoration Case File, Box 321; Technician Fifth Grade James K. Okubo Decoration Case File, Box 319; all in Fifth Army Awards Case Files, RG 338, WNRC. The 442nd Regimental Combat Team was the highly decorated Japanese-American infantry unit that fought in both the Mediterranean and the European Theaters.

92. *Ibid.*

93. Index Card, First Lieutenant James M. Doyle, Box 1639, and Doyle Decoration Case File, Box 314; Index Card, Captain William W. Galt, Box 1639. Doyle's decoration recommendation originated as a Distinguished Service Cross and was approved by the regimental and division commanders for that award. The Fifth Army decorations board recommended a Medal of Honor, and Clark concurred with the upgrade.

94. Headquarters NATO letter for Commanding General Fifth Army, 28 December 1943, "Awards of the Medal of Honor," folder "AG 200.6, Awards and Decorations, Binder 6," Box 321, Fifth Army Awards Case Files, RG 338, WNRC.

95. *Ibid.*

96. Captain William M. Jonas memoranda for deputy chief of staff, 7 January 1944, and 12 January 1944; "S" Note to General Clark, 14 January 1944; and Lieutenant General Mark W. Clark letter to commanding general, NATOUSA, 28 February 1944; all in *ibid.*

97. Lieutenant General Jacob L. Devers letter to the Army adjutant general, 8 March 1944, and AGWAR Message to Devers, 14 May 1944, Box 1349, Decimal 200.6, MTO Adjutant General, Formerly Classified General Correspondence, RG 492, WNRC; G-1 Action Memorandum, 7 April 1944, "Recommendation for the Award of the Medal of Honor," folder "Medal of Honor," Box 351, Decimal 200.6, G-1 Decimal File, 1942–June 1946, RG 165, WNRC.

98. Jonas memorandum for deputy chief of staff, 7 January 1944; "S" Note to General Clark, 14 January 1944.

99. *Ibid.*

100. "War Department Decorations and Awards," 30 June 1947, p. 6.

101. The most important general statements of theater-wide decorations policy were the following: ETO Headquarters letter, 14 September 1943, "Awards and Decorations," folder "200.6/2, Decorations and Awards Policy, 6/30/45–8/7/45," Box 16,

Decimal 200.6, ETO Secretary General Staff, Classified General Correspondence, 1944–45, RG 332, WNRC; ETO Circular 1, 3 January 1944, folder 38, Box 7, ETO Historical Division Administrative File, 1942–Jan 1946, RG 332, WNRC; ETO Circular 32, 20 March 1944, and ETO Circular 56, 27 May 1944, folder "European Command Policy," Box 2, ETO Adjutant General, Records Pertaining to Awards and Decorations, General Correspondence, 1945–46, RG 332, WNRC.

102. For decorations boards, see ETO Headquarters letter, 2 December 1943, "Delegation of Authority to Award Decorations and Decorations Boards," folder "200.6," Box 30, Decimal 200.6, ETO Adjutant General, Classified General Correspondence, 1942–46, RG 332, WNRC; ETO Headquarters letter, 16 December 1943, "Decorations Boards," folder "Policy File of Awards, Vol I," Box 51, Decimal 200.6, 12th Army Group Adjutant General, Administrative Branch Decimal File, 1943-45, RG 331, NA; ETO Headquarters letter, 22 March 1944, "Decorations Boards," folder "Awards and Decorations, 200.6, Committee No. 76," Box 96, ETO General Board, G-1 Section, Correspondence, 1944-45, RG 332, WNRC. For delegation of awards authority, see ETO Headquarters letter, 2 December 1943; ETO Circular 9, 30 January 1944, folder "Distinguished Service Cross 200.6, #2 of 2," Box 41, First Army Awards Case Files, RG 338, WNRC. For the sample decoration submission form, see ETO Headquarters letter, 12 June 1944, "Awards and Decorations," folder "Policy File of Awards, Vol I," Box 51, Decimal 200.6, 12th Army Group Adjutant General, Administrative Branch, Decimal File, 1943–45, RG 331, NA.

103. See, for example, the detailed instructions contained in First Army Circular 66, 18 May 1944, "Awards and Decorations," folder "200.6," Box 29, Decimal 200.6, First Army Adjutant General, General Correspondence, 1940–47, RG 338, WNRC; First Army Circular 2, 4 January 1945, "Awards and Decorations," folder "Miscellaneous Records, 200.6, #1 of 2," Box 44, First Army Awards Case Files, RG 338, WNRC.

104. 12th Army Group Headquarters letter, 31 October 1944, "Awards and Decorations," folder "Policy File of Awards, Vol I," Box 51, Decimal 200.6, 12th Army Group, Adjutant General, Administrative Branch, Decimal File, 1943–45, RG 331, NA; 12th Army Group Headquarters letter 8 January 1945, "Awards and Decorations," folder "Miscellaneous Records, 200.6, #1 of 2," Box 44, First Army Awards Case Files, RG 338, WNRC. The 12th Army Group's major subordinate units included the First, Third, and Ninth Armies and their assigned corps and divisions. Established during the War, the Bronze Star was awarded either for heroic achievement in action or for meritorious service in support of combat operations. When awarded for valor in combat, the Bronze Star ranked in order of precedence just below the Silver Star.

105. *Ibid.*

106. Report of the General Board, United States Forces European Theater, "Awards and Decorations in a Theater of Operations," G-1 Section, Study Number 10, pp. 5–7 (undated, but sometime in late 1945 to early 1946), Box 2, Reports of the General Board, USFET, Records of the U.S. Army, Dwight D. Eisenhower Library, Abilene, Kan.; Colonel John L. Ames letter to Major General Willard S. Paul, 12 August 1946, folder "200.6, 14 June 1946," Box 695, Decimal 200.6, G-1 Decimal File, June 1946–48,RG 165, WNRC.

107. ETO Headquarters letter, 12 June 1944, "Awards and Decorations."

108. First Army Circular 2, 4 January 1945, para 4b and Appendix 1, para 2a.

109. ETO Headquarters letter, 6 March 1945, "Recommendations for Award of Medal of Honor," Box 16, Decimal 200.6, Third Army Adjutant General, General Correspondence, RG 338, WNRC.

110. ETO Circular 32, 20 March 1944, para 8c.

111. Report of the General Board, "Awards and Decorations in a Theater of Operations," pp. 1, 8.

112. Three groups of records—the files of Lieutenant General Benjamin Lear, Eisenhower's deputy theater commander during the first half of 1945; the files of the ETO General Staff secretary; and those of General Omar N. Bradley's 12th Army G-1—were particularly useful in revealing this process. The records contain summaries of many Medal of Honor cases prepared by the headquarters staffs to assist Eisenhower and Bradley in making their own recommendations. These summaries include a narrative description of the heroic act, the results of the action of the theater or army group's decorations board, and the recommendation of each lower echelon.

113. Sergeant Jose M. Lopez Decoration Case File Summary, folder "L," Box 3, Decimal 200.6, ETO Deputy Theater Commander, General Correspondence, 1945, RG 332, WNRC. The War Department did not always go along with unanimous Medal of Honor recommendations. See, for example, the decoration case file summary of Staff Sergeant Edward A. Thielen, Jr., folder "200.6, Decorations and Awards, 8/8/45–10/10/45," Box 16, Decimal 200.6, ETO General Staff Secretary, Classified General Correspondence, 1944–45, RG 332, WNRC.

114. Second Lieutenant Jimmie W. Monteith, Jr., Decoration Case File Summary, folder "Awards and Decorations to Individuals and Units, Volume I," Box 21, 12th Army Group G-1, Morale Branch, Decorations and Awards, 1944–45, RG 331, NA; and folder "200.6, Decorations and Awards, 1944," Box 15, Decimal 200.6, ETO General Staff Secretary, Classified General Correspondence, 1944–45, RG 332, WNRC.

115. First Lieutenant Shirley R. Landon Decoration Case File Summary, folder "L," Box 3, Decimal 200.6, ETO Deputy Theater Commander, General Correspondence, 1945, RG 332, WNRC.

116. Captain Howard H. Ingling Decoration Case File Summary, folder "I," *Ibid.*

117. Sergeant Day G. Turner Decoration Case File Summary, folder "T," Box 2, Decimal 200.6, ETO Deputy Theater Commander, General Correspondence, 1945, RG 332, WNRC; Private First Class Ernest W. Prussman Decoration Case File Summary, folder "Awards and Decorations to Individuals and Units, Volume II," Box 21, 12th Army Group G-1, Morale Branch, Decorations and Awards, 1944–45, RG 331, NA.

118. Among them are Medal of Honor recommendations for at least three members of the 442nd Regimental Combat Team: Private Barney F. Hajiro, Private George T. Sakato, and Sergeant Larry T. Tanimoto. See the decoration case file summaries for each in Boxes 2 and 3, Decimal 200.6, ETO Deputy Theater Commander, General Correspondence, 1945, RG 332, WNRC. None of the three recommendations were favorably endorsed beyond brigade level (the command echelon directly above the 442nd Regimental Combat Team).

119. See the decoration case file summaries for Second Lieutenant Neil M. Chapin, Staff Sergeant Clyde L. Choate, Captain Edward J. Hackett, and Sergeant Edwin J. Masching in Boxes 3 and 4, Decimal 200.6, ETO Deputy Theater Commander, General Correspondence, 1945, RG 332, WNRC; First Lieutenant Theodore R. Ellsworth, folder "200.6, Decorations and Awards, 8/8/45–10/10/45," Box 16, Decimal 200.6, ETO General Staff Secretary, Classified General Correspondence, 1944–45, RG 332, WNRC; and Corporal Dale W. Jeanneret, folder "Awards and Decorations to Individuals and Units, Volume II," Box 21, 12th Army Group G-1, Morale Branch, Decorations and Awards, 1944–45, RG 331, NA.

120. Choate Decoration Case File Summary, and Murphy, *Heroes of WWII*, p. 378.

121. Brigadier General Frederick W. Castle Decoration Case File Summary, folder "200.6, Decorations and Awards, 8/8/45–10/10/45," Box 16, Decimal 200.6, ETO General Staff Secretary, Classified General Correspondence, 1944–45, RG 332, WNRC; and Murphy, *Heroes of WWII*, p. 377.

122. "War Department Decorations and Awards," 30 June 1947, p. 6.

123. United States Army Forces in the Far East (USAFFE) Headquarters letter, 14 December 1941, "Award of Decorations," folder "AG 220.5 (1941)," Box 4381, Decimal 200.6, USAFFE (1), General Correspondence, RG 338, WNRC.

124. The most significant decorations policy statements issued by MacArthur's various headquarters after 1941 were the following: USAFFE Headquarters letter, 24 January 1942, "Award of Decorations," *Ibid.*; General Headquarters Southwest Pacific Area (GHQ SWPA) letter, 1 May 1942, "Award of Decorations," folder "200.63 Pending," Box 2781A, Decimal 200.6, GHQ SWPA Adjutant General, General Correspondence, 1942–45, RG 338, WNRC; GHQ SWPA letter, 3 November 1942, "Substantiation of Actions Constituting Basis for Award of Decorations," folder "200.6–200.63," Box T17, Decimal 200.6, GHQ AFPAC Adjutant General, General Correspondence, 1945, RG 338, WNRC; USAFFE Regulation 10-50, 17 August 1943, "Award of Decorations" (not found); USAFFE Regulation 10-50, 27 May 1944, "Award of Decorations," folder "98 USF1-1.12, Regulations (1-25 thru 20-65)," HQ USAFFE, 1943–45, RG 407, WNRC; and Army Forces Pacific (AFPAC) Regulation 10-50, 25 September 1945, "Award of Decorations," Box T1313, AFPAC Adjutant General, Regulations, RG 338, WNRC.

125. Draft USAFFE Headquarters General Order, January 1945, "Awards and Decorations Board," folder "200.6," Box 3331, Decimal 200.6, GHQ SWPA/AFPAC Adjutant General, General Correspondence, 1944–46, RG 338, WNRC; and R. J. M. [Major General Richard J. Marshall] memorandum, 28 June 1945, folder "200.6-200.62," Box T17, Decimal 200.6, GHQ AFPAC Adjutant General, General Correspondence, 1945, RG 338, WNRC.

126. GHQ AFPAC letter to Commanding General, Tenth Army, 15 August 1945, folder "200.6, Decorations and Awards, Hq Tenth Army," Box 101, Tenth Army Awards Case Files, 1944–46, RG 338, WNRC; and the decorations policy letters and editions of Regulation 10-50 reserving award of the Distinguished Service Cross to MacArthur and delegating award authority for only the Silver Star and lesser decorations.

127. USAFFE Headquarters letter, 24 January 1942, "Award of Decorations."

128. GHQ SWPA letter, 3 November 1942, "Substantiation of Actions Constituting Basis for Award of Decorations"; AFPAC Regulation 10-50, 25 September 1945, "Award of Decorations," para 5c(3) (b & d), settled on one eyewitness if it was the recommender, but two if the recommender was not an eyewitness.

129. USAFFE Headquarters letter, 14 December 1941, "Award of Decorations"; USAFFE Regulation 10-50, 27 May 1944, "Award of Decorations," para 4a; AFPAC Regulation 10-50, 25 September 1945, "Award of Decorations," para 5b. Despite the requirement to include either favorable or unfavorable comments (and the implication that decoration recommendations had to be forwarded to the next-higher echelon if the commander lacked authority), the policy was ambiguous and open to interpretation. In September 1944, the Eighth Army authorized division and corps commanders (and by extension, the Army commander) to disapprove and to return to the initiator even those decoration recommendations for which they did not have award authority (i.e., the Distinguished Service Cross). See Para 7c, Eighth Army Circular 4, 30 September 1944, "Decorations," folder "200.6, 1942-Jul–Dec 1944," Box 100, Eighth Army Awards Case Files, RG 338, WNRC.

130. GHQ SWPA letter, 1 May 1942, "Award of Decorations," para 2b(3).

131. D. Clayton James, *The Years of MacArthur, Volume II, 1941-1945* (Boston: Houghton Mifflin Company, 1975), pp. 125–32; Perret, *There's a War to Be Won*, p. 460.

132. MacArthur message to Marshall, 1 August 1942, WD 172, USAFPAC Correspondence, War Department, RG 4, Douglas MacArthur Memorial Library and Archives, Norfolk, Va.; James, *Years of MacArthur, Volume II*, pp. 150–51.

133. James, *Years of MacArthur, Volume II*, p. 151.

134. Paul Chwialkowski, *In Caesar's Shadow: The Life of General Robert Eichelberger* (Westport, Conn.: Greenwood Press, 1993), pp. 74–75.

135. MacArthur message to AGWAR, 23 August 1943, WD 483, USAFPAC Correspondence, War Department, RG 4, MacArthur Memorial Library; Chwialkowski, *Caesar's Shadow*, pp. 74–75; James, *Years of MacArthur, Volume II*, pp. 275–76.

136. Marshall message to MacArthur, 9 September 1943, WD 523, USAFPAC Correspondence, War Department, RG 4, MacArthur Memorial Library.

137. MacArthur message to Marshall, 11 September 1943, WD 525, *ibid.*

138. WARCOS message to CINCAFPAC, 28 July 1945, folder "200.6 #5," Box 3328, GHQ SWPA/AFPAC, Adjutant General, General Correspondence, 1944–46, RG 338, WNRC.

139. AFPAC Assistant Adjutant General letter to the Army Adjutant General, 11 August 1945, "Recommendations for Award of Medal of Honor," *ibid.*

140. DeWitt's Distinguished Service Cross had been awarded by General Order 52/1944 and Walker's by General Order 24/1942. See Gleim and Harris, *Distinguished Service Cross Awards*, pp. 22, 85.

141. War Department message to CINCAFPAC, 28 September 1945, folder "200.6, #10," Box 3330, Decimal 200.6, GHQ SWPA/AFPAC Adjutant General, General Correspondence, 1944–46, RG 338, WNRC.

142. WARCOS Message to CG USFET Main, CINCAFPAC, CG MIDPAC, CG MTO, 17 May 1946, folder "200.6, 16 Jul 45–31 Jul 45," Box 342, Decimal 200.6, G-1 Decimal File, 1942-June 1946, RG 165, WNRC; Major General W. S. Paul letter to Brigadier General W. A. Beiderlinden, 6 December 1946, folder "200.6, 14 Jun 46," Box 695, Decimal 200.6, G-1 Decimal File, June 1946–48, RG 165, WNRC.

143. Paul letter to Beiderlinden, 6 December 1946.

144. Brigadier General W. A. Beiderlinden letter to Major General W. S. Paul, 29 January 1947, folder "200.6, 14 Jun 46," Box 695, Decimal 200.6, G-1 Decimal File, June 1946–48, RG 165, WNRC.

145. GHQ Far East Command letter to War Department Director of Personnel and Administration, 1 March 1947, "Awards," folder "200.6, Rewards, Badges, Medals, etc., 3/10/47–3/12/47," Box 358, Decimal 200.6, Army Adjutant General, Decimal File, 1946–48, RG 407, NA.

146. Army Adjutant General letters to Commander-in-Chief, Far East, 11 June 1947 and 12 June 1947, folder "200.6, 1 Jan 47–31 Mar 47," Box 693, Decimal 200.6, G-1 Decimal File, June 1946–48, RG 165, WNRC.

*Chapter 4*

# Valor Awards to Black Soldiers in the European Theater of Operations

## Introduction

On the eve of the Normandy invasion in 1944, over 130,000 African-American soldiers were stationed in the British Isles.[1] Dispersed throughout the European Theater of Operations by V-E Day in May 1945, their numbers had doubled to nearly 260,000.[2] Assigned to more than 1,500 units of various types, nearly all were in service units, mostly ammunition, port, quartermaster, and truck companies.[3] There were only 22 black combat units—constituting about 9 percent of African-American troop strength in the theater.[4] Among these, tank battalions, tank-destroyer battalions, field artillery groups and battalions, and antiaircraft battalions experienced the most combat. Moreover, in the last two months of the War, approximately 2,800 black volunteer infantry replacements, usually organized into separate all-black platoons, joined and fought alongside white infantry and armored units.

This small number of combat units, in relation to the aggregate of black units, gives a somewhat misleading picture. Many African Americans in service units were exposed to enemy fire while performing their duties, and some, for short periods, assumed combat roles because of the rapidly changing conditions taking place near the front lines. For example, men of the 57th Ordnance Ammunition Company, who were supporting combat units pursuing German forces across France in 1944, unexpectedly encountered 65 German soldiers. Immediately involved in a firefight, they killed 50 and captured 15. One Silver and one Bronze Star, as well as two French Croix de Guerre, were won by soldiers in the 57th as a result of this action.[5]

Such displays of courage were common. Three African-American combat units—the 761st Tank Battalion, the Third Platoon of Company C of the 614th Tank Destroyer Battalion, and the 969th Field Artillery Battalion—received the Presidential Unit Citation, and many other units earned lesser awards.[6] Individual black soldiers received numerous decorations for valor, beginning with those earned by men of the 320th Anti-Aircraft Artillery Barrage Balloon Battalion and the 582nd Engineer Dump Truck Company on Omaha Beach on D-Day. First Sergeant Norman Day of the 582nd, for example, was awarded the Silver Star, the Purple Heart, and the British Distinguished Service Medal for heroically directing beach traffic under heavy shelling.[7]

Of the highest valor awards, African-American combat and service troops in the European Theater won a small, though significant, number of Silver Stars (about five dozen) and four Distinguished Service Crosses.[8] None received the Medal of Honor, but the names of several were mentioned as prospective candidates, and another one may have been formally recommended for the Medal by his company commander.

## Tank Battalions

Two black tank battalions—the 761st and the 784th—participated in combat in the European Theater. Like other separate armored battalions, these were normally attached to a division for varying periods and were often employed in specialized task forces. Committed to action in late 1944, members of both tank battalions received many decorations for valor. Of the two, the 761st had the more extensive combat role.

About 700 strong and equipped with M4 Sherman tanks, the 761st came ashore onto the Continent early in October 1944 and went into action the first week in November. Although a white officer commanded the unit, most of its other officers, including company commanders, and all of its enlisted men were black. Attached at various times to eight different divisions and three armies, the 761st was actively engaged almost continuously until the end of the War, fighting in France, Belgium, Luxembourg, Holland, Germany, and Austria. The battalion suffered 50 percent casualties from a variety of causes, including 34 killed in action. By the end of 1945, men of the 761st had been awarded 14 Silver Stars, 77 Bronze Stars (most for valor), and 304 Purple Hearts.[9]

The battalion first came under enemy fire on 7 November 1944 near Nancy in northeastern France, less than 50 miles from the German border. During this initial encounter, the commander, Lieutenant Colonel Paul L. Bates, was wounded and had to be evacuated.[10] For the next two weeks, the 761st operated with the 26th Infantry Division and General George Patton's Third Army and engaged in some of the toughest fighting the battalion would experience during the War.[11] In this short period, several of its men performed exceptional feats of heroism.

On 8 November 1944, a column of company A's tanks en route to Vic-sur-Seille ran into a roadblock. Staff Sergeant Ruben Rivers, commanding the lead tank, dismounted under fire, attached a cable from his tank to the roadblock, returned to his tank, and removed the obstacle. For bravery that enabled the company to capture the town that had been its objective, Rivers received a Silver Star.[12]

The next day, First Sergeant Samuel Turley of Company C, and Second Lieutenant Kenneth W. Coleman, one of its platoon leaders, saved the lives of many of their comrades while sacrificing their own. Stopped by a tank ditch and at the mercy of German guns, several of Company C's tanks were set on fire and disabled. Dismounting from their tanks, Turley, Coleman, and others in their tank crews held off the German attack while men from the other tanks retreated to safety under cover of the tank ditch. First Sergeant Turley had removed a .50-caliber machine gun from one of the tanks and, completely exposed to hostile fire, operated the machine gun until he was shot and killed. Both Turley and Coleman received the Silver Star posthumously.[13] Later observers believed the Silver Star awarded to Turley was insufficient recognition for such selfless heroism.[14] In 1948, Trezzvant Anderson, who served with the 761st, wrote to Lieutenant General Willard S. Paul (then the Army's G-1 but on 9 November 1944, the 26th Infantry Division commander) that what Turley had done "would have merited a Congressional Medal of Honor for some others."[15]

On 10 and 11 November, another 761st tanker, Lieutenant (then Sergeant) Warren G. H. Crecy, also earned a Silver Star for repeated acts of heroism under enemy fire while dismounted from disabled tanks.[16] Crecy proved to be one of the most aggressive fighters in the 761st and was much admired by the other men in the battalion. Their tribute to Crecy's warrior qualities was summed up by the caption below his picture in the battalion's unofficial history, *Come Out Fighting*: "... winner of the Silver Star Medal (it should have been the CMH), and holder of the reputation of being the 'baddest man in the 761st!' ... Slew more Germans than any other single man in the battalion."[17] Clearly, those associated with the 761st Tank Battalion believed that the bravery of Turley and Crecy was not sufficiently recognized or rewarded. Though their heroism was given some measure of recognition, as evidenced by the Silver Star, the adequacy of that recognition remains a contentious issue.

Never *officially* acknowledged was the heroism of Ruben Rivers one week after the gallantry he had displayed on 8 November. Major General Paul had pinned Rivers' Silver Star on him in the field for the action of removing the roadblock, even as the 761st's operations against the Germans continued.[18] On 16 November 1944, the tank Rivers was commanding hit a mine at a railroad crossing as Company A advanced toward the town of Guebling, France. Rivers was severely wounded. Though his leg was slashed to the bone, he declined an injection of morphine, refused to be evacuated, took command of another tank, and advanced with his company into Guebling the next day. Repeatedly

**Troops of the 761st Tank Battalion making last-minute adjustments to their weapons, 27 September 1944, at Wimbourne, England, prior to the unit's deployment into combat in France. U.S. Army Photograph, National Archives and Records Administration, courtesy Col. William A. DeShields, U.S. Army (Retired).**

refusing evacuation, Rivers continued to direct his tank's fire at enemy positions beyond the town through the morning of 19 November. At dawn that day, Company A's tanks advanced toward Bourgaltroff, their next objective, but were stopped by enemy fire. Captain David J. Williams, the company commander (who was white), ordered his tanks to withdraw and take cover. Rivers, however, radioed that he had spotted the German antitank positions: "I see 'em. We'll fight 'em." Rivers, joined by another A Company tank, opened fire. Soon Rivers' tank was hit, killing him and wounding the rest of the crew.[19]

Captain Williams maintained in 1994 that immediately after the action, he told Lieutenant Colonel Hollis E. Hunt, who had been sent to command the 761st after Bates was wounded, that Rivers deserved a Medal of Honor. According to Williams, Hunt told him to put it in writing. Williams said that he dictated the recommendation the next morning to Charles P. Ashby, the company clerk, who was responsible for processing decorations for the entire battalion. Both then went to Hunt with the typed recommendation. According to Williams, Hunt told him to dismiss Ashby. Hunt's only comment about the recommendation, according to Williams, was "Well, he's already got the Silver Star!" Hunt otherwise acted indifferently about the proposed Medal of Honor recommendation. When Williams asked him about it a few days later, Hunt replied that it was in channels.[20] Ashby, in an affidavit in 1993, recalled doing the paperwork.[21] Research for this study, however, failed to produce any official documents relating to a Medal of Honor recommendation for Rivers.[22]

Hunt died some years ago, but Williams believes Hunt was a racist who did not like him or seem to care about blacks.[23] Contemporary documents reveal some of Hunt's attitudes toward black soldiers. Interviewed in January 1945 about their performance, Hunt acknowledged some instances of heroism and ability, describing Rivers as an "excellent man." On the other hand, Hunt thought that black officers generally lacked initiative and that only about 15 percent of them met the standard demanded of white officers. In his view, blacks "developed animal foxiness" as they acquired combat experience, but black privates soldiered "only as a necessity"; deficient in their personal appearance and care of equipment, they were "lackadaisical" in observing orders and regulations and possessed a loyalty to superiors akin to "animal loyalty to [the] hand that feeds."[24]

Hunt stayed with the 761st for only three weeks and was replaced by Major John F. George, who commanded the unit until Bates returned on 17 February 1945. Given Williams' belief that Hunt disliked him, and Hunt's racial attitudes, the question arises why Williams did not pursue the matter after Hunt's departure. When asked in 1994 about his failure to do so, Williams explained that he was too busy fighting and that after the war ended, he was too occupied with school, family, and business. For many years, he simply wanted to forget his wartime experience. Then his energies were absorbed in the struggle to win the Presidential Unit Citation for the entire battalion.[25]

If racism influenced the processing of Ruben Rivers' Medal of Honor recommendation, then the poor personal relationship that Williams acknowledged he had with Hunt may also have been a factor. But since Williams could have resubmitted his recommendation after Hunt's departure, racial prejudice or personal animosity were only temporary obstacles. The lack of recognition of Rivers' heroism and the insufficient rewards for the bravery of others in the 761st Tank Battalion may have been the products of the unit's officers, who were aggressive on the battlefield, believed that bravery was the duty of all, and in the stress and chaos of the war and its immediate aftermath, did not always take the initiative to recommend decorations for their men. Williams may indeed have been too busy to follow up on his recommendation, but Lieutenant Colonel Bates, on the other hand, acknowledged that he never submitted any of the soldiers of the 761st for a Distinguished Service Cross or a Medal of Honor. His explanation for not doing so reveals just how

Lunch in England before the fighting, 26 September 1944. Company-grade officers in the 761st, from left to right, are Capt. David J. Williams, Capt. J. R. Lawson, Capt. Irwin McHenry, 1st Lt. Richard W. English, Capt. Ivan H. Harrison, and Capt. August W. Bremer. U.S. Army Photograph, National Archives and Records Administration, courtesy Col. William A. DeShields, U.S. Army (Retired).

crucial a commander's understanding of awards and the decoration process could be: "Frankly, I thought they [the three higher awards] came from God. I had a rough idea what the parameters were but my demands and my expectations and the parameters I used—my expectations—were so great from every damn one of them [the men in the 761st] that later I found out that for God's sake ... we had about eight people who deserved the Congressional Medal of Honor.... We had guys who got Bronze Stars who should have gotten it in terms of what other people got."[26]

Bates was encouraged to submit more recommendations for awards. In April 1945, Major General Willard G. Wyman, Commanding General of the 71st Infantry Division, to which the 761st was then attached, told Bates that men in the 761st had not received the decorations they deserved. He suggested that Bates should reconstruct actions as honestly as possible and submit the decoration recommendations. Wyman would sign them with no questions asked. Bates thereupon initiated about 40 recommendations—some Silver but mostly Bronze Stars.[27]

Whatever the reasons, it is inescapable that Staff Sergeant Ruben Rivers' heroism in action against the enemy from 16 to 19 November 1944—subsequent to his winning a Silver Star and bravery that cost him his life—has never been officially recognized by the Army or the nation. In 1946, Secretary of War Robert Patterson, addressing errors in wartime decorations, had promised, "Where corrective action is found possible and meritorious, you may be sure that it will be taken."[28]

The other black tank battalion employed in the European Theater was the 784th. Formally committed to combat on 1 January 1945, the 784th Tank Battalion fought in Holland and Germany with the Ninth Army and five of its divisions. Commanded entirely by white officers, the 784th suffered 24 killed in action among its 140 battle casualties. By July 1945, 8 Silver Stars and 51 Bronze Stars had been awarded to men of this battalion.[29]

## Tank-Destroyer Battalions

Two black tank-destroyer battalions—the 614th and the 827th—saw combat in the European Theater of Operations. Inadequately trained, the 827th was not prepared for the only combat it experienced for less than a month in January-February 1945. Enough elements of the unit performed so poorly that, following an investigation of its training and disciplinary problems, the 827th was not used in combat for the remainder of the War.[30] In contrast, the 614th Tank Destroyer Battalion compiled a first-rate combat record. One of its platoons earned a Distinguished Unit Citation and one of its black officers a Distinguished Service Cross.

The 614th entered combat at the end of November 1944 attached to the 103rd Infantry Division, with which it fought in France, Germany, and Austria until V-E Day. The battalion had only five white officers, including its commander, Lieutenant Colonel Frank S. Pritchard. Its firepower consisted of three-inch guns towed by half-tracks equipped with .50-caliber machine guns, which gave some protection to each ten-man crew (the soldiers had to dismount from the half-track to position, load, and fire the three-inch gun). In 155 days of combat, the 614th's losses included 17 killed, and 62 wounded in action, and 21 captured.[31]

The 614th earned its Distinguished Unit Citation little more than two weeks after going into combat. On 14 December 1944, Company C's Third Platoon joined a platoon of tanks from the 756th Tank Battalion and a rifle company of the 411th Infantry Regiment, forming a task force to assault the French town of Climbach, five miles from the German border and the Siegfried Line.[32] First Lieutenant Charles L. Thomas, commander of Company C, volunteered to lead the task force in a scout car. Around 2:00 P.M., about 700 yards from the town, the scout car was disabled by artillery fire, wounding

Thomas and another soldier in the vehicle and halting the task force. While helping others to get out of the scout car and directing the placement of the Third Platoon's three-inch guns, Thomas was wounded several more times. Nonetheless, Thomas refused evacuation until he was sure that the platoon commander knew what to do and was ready to carry on the fight. Thomas' brave actions under enemy fire enabled other task force elements to flank German positions in and around the town. For this extraordinary heroism, Thomas received the Distinguished Service Cross—the second awarded to an African-American soldier up to that point in the War and the first in the European Theater.[33]

For four hours, the tank destroyers fired their three-inch guns, .50-caliber machine guns, and small arms from an open field, suffering 50 percent casualties (3 killed, 17 wounded) and losing two of their four three-inch guns to enemy fire. By the time darkness fell, the Germans had withdrawn from the town.[34] The words of the Distinguished Unit Citation underscored the special courage and devotion to duty displayed by the Third Platoon: "During the firefight an ammunition shortage developed, and gun crews were reduced to skeleton size, one man loading, aiming, and firing, while the other men repeatedly traveled a distance of fifty yards through a hail of mortar and small arms fire to obtain shells from a half-track which had been set on fire by a direct hit from an enemy mortar shell. Heedless of possible injury, men continuously exposed themselves to enemy fire to render first aid to the wounded."[35] The Third Platoon's Distinguished Unit Citation was the first awarded to a black ground combat unit during the War and the first won by a unit assigned or attached to the 103rd Infantry Division.[36]

In addition to the Distinguished Unit Citation and Thomas' Distinguished Service Cross, four men in the Third Platoon received Silver Stars (two posthumously) and nine men received Bronze Stars, all for heroism outside of Climbach. One of the Bronze Stars went to Technician Fifth Grade Robert W. Harris, an ammunition truck driver with Company C. Recognizing that the Third Platoon's gun crews were running out of ammunition, Harris drove his fully loaded truck through enemy fire to within 25 yards of the platoon's gun positions even though the task force commander had told him that he would probably be killed. Harris then unloaded the truck and carried ammunition to each gun emplacement.[37]

After this early engagement, the men of the 614th continued to distinguish themselves in combat. For the entire War, they received 8 Silver Stars, 28 Bronze Stars, and 79 Purple Hearts.[38]

## Artillery Battalions

Black artillery units provided fire support and air defense from Normandy beaches to the heart of Germany. Black soldiers in these units—three field artillery groups, seven field artillery battalions, one antiaircraft artillery battalion, and one barrage balloon battalion—earned many individual awards for valor and several unit commendations, including a Distinguished Unit Citation. Word of the heroic performance of one of these soldiers, and the possibility that he was being considered for the Medal of Honor, reached as far as the White House staff.

The ten field artillery groups and battalions were the most numerous of the black combat units in Europe. Equipped with 155-mm howitzers, 8-inch howitzers, or 4.5-inch guns, these heavy-caliber units were used as corps artillery or as reinforcements for one or more divisions. The field artillery groups commanded by black officers often controlled white as well as black field artillery battalions, and the black battalions were directed by both black and white group headquarters, as the tactical situation demanded.[39] The first black field artillery units, the 333rd Field Artillery Group and the 333rd, 578th, and 969th Field Artillery Battalions, entered combat in July 1944; the last unit into combat was the 350th Field Artillery Battalion on 1 March 1945.[40] In comparison to infantry, tank, and tank-destroyer units, field artillery units usually operated at greater distances from the front lines and, with some dramatic exceptions, took correspondingly fewer casualties.

By war's end, the 969th Field Artillery Battalion was among the best known of African-American combat units of any type. Landing on Utah Beach on 9 July 1944, its batteries went into action the next day, firing 28 rounds.[41] By the end of November 1944, the battalion had fired over 20,000 rounds and several of its men would be recognized for heroism.[42] Sergeant Joseph J. Hamilton of Battery A received the Silver Star for gallantry in action in France on 30 July 1944, as did Privates First Class Robert L. S. Foreman and Lawrence Reynolds of Battery B, who were killed by an artillery shell on 1 November 1944 in Luxembourg after they had volunteered to repair several wire communications lines.[43]

In December the 969th, the 333rd Field Artillery Group, and the 333rd and 578th Field Artillery Battalions were caught up in the powerful German drive through the Ardennes Forest, an offensive that began on December 16 and turned into the Battle of the Bulge. All four units took part in the general defense of the besieged and surrounded town of Bastogne, Belgium, from 18 to 27 December 1944.[44] The 333rd Field Artillery Battalion's losses were so great (228 of the approximately 500-man unit were killed, wounded, or captured) that it remained a skeleton outfit for the rest of the War, never returning to combat.[45] The 969th and some of the shattered 333rd's remaining personnel and equipment, attached to the 101st Airborne Division, were inside the approximately half-mile defensive perimeter that had been established around Bastogne. From 21 to 27 December, they were completely surrounded. Because ammunition was short, the battalion fired only on targets seen by observers; at one point, the 101st's lines were within a few hundred yards of the battalion command post.⁴⁶ During the siege, the 969th's losses were 7 killed in action, 12 wounded, and 4 missing.⁴⁷ Summarizing a report on the 969th's role at Bastogne, its commander concluded: "There is no question but that this was our hardest test. The Battalion met the test and proved themselves. In spite of the unusual circumstances—Corps artillery being surrounded, in the midst of infantry fights, short on rations, casualties that hurt—the morale remained good [and] the Battalion as a whole only worked and fought harder. There was no complaining of hardships suffered and always faith that the enemy would be held until aid came."⁴⁸ For its performance at Bastogne, the 969th was commended by Major General Maxwell D. Taylor, the 101st Airborne Division Commander, and in February 1945 received the Distinguished Unit Citation, along with other 101st Division units.⁴⁹

After Bastogne, the 969th and the black 999th Field Artillery Battalion, which had also reached the Continent in July 1944, participated in late January and early February in the reduction of the Colmar Pocket—the German salient protruding into the southern flank of the Allied advance about 50 miles north of where the Franco-German border met Switzerland. For this operation, both were attached to French units.⁵⁰

At about this time, additional African-American field artillery units arrived in Europe. The groups and battalions entering combat after 1 February 1945 were the 349th and 351st Field Artillery Groups and the 350th and 686th Field Artillery Battalions. All of these late-arriving units spent relatively little time in combat.⁵¹

On 25 March 1945, the 349th Field Artillery Group and the 777th Field Artillery Battalion (which had been in action since October) were the first African-American combat units to cross the Rhine River.⁵² Just before crossing, the two black outfits were among the 104 artillery units whose 1,248 guns fired more than 200,000 rounds in a massive barrage. The 777th's gun crews fired 7 rounds in 36 seconds, the artillery pieces becoming so hot that they fired automatically. Of the 777th's 400 men, 2 were killed in action and 6 wounded during the battalion's six months in combat. In all, men of the unit received six Bronze Stars and eight Purple Hearts.⁵³

Of the two African-American air defense battalions engaged in combat in the European Theater, the 452nd Antiaircraft Artillery Automatic Weapons Battalion, commanded and staffed entirely by white officers, was the most active. Deployed to England in October 1943 and equipped with Swedish-made 40-mm Bofors guns, the 452nd defended U.S. installations until June 1944, when it landed at Normandy. On the Continent, the nearly 800-man 452nd principally defended field artillery battalions from air attack but also guarded command posts, bridges, and fuel dumps across France, Luxembourg, and Germany.⁵⁴

The 452nd ranked near the top of all ETO antiaircraft artillery units in downing enemy planes. With 67 German planes destroyed (and another 19 probably destroyed and 11 damaged), the 452nd, a towed unit, stood first among the 60 towed antiaircraft artillery units in the ETO in planes destroyed and third when both towed and self-propelled units were combined.[55] In the 452nd, 13 men were killed and 29 wounded.[56] In addition to Purple Hearts and Bronze Stars (given mostly for meritorious service rather than heroism), members of the battalion earned five Silver Stars, all of which were won by black enlisted men for acts of valor in France in late 1944.[57]

On 27 September 1944, two men from Shreveport, Louisiana—Staff Sergeant William Campbell of Battery C and Technician Fifth Grade Zeno H. Ellis of the 452nd's medical detachment—earned Silver Stars for going to the aid of 171st Field Artillery Battalion men who had been wounded by enemy shelling. While under fire themselves, Campbell and Ellis continued to treat the wounded even though surrounding units were withdrawing.[58] Little more than two months later, Private First Class Willie Jackson and Privates Samuel Johnson and Edward I. Swindell, all of Battery B, received Silver Stars for gallantry in action near Cappel, France, by helping to evacuate five wounded men of the 731st Field Artillery Battalion while under enemy artillery fire.[59]

The 320th Anti-Aircraft Barrage Balloon Battalion was the other African-American air defense unit to experience combat in the European Theater. The only American unit of its type in the theater and the only black combat unit engaged on D-Day, the 320th's mission was to use its silver-colored barrage balloons to help protect friendly troops from attack by low-flying enemy aircraft. On D-Day, elements of the 320th landed on both Omaha and Utah Beaches within four hours of the first assault forces. Though under continuous artillery, machine gun, and rifle fire, which killed and wounded several members of the battalion, the men of the 320th succeeded in getting their balloons ashore and flying. Over the next few days, the 320th's balloons accounted for three German planes destroyed. The unit's performance on the beaches earned the 320th a letter of commendation from General Dwight Eisenhower and individual awards for some of its soldiers.[60]

One of those soldiers, Corporal Waverly B. Woodson, Jr., was wounded in the groin by shrapnel when his LCT hit a floating mine at about 9:30 A.M. on D-Day. Once on shore, and after receiving treatment for his wound, Woodson, one of the 320th's medics, began aiding other wounded soldiers on the beach. For 30 continuous hours while under enemy fire, Woodson cared for more than 200 casualties. Even after being relieved at 4:00 P.M. on 7 June, Woodson gave artificial respiration to three men who had gone underwater during an LCT's landing attempt. Only then did Woodson seek further treatment for his own wound.[61]

Corporal Woodson received a Bronze Star for his heroism on D-Day, but there is some doubt about the kind of award that was originally recommended. The battalion's records reveal only that eight unidentified award recommendations left the unit for higher headquarters by letter on 20 June 1944.[62] After the War, the *Norfolk Journal and Guide* (VA) carried an American Negro Press release stating that the award was for a "Distinguished Service Medal" but had been held up by the 320th's white commander, Lieutenant Colonel Leon J. Reed, until it was too late for action to be taken.[63] The claim that Reed delayed official action beyond the time allowed was not accurate. On 22 August 1944, the 320th's message log referred to correspondence with the Ninth Air Defense Command, an Army Air Forces organization, concerning award recommendations for five men in the 320th, including Woodson.[64]

More intriguing was the note addressed to "Jonathan" and located in the Truman Library in the files of Phileo Nash, who in 1944 was the Special Assistant to the Director of White House Liaison in the Office of War Information (OWI). Although unsigned and undated, the note was probably written by Nash sometime in the late summer or early fall of 1944 to Jonathan Daniels, Administrative Assistant to President Roosevelt. An ETO press release dated 28 August 1944 describing Woodson's actions was attached. Stating that Woodson's commander had originally recommended him for a Distinguished Service Cross, the note's author explained what happened when the recommendation reached Lieutenant General John C. H. Lee's Communications Zone Headquarters (the Services of Supply of the ETO): "Lee's offices said the act merited a Congressional Medal, so the recommendation was reworded. The case is now in the awards committee of ETO. If the committee's action were speeded up, we would soon know whether he [Woodson] will get a Congressional Medal of Honor. This is a big enough award so that the President can give it personally, as he has in the case of some white boys."[65]

Woodson's decoration case file has not been found, and his individual personnel record was apparently destroyed in the fire at the National Personnel Records Center in St. Louis in 1973. A search of other pertinent files and collections yielded no documents about Woodson. Thus, it has not been possible to determine from the official record what award was originally recommended or whether higher echelons considered elevating the award.

## Volunteer Infantry Replacements

The German Ardennes counteroffensive in December 1944 intensified a need for infantry replacements in the European Theater, a need that had been apparent since the preceding summer.[66] To help meet the shortage, General Eisenhower, at Lieutenant General Lee's suggestion, called on black soldiers in European service units to volunteer for additional training and subsequent assignment as front-line infantry. Thousands responded, and many performed heroically on the battlefield. Though none received the Medal of Honor, three earned the Distinguished Service Cross.

Black soldiers of the 161st Chemical Smoke Generating Company, Third Army, laying smoke to cover bridge-building over the Saar River in Germany, 11 December 1944. U.S. Army Photograph, National Archives and Records Administration, courtesy Col. William A. DeShields, U.S. Army (Retired).

The call for troops went out from Lieutenant General Lee's headquarters by letter on 26 December 1944. Because the letter implied that the African-American volunteers would enter infantry units individually as required, Lieutenant General Walter Bedell Smith, Eisenhower's Chief of Staff, feared that it represented a break with the War Department's policy that the Army be segregated. Though General Eisenhower rewrote and reissued the letter, further clarification was needed to determine his intention that the black volunteers were to join white infantry outfits only in segregated units.[67]

Despite this confusion, more than 4,500 African-American soldiers volunteered. Among the requirements for selection were stipulations that the volunteers already had some prior infantry training and were willing to take reductions in rank to private or private first class. Nearly 3,000 received seven weeks' training at the 16th Reinforcement Depot near Compiègne, France. The program included training with the M-1 carbine, Thompson submachine gun, and other light and heavy machine guns, and familiarization with 60-mm and 81-mm mortars and some German weapons. Squad operations received the most emphasis; only one week was devoted to platoon tactics. No time was allotted for company training.[68]

By early March 1945, over 2,250 of the volunteers were ready for assignment to front-line units. Organized into platoons, they were met at the reinforcement depot by white officers and noncommissioned officers who were from the units they were to join and who would lead them in combat. Private First Class Leroy Kemp, in a letter to the colonel who ran the training program, spoke for himself and 11 of his comrades as they prepared to depart: "Sir ... if you are ever asked 'What do you think of the Negro soldier?' Please tell them 'We got tired of giving sweat so we went to give some blood.'"[69]

Including the several hundred men whose training was completed later, about 2,800 African-American soldiers, organized into 53 platoons, went to 8 infantry and 2 armored divisions. Each infantry division received at least 3 platoons, normally assigning one to a company in each of the division's 3 regiments. The Seventh Army got 16 of the platoons (about 800 soldiers), organized them into 4 provisional infantry companies, and assigned the companies to the armored infantry and tank battalions of the 12th and 14th Armored Divisions. The first volunteers reached their divisions in mid-March. Some received additional training; others went immediately into action.[70] Each soldier averaged twenty days in combat by the end of the War.[71]

With respect to battlefield performance, most contemporary—and later scholarly—assessments concluded that the experiment with black infantry volunteers was generally successful.[72] The unofficial history of the 310th Infantry Regiment observed that Company A's black platoon "carried the fight to the Germans with unusual ferocity. We were proud of them."[73] And the 60th Infantry Regiment's unofficial history stated that the black soldiers "eagerly volunteered for every patrol and vied with one another for the more dangerous jobs."[74] Brigadier General H. T. Mayberry, Assistant Division Commander of the 99th Infantry Division, recalled: "They would go anywhere their leaders would take them. Their performance was consistently good."[75]

The soldiers assigned to the 413th, 414th, and 415th Regiments of the 104th Infantry Division were among the most decorated of the black volunteers. Brigadier General Charles Lanham, the Assistant Division Commander, told the black warriors assembled to receive awards at a ceremony in Germany after the war, "I have never seen any soldiers who have performed better in combat than you."[76] At the ceremony, Major General Terry Allen, the 104th Infantry Division Commander, presented three Silver Stars and seven Bronze Stars to men of the black platoons.[77]

The citations for the three Silver Stars reveal the nature of the black soldiers' heroism. On 7 April 1945, Private Ben T. Brown of Company G of the 413th Infantry Regiment crawled 100 yards through machine-gun fire to give first aid to his wounded platoon leader, removed him to temporary cover, returned through the same murderous fire already traversed to find a medic, and then accompanied the medic back to the wounded platoon leader. A week later, Private June Jefferson, Jr., of Company A of the 414th Infantry Regiment, crossed over open terrain swept by fire from a German tank, entered the village where the tank was located, dropped grenades into its turret, and killed the tank's crewmen as they emerged. Returning to friendly lines, Private Jefferson then organized his platoon's successful assault on the enemy riflemen supporting the tank. Finally, on 13 April 1945, Private First Class Claude Pierce, also of the 414th's Company A, traversed open terrain under fire to remove men trapped in a burning tank as enemy artillery shells detonated around him. He then carried the more seriously wounded over 200 yards to safety.[78]

Though the total number has not been determined, there were other Silver and Bronze Star recipients among the black infantry volunteers. For example, Private First Class Edgar E. Zeno, G Company, 39th Infantry Regiment, Ninth Infantry Division, earned a Silver Star for gallantry in action on 7 April 1945 near Siedlinghausen, Germany. When his company encountered heavy machine gun fire, Zeno assaulted the enemy position across open terrain, firing a Browning automatic rifle. When he was 25 yards from the machine gun, Private First Class Zeno hurled a grenade and rushed the emplacement, killing seven Germans and wounding three.[79]

Three of the black soldiers who went into combat as volunteer infantry received the Army's second-highest decoration for heroism—the Distinguished Service Cross. One was awarded to Private First Class Willy F. James, Jr., of the 104th Infantry Division's much-decorated black contingent. Private First Class Jack N. Thomas earned a Distinguished Service Cross while in action with the Ninth Infantry Division's 60th Infantry Regiment. While fighting with the 56th Armored Infantry Battalion, Sergeant Edward A. Carter, Jr., won one of only five Distinguished Service Crosses earned by all personnel in the 12th Armored Division between mid-March and V-E Day (no one assigned to the division received a Medal of Honor in the War).[80] Accounts of the valor of these three black soldiers clearly demonstrated the extraordinary heroism that earned each one of them a Distinguished Service Cross.

After infantry training in France, Private First Class Willy F. James, Jr., became a member of the African-American platoon assigned to Company G of the 413th Infantry Regiment, 104th Infantry Division. On 7 April 1945, the 413th had established a bridgehead across the Weser River in the heart of Germany. To secure and expand the bridgehead, Company G was ordered to capture the town of Lippoldsberg. Private First Class James, first scout of the lead squad in the assault platoon attempting to seize some houses on the town's outskirts, was 150 yards out in front of his squad and the first to draw enemy fire. When joined by his platoon leader, James volunteered to advance farther to pinpoint enemy positions. Under fire the entire time, he made his way 200 yards across open terrain, observed the German positions for more than half an hour, and returned to his platoon with vital information.[81]

Based on the intelligence that Private First Class James had provided, the platoon launched its assault on the outlying buildings that were its original objective. James volunteered again, this time to lead a squad in the attack. During the assault, Private First Class James' platoon leader was hit by enemy sniper fire. Immediately going to his aid, again across open ground, Willy F. James, Jr., was killed by machine-gun fire. The bravery that cost Private First Class James his life inspired his platoon to reach its objective and contributed to the 413th Infantry Regiment's ability to enlarge its bridgehead over the Weser.[82]

Answering the call in December 1944 for volunteer infantry replacements, Private First Class Jack N. Thomas was one of the approximately 40 black soldiers in the separate platoon assigned to Company E of the 60th Infantry Regiment, Ninth Infantry Division.[83] During April 1945, the 60th Infantry Regiment was engaged in operations to reduce the pockets of German resistance in western Germany in the Ruhr Valley and the Harz Mountains. On 9 April, Company E's black platoon, reinforced by a bazooka team for antitank defense, was directed to investigate a German roadblock defended by a tank near the town of Herzgerode. Private First Class Thomas' squad and the bazooka team, with Thomas in the lead, approached to the right of the enemy position to knock out the tank. Deploying into a skirmish line, Thomas and the other men opened fire on the tank to keep enemy soldiers from manning it. Thomas advanced beyond the skirmish line and threw two hand grenades, which wounded several of the enemy. When heavy German fire from automatic weapons and small arms wounded the two bazooka team members, Private First Class Thomas, while under fire, ran to the bazooka position and fired his weapon twice, keeping the Germans away from the tank. As enemy fire continued, Thomas then picked up one of the bazooka men and carried him to safety across a 100-yard clearing.[84]

The recommendation for a Distinguished Service Cross for Private First Class Thomas reached Lieutenant General George S. Patton's Third Army Headquarters late in August 1945. There, the Third Army's decorations board unanimously disapproved the proposed award, recommending a Silver Star instead. General Patton did not agree. The handwritten letters "DSC" followed by the initial "P" are at the bottom of the recommendation.[85]

Assigned to the Seventh Army's Infantry Company No. 1 (Provisional), Staff Sergeant Edward A. Carter, Jr., found himself pressed almost immediately into combat when the company was attached to the 12th Armored Division's 56th Armored Infantry Battalion. At about 8:30 A.M. on 23 March 1945, Carter and his fellow rifle-squad members were riding on a tank advancing toward Speyer, Germany. Suddenly the tank began receiving bazooka and small arms fire from a large warehouse to its left front. After dismounting from the tank and taking cover, Staff Sergeant Carter volunteered to lead a three-man patrol across 150 yards of open field to reconnoiter the warehouse. When one man in the patrol was killed by intense small arms fire, Staff Sergeant

Carter ordered the other two back to a protected position from which they could provide covering fire as he advanced alone. Though one of the men was killed and the other wounded before reaching cover, Staff Sergeant Carter continued on through enemy fire. As he moved forward, Carter was first wounded three times in the left leg, then in an arm and, finally, a hand.[86]

Despite his five wounds, Staff Sergeant Carter, now crawling, kept moving under heavy enemy fire toward the objective. Within 30 yards of the warehouse, he took cover behind an earthen bank. After about two hours, eight German riflemen approached his position. Staff Sergeant Carter killed six and captured the other two. Using the two prisoners as a shield, Carter withdrew across the open field. Even after reaching safety, Staff Sergeant Carter would not let himself be evacuated until he had relayed full information about the enemy's position.[87]

After Carter's Distinguished Service Cross award was announced in October 1945, one African-American newspaper asserted that he had been shortchanged. Erroneously reporting that Carter had been wounded eight times, had destroyed two enemy machine-gun positions, had wiped out a mortar squad, and had killed 50 German soldiers and captured 2, the *Omaha Star* then charged: "The distasteful part of the story is the fact that even the feat and the recommendations of his superior officers that he be awarded the Congressional Medal of Honor brought him only the Distinguished Service Cross.... It would seem that the feat itself would be enough to bring him the top award; but even with the recommendations it didn't. There is some reason why he did not receive it in view of these facts; and the most logical one is that he was a member of the Negro race."[88]

The basis for the *Star*'s claim is unknown. The documentary record shows a recommendation for a Distinguished Service Cross originating with Carter's company commander on 10 July 1945. Given the long lapse between the date of the action (23 March 1945) and the date the award was submitted, it is possible that Carter's award recommendation began as a Medal of Honor and was then changed to a Distinguished Service Cross. Research for this study, however, has found no evidence to support such a hypothesis.[89]

## Conclusion

Fewer than 10 percent of African-American soldiers in the European Theater were in combat units. Since a much higher percentage of all soldiers in the Army served in combat organizations, the black soldier's opportunity, in general terms, to participate in combat and earn awards for valor was significantly less than that of his white counterpart. In spite of the diminished opportunity that flowed from the constraints imposed by segregation, black soldiers distinguished themselves on the battlefield. Indeed, when opportunity was nearly equal, as it was in the case of the volunteer infantry replacements, African-American soldiers earned Distinguished Service Crosses at a rate that matched or exceeded that of white soldiers.

Still, no African-American soldier received a Medal of Honor. Research in the Army's World War II records produced no documentary confirmation or evidence that a black soldier was ever recommended for the Medal. In the wartime period and after, some believed that there were black soldiers who had been recommended for the Medal and others who, by virtue of their heroic acts, should have been recommended for it. That they were not, in this view, was likely the result of racism. Evidence found many years after the War suggests that Staff Sergeant Ruben Rivers, for example, not only may have deserved but was, in fact, officially recommended for the Medal of Honor and that the racial prejudice of the acting battalion commander may have prevented the recommendation from going forward. Racism, however, does not completely explain why Rivers was not considered for the award, since Rivers' unit commanders who acknowledged his heroism and should have recommended him for the award failed to act within the constraints of the allotted time to see that his heroism was recognized.

## Notes

1. War Department Press Release, 13 August 1945, folder "July–August 1945," Box 105, Press and Radio News Releases, 1921–47, News Branch, Public Relations Division, Record Group (RG) 165, National Archives (NA), Washington, D.C.
2. *Ibid.*
3. T/O Colored Units, Continental and Foreign, 7 July 1945, Box 443, Decimal 291.2, G-1 Decimal File, 1942–June 1946, RG 165, Washington National Records Center (WNRC), Suitland, Md.
4. War Department Press Release, 13 August 1945.
5. Ulysses Lee, *The Employment of Negro Troops [United Stated Army in World War II]* (Washington, D.C.: U.S. Government Printing Office, 1966), p. 641.
6. By 1948, recommendations for a Distinguished Unit Citation for the 761st Tank Battalion had been disapproved three times. The unit finally received the award in 1978. See the extensive file of documents extending from 1945 to 1948, "Recommendation for Distinguished Unit Citation to 761st Tank Bn," folder "200.6, Rewards, Badges, Medals, etc., 11/21/45–11/23/45," Box 423, Decimal 200.6, Army Adjutant General Decimal File, 1940–47, RG 407, NA. During World War II, the Distinguished Unit Citation was awarded to units whose collective heroism in action against the enemy was the equivalent of that meriting the award of a Distinguished Service Cross to an individual. See "War Department Policy on Decorations and Awards," 10 January 1946, folder 12, Box 293, Medal of Honor U.S. Army, 1946–48, News Branch, Public Information Division, U.S. Army Chief of Information, RG 319, NA.
7. War Department Press Release, 13 August 1945.
8. Determining the total number of Silver Stars awarded to African-American soldiers in the European Theater would be extremely difficult, if not impossible. General Orders announcing awards did not specify race and often (for security) not even the unit designation. Five dozen is an estimate based on several months working in Army records.

9. War Department Press Release, 21 January 1946, folder "Jan-Mar 46," Box 110, Press and Radio News Releases, 1921–47, News Branch, Public Relations Division, RG 165, NA; Lee, *Employment of Negro Troops*, pp. 661–67; Dale E. Wilson, "The Army's Black Tank Battalions," *Armor*, March-April 1982, pp. 30–31.

10. Lee, *Employment of Negro Troops*, pp. 661-63. Bates did not return to the battalion until 17 February 1945. In the interim, the battalion was commanded until 29 November 1944 by Lieutenant Colonel Hollis E. Hunt, Executive Officer of the 17th Armored Group, and then by Major John F. George.

11. *Ibid.*; Wilson, "Black Tank Battalions," pp. 31–32.

12. 26th Infantry Division General Order 42, 2 December 1944, microfiche #789, Military Awards Branch, Total Army Personnel Command, Alexandria, Va.; Lee, *Employment of Negro Troops*, p. 664.

13. Lee, *Employment of Negro Troops*, p. 665.

14. Trezzvant W. Anderson letter to Lieutenant General Willard S. Paul, 5 February 1948, folder "200.6, Rewards, Badges, Medals, etc., 11/21/45–11/23/45," Box 423, Decimal 200.6, Army Adjutant General Decimal File, 1940–47, RG 407, NA; "Congressional Medal of Honor Conference: Focus on Warren G. H. Crecy, Ruben Rivers, and Samuel Turley," 27 February 1994, 761st Tank Battalion and Allied Veterans Association, Los Angeles, Calif., pp. 10–11.

15. Anderson letter to Paul, 5 February 1948.

16. *Ibid.*; War Department Press Release, 25 December 1944, folder "Releases-Negro-1943–1944," Box 243, Subject File, 1940–47, Civilian Aide to the Secretary, Office, Assistant Secretary of War, RG 107, NA; "Congressional Medal of Honor Conference," 27 February 1994, pp. 6–7.

17. Trezzvant W. Anderson, *Come Out Fighting: The Epic Tale of the 761st Tank Battalion* (Germany: Salzburg Druckerei und Verlag, 1945), pp. 102–3, Box 16792, 761st Tank Battalion, World War II Operations Reports, 1940–48, RG 407, WNRC.

18. Interview of Paul L. Bates and David J. Williams by John A. Cash, Elliott V. Converse III, Daniel K. Gibran, and Richard H. Kohn, 27 January 1994, Raleigh, N.C.

19. After escaping from the tank, one of the wounded crew members, evidently disoriented, ran toward enemy lines. His body was found later. *Ibid.* Affidavit of Theodore Weston, 22 June 1990; Affidavit of Homer A. Bracey, 25 June 1990; Affidavit of David J. Williams, 30 June 1990; all submitted with this report.

20. Interview of Bates and Williams, 27 January 1994.

21. Affidavit of Charles P. Ashby, 13 October 1993, submitted with this report.

22. Rivers' Individual Personnel Record could not be located at the National Personnel Records Center in St. Louis. Such files often contained the initial decoration recommendation as well as the citation for the decoration actually awarded. Rivers' record may have been destroyed in the 1973 fire at the Center.

23. Interview of Bates and Williams, 27 January 1994.

24. Interview of Lieutenant Colonel Hunt by Colonel George W. Coolidge, "Information on Colored Troops," January 1945, War Department Observers Board, folder "Southern Dist. U.K. Reports, 1944–45," Box, Inspection Tours Europe, 1941–45, Papers of Benjamin O. Davis, Sr., U.S. Army Military History Institute, Carlisle Barracks, Penn.

25. Interview of Bates and Williams, 27 January 1994.

26. *Ibid.*

27. *Ibid.*; Citation for Silver Star awarded to Private First Class George C. Blake for gallantry in action on 9 December 1944, 71st Infantry Division General Order 18, 7 May 1945, Box 11395, General Orders, 71st Infantry Division, World War II Operations Reports, 1940–48, RG 407, WNRC; War Department Press Release, 2 July 1945,

folder "July 45," Box 104, Press and Radio News Releases, 1921–47, News Branch, Public Relations Division, RG 165, NA.

28. Secretary of War Robert P. Patterson letter to Senator Joseph F. Guffey, 29 November 1946, folder "200.6, Rewards, Badges, Decorations, and Citations," Box 203, Decimal 200.6, Office, Administrative Assistant to the Secretary of War, Coordination and Records, Decimal File, Feb 1946–Jun 1947, RG 107, NA.

29. 784th Tank Battalion Report of Operations, 2 July 1945, folder "ARBN-784-0.3 (14641) Opn Rpt-784 Tank Bn, Jan-Jun 45," Box 16822, 784th Tank Battalion, World War II Operations Reports, 1940–48, RG 407, WNRC; Coolidge, "Information on Colored Troops"; Lee, *Employment of Negro Troops*, pp. 675–78.

30. Lee, *Employment of Negro Troops*, pp. 679–86. One member of the 827th earned a Silver Star. See 79th Infantry Division General Order 36, 8 March 1945, folder "TDBN-827-0.7 Journal 827th Tank Dest Bn," and folder "TDBN-827-0.3 (29841) Unit History Narratives - 827th Tank Dest Bn," in Box 23871, 827th Tank Destroyer Battalion, World War II Operations Reports, 1940–48, RG 407, WNRC.

31. Coolidge, "Information on Colored Troops"; War Department Press Release, 10 September 1945, folder "Aug-Sep 45," Box 106, Press and Radio News Releases, 1921–47, News Branch, Public Relations Division, RG 165, NA; 614th Tank Destroyer Battalion Initial Information Report, 9 July 1945, folder "TDBN-614-0.1, History 614th TD Bn, Jan 43-Nov 46," Box 23574, 614th Tank Destroyer Battalion, World War II Operations Reports, 1940–48, RG 407, WNRC; Lee, *Employment of Negro Troops*, pp. 667–74.

32. First Lieutenant Charles L. Thomas Decoration Case File, folder "200.6, 7th Army HQ Recommendation for Award, 1944 and 1945 (T)," Box 78, Seventh Army Awards Case Files, RG 338, WNRC.

33. Seventh Army General Order 58, 20 February 1945, folder "107-1.13, General Orders, Jan 1945-Mar 1946," Box 2581, Seventh Army, World War II Operations Reports, 1940–48, RG 407, WNRC; First Lieutenant Charles L. Thomas Decoration Case File; 614th Tank Destroyer Battalion Narrative Report, 14 December 1944, and S-3 Journal, 14 December 1944, both in Box 23574, 614th Tank Destroyer Battalion, World War II Operations Reports, 1940–48, RG 407, WNRC; War Department Press Release, 19 March 1945, folder "Mar 45," Box 97, Press and Radio News Releases, 1921–47, News Branch, Public Relations Division, RG 165, NA; Lee, *Employment of Negro Troops*, pp. 668–70. In 1943 in the Pacific, Private George Watson was posthumously awarded the first Distinguished Service Cross earned by an African-American soldier in World War II. See chapter 6.

34. War Department General Order 37, 1945, Box 23574, 614th Tank Destroyer Battalion, World War II Operations Reports, 1940–48, RG 407, WNRC; 614th Tank Destroyer Battalion Narrative Report, 14 December 1944; Lee, *Employment of Negro Troops*, pp. 668–70.

35. War Department General Order 37, 1945.

36. Lee, *Employment of Negro Troops*, p. 670.

37. 103rd Infantry Division General Order 88, 27 December 1944, and General Order 89, 28 December 1944, folder "TDBN 614-0.3 (21964)," Box 23575, 614th Tank Destroyer Battalion, World War II Operations Reports, 1940–48, RG 407, WNRC.

38. 614th Tank Destroyer Battalion Initial Information Report, 9 July 1945.

39. Lee, *Employment of Negro Troops*, p. 644. The field artillery group was a headquarters normally controlling three separate battalions.

40. *Ibid.*, pp. 644, 657.

41. 969th Field Artillery Battalion Unit Journal, 9 and 10 July 1944, folder "FABN 969-0.3 (6697), A/A Rpt 969 FABN, July-Aug 44, Oct-Dec 44," Box 20337,

969th Field Artillery Battalion, World War II Operations Reports, 1940–48, RG 407, WNRC.

42. Report After/After Action Reports from 1 to 30 November 1944, *ibid.*

43. 969th Field Artillery Battalion Unit Journal, 13 September 1944; Report After/After Action Reports from 1 to 30 November 1944; 969th Field Artillery Battalion Unit Journal, 1 November 1944; Report After/After Action Reports for the month of April 1945, folder "FABN 969-0.3 (6697), A/A Rpt 969 FABN, Jan-May 45," Box 20337, 969th Field Artillery Battalion, World War II Operations Reports, 1940–48, RG 407, WNRC; War Department Press Release, 18 June 1945, folder "June 45," Box 103, Press and Radio News Releases, 1921–47, News Branch, Public Relations Division, RG 165, NA.

44. Lee, *Employment of Negro Troops*, pp. 646–51. A total of 13 artillery units took part in the defense of Bastogne.

45. *Ibid.*, p. 651.

46. Report After/After Action Report for the month of December 1944, 6 January 1945, folder "FABN 969-0.3 (6697), A/A Rpt, 969 FABN, July-Aug 44, Oct-Dec 44," Box 20337, 969th Field Artillery Battalion, World War II Operations Reports, 1940–48, RG 407, WNRC.

47. *Ibid.*

48. *Ibid.*

49. Extract, Third Army General Order 31, 7 February 1945, folder "FABN 969-0.3 (6697), A/A Rpt 969 FABN, Jan-May 45," Box 20337, 969 Field Artillery Battalion, World War II Operations Reports, 1940–48, RG 407, WNRC; Lee, *Employment of Negro Troops*, pp. 651–52.

50. Lee, *Employment of Negro Troops*, pp. 654–56.

51. *Ibid.*, pp. 657–58.

52. *Ibid.*, p. 658.

53. War Department Press Release, 3 September 1945, folder "Aug-Sep 45," Box 106, Press and Radio News Releases, 1921–47, News Branch, Public Relations Division, RG 165, NA.

54. Battalion History of the 452d Antiaircraft Artillery Auto Wpns Bn (Mbl) for the period 1 January 1944–31 December 1944, folder "CABN-452-0.1 (7115), History-452d AAA (AW) Bn, Yr 44," Box 17174, 452nd AAA (AW) Battalion, Coast Artillery, World War II Operations Reports, 1940–48, RG 407, WNRC; Coolidge, "Information on Colored Troops"; War Department Press Release, 15 October 1945, folder "Sep-Oct 45," Box 107, Press and Radio News Releases, 1921–47, News Branch, Public Relations Division, RG 165, NA; Lee, *Employment of Negro Troops*, pp. 658–60.

55. War Department Press Release, 15 October 1945.

56. *Ibid.*

57. *Ibid.*; Battalion History of the 452d Antiaircraft Artillery Auto Wpns Bn (Mbl) for the period 1 January 1944–31 December 1944.

58. XII Corps General Order 4, 13 January 1945, folder "CABN-452-0.1 (7115), History-452d AAA (AW) Bn, Yr 44," Box 17174, 452nd AAA (AW) Battalion, Coast Artillery, World War II Operations Reports, 1940–48, RG 407, WNRC; Battalion History of the 452d Antiaircraft Artillery Auto Wpns Bn (Mbl) for the period 1 January 1944–31 December 1944; War Department Press Release, 15 October 1945; Lee, *Employment of Negro Troops*, p. 659.

59. Extract, XII Corps General Order 3, 9 January 1945, folder "CABN-452-0.1 (7115), History-452d AAA (AW) Bn, Yr 44," Box 17174, 452nd AAA (AW) Battalion, Coast Artillery, World War II Operations Reports, 1940–48, RG 407, WNRC; 452nd AAA (AW) Battalion Unit Journal, 3 December 1944, folder "CABN-452-0.3

(29142), A/A Rpt 452d AAA Auto Wpns Bn (Mbl), June-December 1944," Box 17174, 452nd AAA (AW) Battalion, Coast Artillery, World War II Operations Reports, 1940–48, RG 407, WNRC; Battalion History of the 452d Antiaircraft Artillery Auto Wpns Bn (Mbl) for the period 1 January 1944–31 December 1944; Lee, *Employment of Negro Troops*, p. 659.

60. Folder "CABN-320-0.1 (23102), 320th AA Balloon Bn-VLA, Unit History," Box 17061, 320 Antiaircraft Artillery Balloon Battalion, VLA, Coast Artillery, World War II Operations Reports, 1940–48, RG 407, WNRC; Major General W. S. Kean letter to Lieutenant General Walter Bedell Smith, 15 July 1944, enclosing Colonel C. G. Patterson memorandum to Chief of Staff (Major General W. S. Kean), 10 July 1944, Frames 1360 and 1366, Microfilm Roll 7, Supreme Headquarters Allied Expeditionary Force (SHAEF), Secretary General Staff Records, 1943–45, Dwight D. Eisenhower Library, Abilene, Kans.; General Dwight D. Eisenhower letter to Commanding Officer, Officers, and Men of the 320 A.A. Balloon Battalion, "Commendation," 26 July 1944, Frame 1349, Microfilm Roll 7, SHAEF, Secretary General Staff Records, 1943–45, Eisenhower Library; War Department Press Release, 13 August 1945.

61. Interview of Waverly Woodson by John A. Cash, 18 November 1993, Clarksburg, Md. See also Headquarters European Theater of Operations Press Release, 28 August 1944, folder "1942, 1943, 1944," Box 29, Papers of Phileo Nash, Harry S Truman Library, Independence, Mo.

62. Entry, 20 June 1944, folder "CABN 320-0.7, Message Center Log, 320 AA Balloon Bn, VLA, 11 May 44–19 May 45," 320 Antiaircraft Artillery Balloon Battalion, VLA, Coast Artillery, World War II Operations Reports, 1940–48, RG 407, WNRC.

63. Report of Trends in the Negro Press (week ending 19 December 1945), 5 January 1946, Analysis Branch, News Division, U.S. Army Bureau of Public Relations, folder "Press Analysis," Box 238, Subject File, 1940–47, Civilian Aide to the Secretary, Office, Assistant Secretary of War, RG 107, NA.

64. Entry, 22 August 1944, folder "CABN 320-0.7, Message Center Log, 320 AA Balloon Bn, VLA, 11 May 44–19 May 45," 320 Antiaircraft Artillery Balloon Battalion, VLA, Coast Artillery, World War II Operations Reports, 1940–48, RG 407, WNRC.

65. Unsigned Note to Jonathan, undated, folder "1942, 1943, 1944," Box 29, Papers of Phileo Nash, Truman Library. The Communications Zone, or "COMZ," was the European Theater's Services of Supply organization, and Lee, until early 1945, was Eisenhower's deputy theater commander.

66. Lee, *Employment of Negro Troops*, p. 688.

67. *Ibid.*, pp. 688-93.

68. *Ibid.*, pp. 691-95; Headquarters 99th Infantry Division letter to Commanding General XII Corps, 21 June 1945, "Reports on Negro Platoons," folder "Army Ground Forces Report on Negro Troops," Box 183, Decimal 291.2, Headquarters Army Ground Forces Correspondence, 1942–48, RG 337, NA.

69. Lee, *Employment of Negro Troops*, pp. 693–95; PFC Leroy W. Kemp and Eleven Others Letter to Colonel George, undated, folder "Bureau of Public Relations," Box 183, Subject File, 1940–47, Civilian Aide to the Secretary, Office, Assistant Secretary of War, RG 107, NA.

70. Lee, *Employment of Negro Troops*, pp. 695–700.

71. Headquarters U.S. Forces, European Theater (Main) letter to Adjutant General, War Department, 1 October 1945, folder "AG 291.2, Participation of Negro Troops in the Postwar Military Establishment, 23 May 45," Box 1507, Decimal 291.2, Army Adjutant General Classified Decimal File, 1943–45, RG 407, NA.

72. See the collection of field unit reports attached to OPD, War Department Staff Disposition Form to G-3, SPD, 3 August 1945, "Employment of Negro Rifle Platoons (ETO)," in folder "Army Ground Forces Report on Negro Troops," Box 183, Decimal 291.2, Headquarters Army Ground Forces Correspondence, 1942–48, RG 337, NA; Lee, *Employment of Negro Troops*, pp. 696–702.

73. *Roer, Rhine, Ruhr: History of 310th Infantry Regiment*, p. 105, Box 11818, 78th Infantry Division, 310th Infantry Regiment, World War II Operations Reports, 1940–48, RG 407, WNRC; War Department Press Release, 30 April 1945, folder "Apr–May 45," Box 100, Press and Radio News Releases, 1921–47, News Branch, Public Relations Division, RG 165, NA.

74. *Follow Through*, p. 110, folder "309-INF (60)-0, World War II, 60th Infantry Regiment, June 1917-9 May 1945," Box 7535, 60th Infantry Regiment, Ninth Infantry Division, World War II Operations Reports, 1940–48, RG 407, WNRC.

75. Interview of Brigadier General H. T. Mayberry, 6 July 1945, by Major Bell I. Wiley, Papers of Edward M. Almond, U.S. Army Military History Institute.

76. War Department Press Release, 18 June 1945, folder "June 45," Box 103, Press and Radio News Releases, 1921–47, News Branch, Public Relations Division, RG 165, NA.

77. *Ibid.*

78. *Ibid.*

79. War Department Press Release, 13 August 1945.

80. For a listing of Distinguished Service Crosses, see Albert F. Gleim and George B. Harris III, *Distinguished Service Cross Awards for World War II*, rev. 2d ed. (Fort Myer, Va.: Planchet Press, 1991). U.S. Army infantry regiments in World War II had about 3,000 men at full strength. War Department policy was to maintain combat units at full strength rather than create new units, and a review of strength reports for several regiments in the spring of 1945 bears this out. Thus the number of individuals in the 24 regiments in the eight infantry divisions to which black platoons were assigned totaled approximately 72,000. No more than 2,000 African-American soldiers were assigned to these regiments beginning in mid-1945 (the other 800 went to the 12th and 14th Armored Divisions). Comparison of totals of Distinguished Service Crosses awarded to white and black soldiers in these 24 regiments (for actions on or after 12 March 1945, the earliest date that African-American soldiers reached these units) shows that black soldiers received 4.3% of the Distinguished Service Crosses (2 of 46) though they represented only 2.8% of the total strength of the 24 regiments (2,000 of 72,000). When Distinguished Service Crosses awarded to officers are eliminated (there were no black officers in the volunteer infantry replacement program), the percentage rises to 7.4% (2 of 27).

81. Private First Class Willy F. James, Jr., Decoration Case File, Box 74, Seventh Army Awards Case Files, RG 338, WNRC; Seventh Army General Order 512, 14 September 1945, folder "107-1.13, General Orders, Jan 1945–Mar 1946," Box 2581, Seventh Army, World War II Operations Reports, 1940–48, RG 407, WNRC.

82. *Ibid.*

83. Private First Class Jack N. Thomas, Decoration Case File, folder "Vol. 70, Case 49," Box 34, Third Army Awards Case Files, RG 338, WNRC; Third Army General Order 255, 18 September 1945, folder "General Orders," Box 2036, Third Army, World War II Operations Reports, 1940–48, RG 407, WNRC; War Department Press Release, 8 November 1945, folder "Decorations and Awards," Box 199, Subject File, 1940–47, Civilian Aide to the Secretary, Office, Assistant Secretary of War, RG 107, NA; Discharge Document, 31 January 1946, Jack N. Thomas Individual Personnel Record, National Personnel Records Center, St. Louis, Mo. This is the only document in Thomas' personnel file.

84. Private First Class Jack N. Thomas, Decoration Case File.

85. *Ibid.*

86. Staff Sergeant Edward A. Carter, Jr., Decoration Case File, folder "200.6 1945," Box 34, Seventh Army Awards Case Files, RG 338, WNRC; Seventh Army General Order 580, 4 October 1945, folder "107-1.13, General Orders, Jan 1945–Mar 1946," Box 2581, Seventh Army, World War II Operations Reports, 1940–48, RG 407, WNRC; 56th Armored Infantry Battalion Operations History, March 1945, folder "612-INF (56)-0.3, A/A Report, 56th Inf Bn, 12th Armored Division, March 45," Box 16234, 56th Armored Infantry Battalion, 12th Armored Division, World War II Operations Reports, 1940–48, RG 407, WNRC; War Department Press Release, 15 November 1945, folder "Decorations and Awards," Box 199, Subject File, 1940–47, Civilian Aide to the Secretary, Office, Assistant Secretary of War, RG 107, NA.

87. Staff Sergeant Edward A. Carter, Jr., Decoration Case File.

88. Report of Trends in the Negro Press (week ending 1 November 1945), 7 November 1945, Analysis Branch, News Division, U.S. Army Bureau of Public Relations, folder "Negro Press," Box 223, Subject File, 1940–47, Civilian Aide to the Secretary, Office, Assistant Secretary of War, RG 107, NA.

89. Staff Sergeant Edward A. Carter, Jr., Decoration Case File.

*Chapter 5*

# Valor Awards to Black Soldiers and Airmen in the Mediterranean Theater of Operations

## Introduction

With the invasion of North Africa in November 1942, the Allies began offensive operations that would continue in the area of the Mediterranean Sea until Germany's defeat in May 1945. At peak strength in the fall of 1944, approximately 85,000 African Americans were among the more than 1 million American soldiers and airmen who fought from North Africa to Sicily to Italy, in what was first designated the North African, and later the Mediterranean, Theater of Operations.[1] About one-fourth of these black soldiers and airmen were in combat and combat support units, with the remainder in service units.[2] When compared with the European Theater, the Mediterranean had a much higher percentage of blacks in combat units, reflecting the nearly 15,000 men in the 92nd Infantry Division, which deployed to Italy in late summer 1944, and also the presence of the all-black 366th Infantry Regiment, a tank battalion, a tank-destroyer battalion, a handful of antiaircraft artillery units, a chemical company, and the four squadrons of the all-black Army Air Forces 332nd Fighter Group.[3]

Though engaged in relatively little fighting, the 450th Anti-Aircraft Artillery Battalion was the first African-American unit to arrive in North Africa, in March 1943, and in Italy, nine months later.[4] Airmen of the all-black 99th Pursuit Squadron disembarked in North Africa at the end of April 1943, entered combat in June 1943, and shot down their first enemy aircraft on 2 July 1943.[5] Ironically, however, the first Silver Stars awarded to African Americans in the Mediterranean Theater did not go to soldiers or airmen in a combat unit but to men assigned to service units.

On 8 November 1943, north of Naples in southern Italy, Private Woodall Marsh of the 3404th Quartermaster Truck Company earned a Silver Star for heroism while driving his truck through enemy mortar and artillery fire to evacuate 12 wounded paratroopers from the front lines. The road was in such bad condition that Marsh had to stop the truck and improve the roadbed as he went along.[6] In March 1944, on the Anzio beachhead, Staff Sergeant Jimmie L. Mills and Sergeants Oren B. Boyd and Harris Madison of the African-American 387th Engineer Battalion also received Silver Stars for gallantry in action. When they observed a landing craft that had been hit by bombs near shore, they left cover and, under continuous bombing and shellfire, organized working parties to secure the boat; they constructed a temporary bridge to the sinking vessel and devised measures to keep it from overturning while they evacuated the wounded.[7]

Black soldiers in service units won only a small fraction of the highest valor awards, however. Of the total of such decorations awarded to African Americans in the Mediterranean Theater, over 90 percent went to personnel in combat units, including two Distinguished Service Crosses and approximately 100 Silver Stars.[8] One witness claims to have typed a Medal of Honor recommendation for a black officer assigned to the 92nd Infantry Division; this is the only evidence to indicate that any African American was formally recommended for the Medal of Honor in the Mediterranean Theater.

## 92nd Infantry Division

Activated at Fort McClellan, Alabama, in October 1942, the 92nd Infantry Division trained for six months in smaller units at camps in Alabama, Arkansas, Indiana, and Kentucky. In May 1943, the Division assembled at Fort Huachuca, Arizona, and trained both there and in Louisiana until its deployment to northern Italy in the summer of 1944. The Division's 370th Regimental Combat Team entered the line on 24 August 1944; the remaining elements were committed during the first two weeks of November. Anchoring the Fifth Army's western flank from the Ligurian Sea up to 30 miles inland, the Division's mission until April 1945 was essentially defensive.[9]

The Division's organic combat elements included the 365th, 370th, and 371st Infantry Regiments; the Division Artillery Headquarters Battery and the 597th, 598th, 599th, and 600th Field Artillery Battalions; the 92nd Cavalry Reconnaissance Troop; and the 317th Engineer Combat Battalion.[10] Except in the all African-American 597th and 600th Field Artillery Battalions, the Division's senior command and staff positions were held by white officers even though nearly 70 percent of the total officer complement was African American.[11]

Nearly 50 units of all kinds, including British, Indian, and Italian forces, were attached to the 92nd Division at one time or another, often giving it an operating strength close to 25,000.[12] Among the attached units were the all-black 366th Infantry Regiment, as well as the 758th Tank and 679th Tank

Destroyer Battalions (both also African-American units but with white officers in senior positions). In March 1945, the Japanese-American 442nd Regimental Combat Team and the white 473rd Infantry Regiment (which had been formed from antiaircraft artillery personnel) were attached to the Division, replacing, for all practical purposes, the 365th, 366th, and 371st Infantry Regiments. This reorganization deprived the 92nd Division of its overwhelmingly African-American composition for the last month of the war.[13]

Early in July 1945, Major General Edward M. Almond, the 92nd's commander, declared that his attempt to create a combat infantry division of African-American units had been a "failure."[14] Even though Almond acknowledged the skill and heroism of some black soldiers, he gave the principal reasons for this outcome as the supposed deficiencies that he and other top 92nd commanders attributed to inherent racial characteristics of black infantry officers and enlisted men.[15]

Truman Gibson, Civilian Aide to the Secretary of War on Negro Affairs, had visited the 92nd in Italy in March 1945 and had already expressed a different view. In his official report, Gibson conceded that "melting away" under fire was a "tendency of many" (though certainly not a majority) and that there had been "many withdrawals by panic stricken Infantrymen." Very obliquely, Gibson suggested that discriminatory racial attitudes and practices within the Division—not any alleged characteristics of black soldiers—had been an important factor in the 92nd's poor performance up to that point.[16] Many African-American newspapers, which had fought hard against segregation in the Army and had vigorously protested War Department foot-dragging in letting African-American units enter combat, blasted Gibson after he seemed to criticize black soldiers at a press conference conducted in Italy.[17] In April 1945, Gibson reacted: "It is hard for me to see how some people can, on the one hand, argue that segregation is wrong, and on the other, blindly defend the product of that segregation."[18]

Most historians have followed Gibson's interpretation. While generally accepting the verdict passed by the military commanders on the performance of the Division and its soldiers, they have pointed to racism and segregation as the underlying causes.[19] Ulysses Lee, in the Army's official history of African-American soldiers in World War II, identified many problems in the 92nd but related most to segregation and racial prejudice, particularly "an all pervading lack of trust" among its men.[20] Ernest Fisher, in his official history of the campaign in northern Italy, echoed Lee's view in characterizing units of the 92nd Division as "plagued ... with a long-standing malaise growing from mutual distrust between mainly white officers and black enlisted men."[21] Similarly, Bernard Nalty, in his history of blacks in the American military, described the 92nd Division's performance as "sluggish"; he claimed, "Racial segregation and its consequences hamstrung the division, inflicting more serious damage to its effectiveness than did the enemy."[22] Finally, Morris MacGregor's *Integration of the Armed Forces, 1940–1965* also endorsed the theme of poor performance caused by segregation.[23]

The emphasis placed by historians on the destructive impact of segregation and racial prejudice on the 92nd Infantry Division may have unintentionally prevented a more balanced assessment. Hondon Hargrove, a black veteran who served as a battery commander in the 92nd's 597th Field Artillery Battalion, acknowledged racism's divisive role but also presented, to a much greater extent than other historians, other factors that influenced the Division's combat performance. Through careful and detailed analysis of the Division's combat actions, Hargrove showed quite clearly that black soldiers repeatedly went forward into battle and that many (not just a few) fought heroically. If there were failures in performance, then racism's debilitating effect was but one factor. Hargrove gave full attention to the difficulties presented by the rugged mountainous terrain and the extensive and well-prepared defenses of the German Gothic Line, especially minefields and long-range coastal guns not silenced until late April 1945. He also suggested that the Division's practice of shifting officers and men in and out of units and parceling out units or elements of units weakened cohesion. Finally, in Hargrove's view, the Division's leadership employed unimaginative and sometimes questionable tactics, particularly in ordering repeated frontal assaults.[24]

The purpose of this study is not to evaluate the 92nd's combat effectiveness or to reach a conclusion about the overall performance of its soldiers, but rather to investigate valor awards relating to the Medal of Honor for African Americans. But the attitudes of the Division's top commanders—the officers exercising a determining influence over awards—on the issues of race and combat performance are critical to this analysis.

Evaluating and reporting the performance of a unit's personnel was a key responsibility for any commander. What distinguished this function in the 92nd Infantry Division was that most of its officers and enlisted men were African Americans and that this was the central focus of the reports prepared by the Division's commanders. Indeed, though unquestionably serving as part of the Division and sharing the dangers of combat, its senior officers were also separated from their men, beyond even the distance created by race, rank, or position. The leadership of the 92nd saw itself as reporting the results of an experiment. "The constant objective of top commanders of the 92nd Division," said General Almond soon after the war's end, "has been to collect, evaluate, and draw conclusions from reliable first-hand and at-the-time data which could be relied upon by the War Department in future employment of negro military manpower."[25] As a consequence of this perspective, the 92nd's leaders viewed their soldiers first as African Americans and second as soldiers whose performance was one among several factors bearing on a unit's success or failure in battle.

Racial tension and conflict flared in the 92nd Division during both training and combat. Truman Gibson recalled witnessing the troops booing General

Almond on an inspection visit to Fort Huachuca.[26] Former Maryland Congressman Parren Mitchell, who served as a company commander in the 370th Infantry Regiment, remembered initially being refused service at the white officers' mess on the day in 1943 that he reported to the Division.[27] Vernon Baker, a platoon leader in the 370th who later won a Distinguished Service Cross, stated that black officers knew not to enter Division headquarters at Fort Huachuca through the front door.[28]

Some black soldiers struck back during training, occasionally with violence. Enlisted men stoned a car occupied by white officers, and a white lieutenant was hit in the head with a shovel while asleep in his tent.[29] Other soldiers resisted passively. By the time the Division was ready for overseas deployment in the summer of 1944, over 2,000 of its soldiers, men deemed physically or psychologically unfit for combat, were in the Division's "Casual Camp."[30] One black veteran of the 92nd, who described himself as a "game player" in "the white man's Army" but who was not a "casual," gave the following description of the men assigned to the Casual Detachment:

> There was a group of fellows in the 92nd called the Casuals. Some of the guys in this unit were ASTP [Army Student Training Program] men. Now actually these guys were malingerers and there was nothing, I mean *nothing*, the army could do with them. They were actually an embarrassment to the military. Yet the 92nd had to carry them because they needed those high IQ's for the division's files. That the command did not recognize a tremendous morale problem in the division with so many highly intelligent men in the Casual group gives you an idea of the brain power in charge of the 92nd Division. It seems that the whites were completely blind at this point in history. The only sickness those Casuals had was one of morale. If they had been treated as human beings, as soldiers in the United States Army, they would not have become a problem.[31]

Though perhaps exaggerated, this reminiscence and other evidence suggests that many of these soldiers were responding to the environment of segregation and prejudice in the 92nd. More than 800 "casuals"—soldiers psychologically but not physically unfit—sailed with the Division to Italy.[32]

Racial incidents continued in the combat zone. Shortly after arriving in Italy, a white officer in the 317th Engineer Combat Battalion was shot in the foot while asleep in a tent. The investigating officer, a captain from the Division's Inspector General Section, was unable to discover the assailant's identity but unambiguously described the battalion's dismal morale: "The EM [enlisted men] dislike their officers; the officers dislike each other; and they all seemingly dislike their Bn [battalion] Commander." The captain's report made it clear that perceptions of racial discrimination were an important, though not the only, factor contributing to the explosive situation in the battalion. He recommended that the 317th's commander, Lieutenant Colonel Edward L. Rowny, be relieved, but General Almond declined to take this action.[33]

Racism also touched a black officer assigned to the Division's General Staff. In February 1945, Captain Leroy Clay, an African American assigned to the G-3 (Operations) Section, was convicted by court-martial for disobeying an order. Lieutenant Bert Cumby, an African American assigned to the Adjutant General Section, refused to testify on Clay's behalf at the court-martial and subsequently received a letter threatening his life:

> You should be ashamed of yourself.... We know that if any Negro Officer in the 92nd Division, knows the inner-workings of the division's vicious circle, you do. We know that you have been exposed to more trickery in the 92nd Division than any other Negro Officer in the division.... The 92nd Division has a world-wide reputation for its injustices to the Negro Officer and enlisted man. It was that way in the United States ... and it will continue to be a slave unit for white masters as long as weak and indifferent Negro officers like yourself, continue to watch justice raped, and say, "I don't know the facts in the case." ... We have just begun to fight, not for a bunch of incompetents who dictate life and death to us in the lily-white 92nd Division, but for ourselves. We know now too well, who our enemies are, and they are not only Germans. Our enemy is that race-hating white man, the kind and type the Army has selected to "command" the "Negro Division", and the 92nd Division. You will never be able to stand between our cause and justice again. Over here life is cheap, very cheap. The cheapness of you, as an officer makes your own life, in our sight, cheaper.[34]

Signed only with a cross, the letter is important not only because it describes the racial prejudice perceived in the Division by black soldiers but also because it reveals a level of suspicion and hatred high enough to divide black soldiers from each other.

Contemporary observers noted that the Division's leadership seemed unaware of the damage that racial conflict was doing. Following a visit to the Division in the summer of 1943, Brigadier General Benjamin O. Davis, the only black general officer in the U.S. Armed Forces at the time, reported to the War Department: "General Almond has ... overlooked the human element in the training of this Division.... Apparently not enough consideration has been given to the maintenance of a racial understanding between white and colored officers and men."[35] In his March 1945 report, Truman Gibson commented on the accounts of undisciplined withdrawals by black infantrymen under fire: "The underlying reasons are quite generally unknown in the Division."[36]

The racism and segregation marking much of American society in the 1940s was reflected in the Army and in the 92nd Infantry Division. These racial policies and practices produced a heavy burden of distrust that white and black officers and black enlisted men carried with them into battle. This was the context in which the reports on the overall performance of black soldiers authored by the Division's senior commanders were produced, and it is also the context in which the awards process within the 92nd must be evaluated.

The reports contained an underlying thesis about black infantrymen, one that evolved over the course of the Division's participation in combat between August 1944 and May 1945. Briefly stated, this interpretation held that African-American infantry officers, noncommissioned officers, and enlisted men lacked the personal attributes required to perform effectively in combat and behaved unsatisfactorily on the battlefield. Furthermore, their deficiencies were so great—some inherent characteristics of their race and others a product of their history and place in American society—that it was unlikely that they could be made into effective infantry for generations to come. Although some black soldiers fought well and heroically, they were too few in number to exercise any appreciable influence over the mass of the others. In short, they were exceptions that proved the rule.

The 370th Regimental Combat Team was the only 92nd Division unit in combat from the end of August through early November. During this period, the 370th was attached initially to the First Armored Division and later to Task Force 92, commanded by Brigadier General John E. Wood, the 92nd's assistant commander. (Almond, still en route to Italy, did not assume command until 5 October.) The 370th enjoyed early success as it attacked across the Arno River, pursuing and clashing with lightly-resisting German units that were withdrawing north to prepared positions in the so-called Gothic Line. After Almond's arrival, the 370th attacked the now-entrenched Germans but made little progress and failed to take some objectives or hold others once taken.[37]

In keeping with the 370th's successful advance in September, General Wood's first assessments of the Division's black soldiers were optimistic. In several reports during the month, Wood told Almond that although the troops were not aggressive, they willingly followed their officers and held fast when led. Junior officers and noncommissioned officers had also done well in combat, but they seemed reluctant to require high standards of performance from their men. Nonetheless, said Wood, the 370th's execution of combat missions had been "highly creditable," with many men "deserving of more recognition in the way of awards than specific knowledge has permitted"; the improvement after a month of combat was "little short of amazing."[38]

In October, after the 370th had assaulted well-defended German positions in mountainous terrain and had experienced difficulty, assessments by senior officers began to include pejorative generalizations about African-American soldiers. Lieutenant Colonel John Phelan, the 370th's executive officer who had only recently joined the regiment after six months' experience in Italy with white units, did not think black soldiers lacked courage: "I have seen or heard of just as many acts of individual heroism among negro troops as among white. There is no reason to believe that there is any greater lack of individual guts among them." On the other hand, after witnessing two companies that repeatedly refused to advance or that broke and ran under fire, Phelan also reported that African-American troops had a greater "tendency to

Two columns of Company I, Third Battalion, 370th Regimental Combat Team, 92d Infantry Division, fording the Arno River unopposed in the Cascina area of Italy, 1 September 1944. U.S. Army Photograph, National Archives and Records Administration, courtesy Lt. Col. Major Clark, U.S. Army (Retired).

mass hysteria or panic" than white troops and in general, had a lessened feeling of individual pride than white soldiers. There were also not enough blacks who were officer material "by virtue of birth, education, occupational environment, or inherent characteristics."[39]

Colonel Raymond G. Sherman, the 370th's commander, had also begun negative characterizations. Agreeing with Phelan, he told the IV Corps G-1 (the Corps' senior personnel officer) that in comparison with whites, black soldiers panicked more and possessed less self-pride. There were some good black officers, but as a whole they were not as good as their white counterparts. Black officers' dependability, in his view, was "definitely questionable." Black enlisted men, he believed, did not trust each other. Although Sherman recognized that, in contrast to the conditions during the successful advance in September, the terrain was now more rugged and German resistance more determined, he thought his soldiers were exaggerating the difficulties. He cited reports from one platoon claiming to have been pinned down by a sniper and others from a company immobilized by a machine gun. Sherman doubted that either situation was possible. Still, he noted, "We have been making attacks and carrying out the mission." It was "too early to definitely state whether or not negro troops could be made good combat soldiers."[40]

By mid-November, the balance of the 92nd Division, including the 365th and 371st Infantry Regiments, had taken up positions in the line and entered combat. On 24 November, the three rifle companies of the 370th's Second Battalion, after being hit by fire from their own tanks as well as from enemy mortars and artillery, dissolved before reaching their objectives, with many men retreating pell-mell from the firing line.[41] The next day, General Wood sent General Almond another assessment, this one laced with racist language. Although he denied having yet reached a "crystallized conclusion," Wood asserted that "Negroes as a race" were "careless," "sluggish in mental reactions," and oblivious to the "necessity for or virtue of cleanliness." Additionally, they preferred self-inflicted wounds or imprisonment to the hazards of battle. "They know that post-war crusades will restore to them all rights forfeited by military sentences." Articulating a critical feature of the thesis developing among the Division's white leadership, Wood argued that although there were "notable exceptions" to his generalizations about black soldiers, the percentage was too small to contradict them. "In my opinion," he concluded, "the negroes known to me have not been suitable for combat duty with lettered infantry companies."[42]

With Wood's and Sherman's reports in hand, General Almond forwarded his first formal evaluation of the Division to Lieutenant General Mark W. Clark, the Fifth Army Commander, on 27 November. Performance of the Division's personnel, particularly in support units such as artillery, had been "excellent," wrote Almond. There were, however, two "outstanding deficiencies" among the infantry: inadequate squad and platoon leadership (almost all African-American in the 92nd), and "the tendency of many men to 'melt away' to avoid enemy shelling." Almond went on to list several "traits of character" lacking among the black officers and noncommissioned officers, including pride, aggressiveness, responsibility, and reliability. Enlisted men were afraid of the dark and of fire from weapons they could not see (artillery and mortars); they tended to panic, exaggerated dangers, and lacked "mutual confidence and trust." His remarks, Almond wrote Clark, were "not offered as conclusions on the battle efficiency of the Division but as facts and observations which later will be continued."[43]

At the end of November, the Fifth Army attached the entirely African-American 366th Infantry Regiment to the 92nd Division. In Italy since 1944, the 366th had been providing air base security. Thus augmented by a fourth infantry regiment, the 92nd Infantry Division faced two key battle tests in the winter of 1944–45. On 26 December, the Germans launched a limited objective attack against Division positions in the Serchio Valley, and early in February the 92nd conducted its own limited offensive along the length of its front. During the two-day German attack in late December, the 366th's Second Battalion, attached to the 370th, dissolved under enemy pressure, opening a gap in the 92nd's lines. As a result, to prevent a German breakthrough, the 370th and the 366th's Second Battalion were temporarily withdrawn and were replaced by troops from the Eighth Indian Division.[44]

By the beginning of February 1945, all of the 92nd's regiments were now back in the line (the 365th had been attached to the 88th Infantry Division from 4 December to 10 January), and the African-American 758th Tank Battalion was attached to the Division. Early in the month, the 92nd undertook a limited attack across its front. A diversionary attack, starting on 4 February, initiated the offensive, but the main effort, which included the disastrous attempt to cross the Cinquale Canal at its mouth on the coast, took place from 8 to 10 February. Almond halted the attack on the tenth, telling Lieutenant General Lucian K. Truscott, now the Fifth Army Commander, that the Division had been unable to meet its limited objectives and that, except for an 800-yard gain in one sector, the Division's lines were the same as before the attack. The reason for the operation's failure, Almond explained to Truscott, was "due almost entirely to the unreliability of the infantry units as shown by their repeated withdrawals in the face of enemy fire and small, though determined, hostile counterattacks; the withdrawals by our infantry take the form of panics, or disorderly retirements with little heed to command and leadership, particularly the weak leadership in the platoon echelons. Little if any determined offensive spirit to meet the enemy at close quarters existed in most of the infantry units." Almond had "nothing but praise" for the Division's regimental and battalion leadership. Therefore, in Almond's view the 92nd's soldiers were responsible for the failure.[45]

Following the two winter setbacks, more reports flowed from the Division's regimental commanders, and the Division's inspector general conducted three investigations (two prompted by General Wood) of the 366th Infantry's battalions. Both Colonel Raymond G. Sherman, 370th Infantry Commander, and Colonel James Notestein, 371st Infantry Commander, had made up their minds about their black officers and men. In lengthy assessments, both repeated familiar refrains regarding the paucity of initiative, aggressiveness, dependability, responsibility, and courage exhibited by African-American infantry officers and noncommissioned officers. The exceptions were very few. Enlisted men, they reported, lacked pride, and were careless, afraid of combat, and prone to panic. Sherman unambiguously concluded, "Negro troops are not suitable for use as troops in rifle companies." Notestein thought that it would take 60 years before "the essential qualities of character and stamina to produce riflemen [could] be bred into the race." He no longer believed that "the combat capabilities of the bulk of the riflemen in this regiment [could] be substantially increased by any amount of training, experience, or any other means."[46]

The evaluations submitted to General Almond by Colonel J. D. Armstrong, 365th Infantry Commander, and Lieutenant Colonel Alonzo Ferguson, the African-American commander of the 366th Infantry Regiment, did not conform to the rapidly crystallizing thesis prevailing among the other commanders. Armstrong had some criticisms of his black officers and enlisted

Men of Company C of the 365th Infantry Regiment, 92nd Infantry Division, carrying ammunition to the assault companies and pinned down by a sniper who had infiltrated through the lines, 10 January 1945. U.S. Army Photograph, National Archives and Records Administration, courtesy Lt. Col. Major Clark, U.S. Army (Retired).

men: officers were short of the desired levels of initiative and responsibility; enlisted men were careless with equipment (though not their weapons), did not follow orders and regulations unless forced, and were "lacking in devoted loyalty." Nevertheless, officers had overcome initial timidity in combat, and enlisted men had also "conducted themselves fairly well." In fact, Armstrong estimated that 90 percent of his black officers measured up well in combat in all respects and 85 percent as leaders generally. He rated the overall soldierly proficiency of 80 percent of the enlisted men as "good." Yet for some reason, Armstrong ended his generally very positive assessment with a curiously negative conclusion: "While the Regiment apparently has done well, I am not convinced that it has good potential value despite the favorable comments of the Battalion Commanders as to the fighting ability of these troops."[47]

Though he did not comment on the combat performance of his enlisted men, Lieutenant Colonel Ferguson, commanding the all-black 366th Infantry Regiment, presented a favorable evaluation of the unit's officers and noncommissioned officers. Though "not what had been hoped for," he judged his officers' initiative as "satisfactory as a whole." He found no instance of any officer "unable to stand the gaff of battle" and added that 75 percent were aggressive (the remainder lacking only experience). All were unquestionably loyal to their superiors. His noncommissioned officers were "on par with other outfits."[48]

Questionable performance and a shortage of African-American infantry replacements forced a reorganization of the 92nd Division during February and March 1945. The 366th Infantry was detached from the Division and eventually converted into a general-service engineer regiment; the 365th and 371st were moved to quieter sectors; the Japanese-American 442nd Regimental Combat Team and the white 473rd Infantry Regiment were attached to the Division. To strengthen the 370th Infantry, dozens of officers and more than 1,300 enlisted men—the most proficient soldiers from the 365th and 371st (some with decorations for heroism)—were transferred into the 370th, and an approximately equal number of the weakest officer and enlisted performers were sent to the 365th and 371st. In mid-March, the 679th Tank Destroyer Battalion, an African-American unit commanded by white officers, was also attached to the Division.[49]

The reorganized 92nd, along with the rest of the Fifth Army, began the final offensive of the war in Italy on 5 April. The 370th Infantry, however, was unable to advance and achieve the objectives set for it during the offensive's first two days. Units became disorganized, and there was much straggling.[50] In a postwar report to Almond on the 370th's performance at the outset of the offensive, Colonel Sherman wrote that his soldiers' "melting away" was "inexcusable." Some men did well, but "the majority of negro infantrymen have no heart for combat." He pointed out that units disintegrated when platoon and squad leaders became casualties. "I am now completely convinced," he said, "that the great majority of negroes cannot be made into good infantry soldiers or even satisfactory ones. They have on every occasion clearly demonstrated that they are entirely undependable."[51]

Other commanders in the 92nd also submitted reports after the war ended in Italy.[52] Only Colonel Armstrong, the 365th's commander, had changed his view of African-American infantry. This man, who had told Almond soon after the February offensive that 80 to 90 percent of his African-American officers and men had done well in combat and were good soldiers, now in June did an about-face. Except for a few officers who were "exemplary" in combat, Armstrong reported that the remainder lacked "initiative, a sense of responsibility, and aggressiveness." The black enlisted man did not "possess those qualities of aggressiveness, determination, and ability to bear hardship to make him a good soldier."[53]

Armstrong's generalizations, however, were not only inconsistent with his previous evaluation but also badly distorted when measured against the actual combat activity of the 365th during the last two months of the War. To be sure, Armstrong had lost many of his best people to the 370th during the 92nd's reorganization and had received, in return, many of the 370th's worst, a situation he lamented.[54] Still, his report praised the combat performance of the 365th's First Battalion during periods of attachment to the Tenth Mountain Division and the 371st Infantry in March and April. Moreover, as he himself pointed out, the 365th had only a minor role in the April offensive.[55] In fact, the Regiment suffered only 28 casualties in March and April, in contrast to the nearly 400 it had taken between November and February.[56] What Armstrong's June report really revealed was the complete dominance of the Division leadership's thesis about African-American infantry; the 365th's commander was simply getting on board with the other senior officers.

At the end of June 1945, in response to a request from General Joseph T. McNarney, Mediterranean Theater Commander, General Almond formed a board of the Division's top commanders to prepare a report on the 92nd for the War Department, then studying the postwar use of African-American soldiers. Presided over by General Wood, the Board's members included the regimental commanders Armstrong, Notestein, and Sherman; Colonel William J. McCaffrey, the Chief of Staff; and Major A. D. Wilder, Jr., who had succeeded Lieutenant Colonel Rowny in mid–May as commander of the 317th Engineer Combat Battalion. They met on 24 and 25 June and put together a 25-page report that appended 15 reference documents. After receiving the report, General Almond added a long covering letter and forwarded, on 2 July 1945, the whole study to General McNarney through Lieutenant General Truscott, the Fifth Army Commander.[57]

The report, the findings of which Almond fully endorsed in his covering letter, was a lengthy elaboration of the white leadership's thesis about black soldiers. The document was remarkable not only for its thoroughgoing racism but also for the white leadership's rejection of its own personal responsibility for the Division's performance. The report possibly constitutes the only instance in American military history in which all of the top commanders of a division placed the blame for failure completely on their soldiers, rather than accepting responsibility themselves.[58]

In the report, the 92nd's commanders alleged characteristics that, in their judgment, made African Americans unsuitable as combat infantry, but they dismissed or minimized other factors that might have explained the Division's performance. The 92nd's training, they argued, had been the best the Army could provide. Yet in the training phase, there was an "epidemic of straggling" after long marches, involving over time as many as 2,000 men. "This probably was the first indication," said the Board members, "of racial instability and for disinclination to enter combat."[59] The senior officers did not think that standard measures of ability, such as test scores and educational levels (much below those in an average white division), could account for their soldiers' "instability" in combat.[60] Additionally, the 92nd's senior officers minimized the impact of the northern Italian terrain (by then "difficult but familiar") on the

Division's combat performance during the February offensive and made light of the quality of enemy opposition.⁶¹ That the German troops facing the Division "were by far not the most reliable in Italy," they suggested, was demonstrated by the large number of desertions from German units and by captured prisoners' references to the German 148th Infantry as the "Polish" Division.⁶²

Disparaging the capabilities and performance of black officers, the report's authors praised the quality and behavior of the Division's white officers. In an irony that apparently never occurred to the Board members, the report recommended that there be few independent African-American commands in the future because of black officers' "incapacity for self criticism."⁶³

In a long litany of supposed deficiencies of African-American officers and enlisted men, the Board's report advanced overtly racist interpretations. The African-American officer was viewed as a "by-product of his race" in whom "servility" had been "bred ... for generations." For this reason, he could not be an aggressive troop leader. Moreover, the black officer's "love of exhibitionism," which stemmed from "an inherent inferiority complex," prevented him from inspiring confidence in his men. The black enlisted man, said the Board, had "no loyalty to fellow soldiers and abandon[ed] them on the battlefield to seek his personal safety." Moreover, he was "prone to distort facts or prevaricate to gain any personal advantage." Not for at least three generations, predicted the Board, would "the essential qualities of character and stamina to produce Infantrymen ... be bred into the Negro Race."⁶⁴

Almond and the officers on the Board conceded that some African-American infantrymen did not fit the general pattern. During the Division's combat operations, Almond wrote, there had been "many individual cases of valor or outstanding performance." He added, "However, such cases are the exceptions: the Dr. Carvers, Booker T. Washingtons, and Marian Andersons of the Negro Race; they do not represent the average ability of the negro in combat."⁶⁵ This element of the senior white officers' thesis about African-Americans in combat—heroic acts that were "exceptions" to the norm—is central to understanding the Division's awards policies and practices.

During the period of the War, one of the Division's white officers was formally recommended for the Medal of Honor, and three officers (two white and one black) earned Distinguished Service Crosses.⁶⁶ The Division awarded 102 Silver Stars and 753 Bronze Stars to personnel assigned to its organic units.⁶⁷ Standing alone, these figures mean little. Many black veterans who served with the 92nd in Italy believe that some black soldiers were not appropriately recognized by the Division for their heroism—that in fact an unwritten policy, or at least a mindset, existed among the Division's white leaders and limited both the number and the level of valor awards for African-American officers and enlisted men.⁶⁸ Dennette Harrod, an officer in the 366th Infantry Regiment, claims, for example, that someone overheard Lieutenant Colonel Carthal F. Mock, the Division's G-1 and a key figure in the Division's awards

Maj. Gen. Almond laying a wreath on the grave of one of the 92nd Infantry Division's dead during a memorial service on Easter, 1 April 1945, at Castelfiorentino, Italy. U.S. Army Photograph, National Archives and Records Administration, courtesy Lt. Col. Major Clark, U.S. Army (Retired).

approval process, say, "Under no circumstances will a nigger get a Congressional as far as I'm concerned."[69] Though hearsay, Mock's reputed declaration was entirely consistent with the deep suspicions that many black veterans had then, and still have today, of the 92nd's white leadership.

General Almond apparently issued policy letters concerning awards, but research for this study failed to find any in the Division's World War II files. Other 92nd and Army records, however, reveal the Division's awards policy. A draft document titled "Citations" in the Division's files states that the 92nd's policy from the beginning was to emphasize awards and decorations. It quotes General Almond as saying his aim was to "recognize heroic acts" as they occurred.[70] Almond also discussed awards with the Mediterranean Theater's Army Ground Forces observer and indicated another important purpose for awards: "Whenever a colored officer or soldier performed any outstanding act in contact with the enemy, he has received an award commensurate with the act. I was in hopes by this method and also by appealing to pride of race and what the colored people in America expected of them, that they would go forward in battle." But, said Almond, this didn't work: "They have failed me and have not only failed to go forward but have run from the enemy in groups as large as a battalion."[71]

The awards approval process in the 92nd Division functioned much the same way as it did throughout the Army. When an award recommendation was received at Division Headquarters, it went first to the Adjutant General Section, which checked that the recommendation met administrative requirements. The proposed decoration was then passed to the Division's Awards and Decorations Board, which recommended approval or disapproval. The awards package next went through the G-1 and the chief of staff, each of whom made a recommendation, and then to the Division commander for final action. Once the 92nd's commander made a decision, the paperwork went back through the G-1 to the adjutant general, who sent the medal and citation to the awardee's unit or held them for later presentation by the Division commander at a ceremony. The adjutant general also published the award in General Orders. If the Division did not have the authority to make the award, as in the cases of a Distinguished Service Cross or a Medal of Honor, the adjutant general forwarded the Division's recommendation to the next-higher command echelon.[72]

Certainly the awards policy as stated by General Almond and the approval process as described in the Adjutant General Section's report may not have represented actual practice. An analysis of the Division's awards records indicates the extent to which policy coincided with practice. Only 9 of the 115 General Orders published by the Division from August 1944 through November 1945 could not be located.[73] Thus, it is possible to identify the name, rank, and unit of virtually all of the individual award recipients and to determine, with some precision, the total number of each type of award. Because the General Orders do not specify the race of the awardee, that information must be obtained in other ways.[74]

Unfortunately, there are huge gaps in other award records. Few of the 92nd Division's awards case files, which normally contained the decoration recommendation, approval/disapproval actions, and proposed citation, still survive. Only two folders, pertaining principally to Bronze Star awards, were found during research for this study.[75] The extensive Fifth Army awards case files (more than 20 cartons of records) contain some 92nd Division case files, notably those involving Distinguished Service Cross recommendations.[76] The case files are especially important because they show not only the approved award but also the one originally recommended. Individual personnel records ("201 files"), housed at the National Personnel Records Center in St. Louis, are useful because during World War II, a copy of the award recommendation was often included along with a copy of the award citation. Regrettably, too few of the individual personnel files survived the 1973 fire at the National Personnel Records Center to make up for the absence of the 92nd's awards case files.[77] Yet despite the loss of many important records, it is still possible, with the records that have been preserved, to partially reconstruct the 92nd Infantry Division's award practices.

The important first question is: how many of the highest valor awards (Silver Star and Distinguished Service Cross) did black soldiers receive of the total awarded? Of the approximately 260 Silver Stars awarded by the Division, African Americans from both assigned and attached units earned 87, about one-third of the total (the race of seven has not been identified).[78] This apparently low percentage of the whole is misleading because the total includes awards to all assigned and attached units, most notably the Japanese-American 442nd and the white 473rd Infantry Regiments, which constituted two-thirds of the Division's infantry force beginning with the offensive in early April 1945. If awards, as General Almond maintained, were used in part to inspire the Division's black soldiers to perform well, then a more illustrative breakout might be the number of Silver Star awards announced before the war ended on 2 May 1945 (also, coincidentally, before Silver Stars for members of the 442nd and 473rd began to show up in General Orders). Using this measure, black soldiers received about two-thirds of the total, that is, 45 of 71 Silver Stars (the race of two has not been identified).[79]

As noted earlier, two white officers and one black officer received Distinguished Service Crosses. The two white officers were Captains Gilbert S. Holbrook and John F. Runyon; Captain Philip Thayer, another white officer from the 92nd's organic units, was recommended by the Division but did not receive the award.[80] Lieutenant Vernon J. Baker of the 370th Infantry Regiment was the only black in the 92nd to receive a Distinguished Service Cross during the war.[81] The Division, however, had recommended four other African Americans, all enlisted men, for the Distinguished Service Cross: Staff Sergeant Fred D. Rhodes, Private Henry D. Roberts, and Private Jake McInnis, all of the 370th Infantry, and Private First Class Herman E. Rochelle of the 597th Field Artillery Battalion. The Fifth Army disapproved all four recommendations.[82]

Three of the four enlisted Distinguished Service Cross recommendations were for heroic feats that occurred during the 370th Infantry Regiment's early success on the battlefield in late summer and early fall 1944. On 16 September, Staff Sergeant Rhodes, while on a nighttime motorized patrol, dismounted from a truck that had been halted by the enemy and opened fire from an exposed position on the highway, enabling the rest of the patrol to take cover. Then, firing from the doorway of a nearby building, Rhodes covered the successful evacuation of the patrol's wounded. Though eventually wounded himself, Staff Sergeant Rhodes kept on firing, inflicting enemy casualties before exhausting his own ammunition and that from a recovered enemy weapon.[83]

Two days later, Private Henry Roberts, whose advancing platoon had been pinned down by two enemy machine guns, crawled across open terrain under heavy fire and, assisted by another member of the platoon, attacked one of the machine gun positions, killing two Germans and forcing the remainder to withdraw. He then waited alone at the machine-gun position, repulsed the enemy's attempt to recapture it, and then destroyed the weapon. Roberts' courage enabled his platoon to continue its advance.[84]

The Distinguished Service Cross recommendation for Private Jake McInnis demonstrated the connection General Almond made between successful unit performance and recognition for individual heroism. When Almond assumed command of the 92nd on 5 October, the 370th began to attack the German Gothic Line defenses. Though the 370th reached the summit of tactically important Mount Cauala on its second attempt, it could not hold the position. On the third attempt, the 370th's Company K reached the mountain's crest on the night of 11 October and held on through much of the following day.[85] Private McInnis, operating a machine gun on the summit, threw back six German counterattacks. When McInnis discovered that his machine gun's traverse would not cover the advancing Germans, he removed the weapon from its tripod, wedged it between two rocks, and continued firing. Finding that even this method would not do the job, Private McInnis left his protected position and, while exposed to enemy fire, began using his M-1 rifle. Throughout the day, McInnis was responsible for at least a dozen German casualties.[86]

The Division's award recommendation for McInnis was unusual for two reasons. First, the original recommendation was for a Bronze Star; General Almond elevated it to a Distinguished Service Cross. Second, Almond personally signed the write-up. Normally, he simply endorsed recommendations submitted to him by other officers. The first and last sentences of the proposed citation illustrated Almond's criteria for a Distinguished Service Cross: "Private McInnis, as a member of Co K, on the morning of 12 October 1944 was manning a machine gun position *on the crest atop Mount Cauala*.... This conspicuously gallant act ... *materially contributed to repelling the enemy from the mountain*, and *served as an incentive to his comrades* in maintaining their excellent morale during the battle" (emphasis added).[87] Late in the afternoon, however, the 370th was once again forced off Mount Cauala. Still, Private McInnis' heroism, combined with the success of reaching and defending the top of the mountain, represented the kind of example General Almond hoped would inspire the 92nd's black soldiers.

The degree of battlefield success Almond desired for the 92nd Division never materialized. Not until the first hours of the April offensive would another African-American infantryman achieve the combination of heroism and accomplishment in the field that General Almond thought merited a Distinguished Service Cross, let alone a Medal of Honor.

Nowhere was General Almond's linking of awards for valor to unit performance in battle more apparent than in the outcome of the awards proposed for two officers in the 366th Infantry Regiment. Relations between the 366th and the 92nd's leadership were poor from the start. Almond seemed not to have wanted the regiment in the first place.[88] When he pushed it piecemeal into the front line within days of its arrival and before its African-American commander, Colonel Harold D. Queen, thought the unit was ready, Queen requested to be relieved of command. He was succeeded by Lieutenant Colonel Alonzo G. Ferguson, the Regiment's executive officer.[89]

On 5 December, Company B of the 366th, commanded by Captain Walter E. Dabney, became disorganized under heavy enemy fire. Dabney, though wounded, reorganized his men, who then resumed fire, killing and capturing more than a dozen Germans before withdrawing in good order through the lines of the 371st Infantry Regiment, as they had been directed. For his gallantry in action, Captain Dabney was recommended for a Silver Star.[90]

General Almond had a much different view of the engagement and ordered the 371st's commander to investigate the company's performance.[91] Colonel Notestein reported back to Almond: "I am convinced that the only deficiency in the combat performance ... was loss of control when the company came under fire the first time. This was more than offset by the commendable action of the company commander in organizing maneuver against an enemy machine gun."[92] Almond was not satisfied, telling Notestein that the "meagre information" Almond possessed indicated that only about 10 percent of the men did their duty and that the remaining officers and men "completely dissolved for unjustifiable reason." Almond directed Notestein to investigate again, this time using the Division's inspector general.[93] The same captain who had looked into the turmoil in the 317th Engineer Combat Battalion conducted the investigation and reached the same conclusion as Notestein. Moreover, the officer recommended that "Captain Dabney be commended for his actions which were a source of inspiration to those around him."[94]

General Almond stubbornly refused to change his mind and several times disapproved Dabney's Silver Star recommendation. Sometime in the spring of 1945, Dabney formally complained to the Fifth Army that he had been wrongly denied the decoration. In June, the Fifth Army investigated. Colonel McCaffrey told the investigating officer that the "results of the mission were unsatisfactory to the Division Commander." Furthermore, stated the chief of staff, the investigation conducted by the 92nd's Inspector General Section "convinced the Division Commander that the acts specified did not justify the award."[95] Thus, Captain Dabney's valor in combat, impressive to everyone but Almond, went unrecognized probably not from any lack of individual heroism but from Almond's belief that Dabney's acts occurred within the context of overall mission failure.

However incongruous and unjust General Almond's decision appeared, it was within his authority to disapprove Captain Dabney's Silver Star. But in the case of the Distinguished Service Cross recommendation for First Lieutenant John R. Fox, another infantry officer assigned to the 366th, General Almond may have exceeded his authority.

During the night of 25–26 December 1944, enemy personnel dressed as civilians infiltrated the village of Sommocolonia in the Serchio Valley. Occupied by two platoons of the 366th Infantry Regiment and Italian partisans, the village was attacked between 5:00 and 7:00 A.M. by uniformed German and Italian Fascist forces following a mortar and artillery barrage. Several hours of street fighting followed.[96]

Lieutenant Fox, assigned to the 366th's Cannon Company and acting as a forward observer for the 598th Field Artillery Battalion, took a position, along with other members of his observer party, on the second floor of a house in the village from where he could best observe the enemy forces and direct friendly artillery fire. At eight o'clock, Fox began to call for defensive artillery fire. Soon enemy troops reached his location; he could hear them attempting to enter the building. Fox continued to adjust close-in fire until the shells were landing very near to the house. He then radioed the 598th's Fire Direction Center (FDC), "That [last] round is just where I want it—bring it in sixty more yards." The FDC duty officer called the 598th commander to inform him of Fox's request; he, in turn, radioed Fox to verify that the request had been called correctly. Fox answered: "Fire it! There are more of them than there are of us. Put fire on my OP [Observation Post]." Thereupon the 598th fired a battery volley (12 rounds of 105-mm high explosive), destroying the building and killing Fox and the other men in the observer party as well as dozens of enemy soldiers.

For his extraordinary valor in Sommocolonia, Lieutenant Fox was recommended for the Distinguished Service Cross. Several witnesses, among them Brigadier General William H. Colbern, the 92nd Division's Artillery commander, maintain that they saw the recommendation. General Colbern even stated, in an interview on 2 July 1945, that he had recommended Fox for the award.[98]

Thus, neither Lieutenant Fox's heroism nor the existence of a recommendation for the Distinguished Service Cross is at issue. What has never been adequately explained is why the recommendation was not forwarded from the Division to the Fifth Army. Some have suggested that it was inadvertently lost or not acted on. Others think the omission was deliberate—either because Fox was black or because commanders wanted to cover up the bombing of the American troops in the village by Allied aircraft.[99] Although what happened to Lieutenant Fox's award recommendation will never be known with certainty, another explanation, quite consistent both with General Almond's apparent criteria for the top valor awards and with the developing thesis about black infantry, may answer the question.

On 31 December 1944, Colonel McCaffrey sent a memorandum to General Almond summarizing the German attack in the Serchio Valley, including the fighting in Sommocolonia and the dissolution of the 366th's Second Battalion, which had opened the gap in the 92nd's lines.[100] McCaffrey attached to his memorandum a report by a IV Corps Office of Strategic Services (OSS) officer who related the partisans' account of the battle in Sommocolonia:

> Partisans withdrew from Sommocolonia at 1200A after continuous street fight lasting about 6 hours. During this period they received no help from American troops. American troops closed themselves in houses and when Partisans came to help them out, refused to leave. In one instance groups of 6 Partisans went so far as to lean a ladder against a second story window to facilitate the escape of 17 American troops, they refused to come out. Partisans report 60 Germans and Italians killed, many wounded. Allied Arty was very effective against the enemy.[101]

McCaffrey's memorandum did not mention Fox or his call for artillery fire on his own position. Perhaps neither McCaffrey nor Almond had yet learned of Fox's heroism. Surely General Almond found out when he received the award recommendation endorsed by General Colbern, and certainly he knew no later than 4 March 1945, when he received a report he himself had requested from the 370th Infantry Regiment on the events in the Serchio Valley. That report clearly described Fox's actions.[102]

Exactly when General Almond learned about Lieutenant Fox's heroism, however, was probably irrelevant because, as in Captain Dabney's case, Fox's valor occurred during what Almond undoubtedly saw as a disastrous mission failure, including African-American infantry in Sommocolonia who, in the opinion of partisans, refused to come out and fight, and the disorderly withdrawal of the 366th's Second Battalion. For this reason, General Almond may have declined to endorse favorably a Distinguished Service Cross recommendation for Fox or even to forward it recommending disapproval to the Fifth Army.[103]

The ill-starred 366th and the Division's three organic infantry regiments were fully engaged in the week-long February offensive—a failure "due almost entirely to the unreliability of the infantry units" according to Almond. The operation cost the Division 815 men killed and wounded in action (about 30 percent of its total combat casualties in the war).[104] Following the offensive, the Division recommended three men for Distinguished Service Crosses: Captain Gilbert S. Holbrook, a white infantry officer assigned to the Division's G-3, but operating with the task force attempting to cross the Cinquale Canal; Captain Philip Thayer, a white company commander in the 370th Infantry; and Private First Class Herman E. Rochelle, an African American assigned to the 597th Field Artillery Battalion.[105] Although at least 30 black infantrymen received Silver Stars for gallantry in action during the February offensive (about 30 percent of the total Silver Stars the Division awarded to its own personnel in the war), not one was recommended by the Division for a Distinguished Service Cross.[106]

As a result of extraordinary heroism demonstrated during the first two days of the April offensive, a black soldier from the Division would finally win the nation's second-highest award for valor. At 5:00 A.M. on 5 April 1945, Second Lieutenant Vernon J. Baker, assigned to the 370th Infantry Regiment's Company C, advanced at the head of his weapons platoon and, along with the rest of Company C's three rifle platoons, moved toward their objective, Castle Aghinolfi—a German mountain strongpoint on the high ground just east of the coastal highway and about two miles from the 370th's line of departure.[107]

Moving more rapidly than the rest of the company, Lieutenant Baker and about 25 men reached the south side of a draw some 250 yards from the castle within two hours. In reconnoitering for a suitable position to set up a machine gun, Lieutenant Baker observed two cylindrical objects pointing out of a slit in a mount at the edge of a hill. Crawling up the hill and under the mount's opening, he stuck his M-1 rifle into the slit and emptied his clip, killing the observation post's two occupants. Moving to another position in the same area, he stumbled upon a well-camouflaged machine-gun nest, the crew of which was eating breakfast. Baker shot and killed both enemy soldiers.[108]

After Captain John F. Runyon, Company C's commander, joined the group, a German soldier appeared from the draw and hurled a grenade, which failed to explode. Lieutenant Baker shot the enemy soldier twice in the back as he tried to escape back into his dugout. Baker then went down into the draw alone. There he blasted open the concealed entrance of another dugout with a hand grenade, shot one German soldier who emerged after the explosion, tossed another grenade into the dugout, and entered, firing his submachine gun and killing two more Germans.[109]

As Lieutenant Baker climbed back out of the draw, enemy machine-gun and mortar fire began to inflict heavy casualties on the group of 25 soldiers, killing or wounding about two-thirds of them. When expected reinforcements did not arrive, Captain Runyon ordered a withdrawal in two groups. The company commander led the first group of mostly walking wounded; Lieutenant Baker volunteered to cover its withdrawal and to remain to assist in the evacuation of the more seriously wounded. During the second group's withdrawal, Lieutenant Baker, supported by covering fire, destroyed two machine-gun positions, previously bypassed during the assault, with hand grenades.[110]

On 5 April 1945, the men of Company C had killed 26 Germans, wounded many others, and destroyed six machine-gun positions, two observer posts, and four dugouts. Baker himself had accounted for 9 of the dead enemy soldiers, three of the machine-gun nests, an observer post, and a dugout. The position above the draw in front of the castle, however, was the high tide, not only of Company C's advance but of the 370th Regiment's. In fact, the bulk of the Regiment never really got going during the first two days of the offensive.[111]

For showing extraordinary heroism and leadership on 5 April, and for leading a battalion advance through enemy minefields and heavy fire the next day, Captain Runyon recommended Lieutenant Baker for the Distinguished Service Cross. Warrant Officer Robert Millender, the 370th's assistant adjutant, recalled, nearly 30 years after the war, preparing a different award for Baker at regimental headquarters: "Now I had personally written up the citation, the recommendation of our commanding officer, for a Congressional Medal of Honor. One never forgets a thing like that; at last a black man was going to receive the Medal of Honor in this war. But the higher ups decreed otherwise and he ended up with the DSC."[112] Runyon recently stated that he had recommended Baker for a Distinguished Service Cross, not a Medal of Honor, but it is possible that either Lieutenant Colonel E. V. Murphy, the First Battalion Commander, or Colonel Sherman, the 370th Regiment Commander, elevated Runyon's original recommendation from a Distinguished Service Cross to a Medal of Honor.[113] Other than Millender's testimony, however, no corroborating evidence has been uncovered for a Medal of Honor recommendation for Baker.[114] The Division forwarded a Distinguished Service Cross recommendation to the Fifth Army, which approved and announced Lieutenant Baker's award in General Orders on 10 June 1945.[115]

During a personal conference with Baker, most likely around 10 June, General Almond asked the lieutenant to prepare a written report of the events of 5 April. Baker submitted his account on 12 June.[116] A few days later, General Almond wrote a note to Colonel McCaffrey, expressing his dissatisfaction with Lieutenant Baker's effort: "Send for Runyon and have him write an account of what happened to Co. C ... Baker's report says nothing except 'What I did!'"[117]

Captain Runyon's report, written during the next two weeks, was dated 1 July 1945.[118] Both his and Baker's accounts appear as 2 of the 15 reference papers appended to the Division Board's report on African-American soldiers, prepared in the last week of June. The version of Runyon's report attached to the Board's study, however, had been edited, retyped, and backdated to 12 April 1945.[119]

The reasons for this lapse in reporting integrity are readily apparent. Captain Runyon's 1 July report was backdated because the Division's commanders had already finished their report on the 92nd's black soldiers. Much of what Runyon had written in his report supported their thesis about African-American infantry. But to avoid the appearance that Runyon's account had been manufactured for that purpose, it was backdated. Since, however, some of Runyon's report contradicted the prevailing view at the top of the Division, it also had to be edited.

The edited and backdated version of Runyon's account that was appended to the Board's report offered strong support by a junior officer, not part of the high command, for the leadership's thesis. Runyon, of course, described Baker's heroism in his report—Baker was a clear example of the outstanding

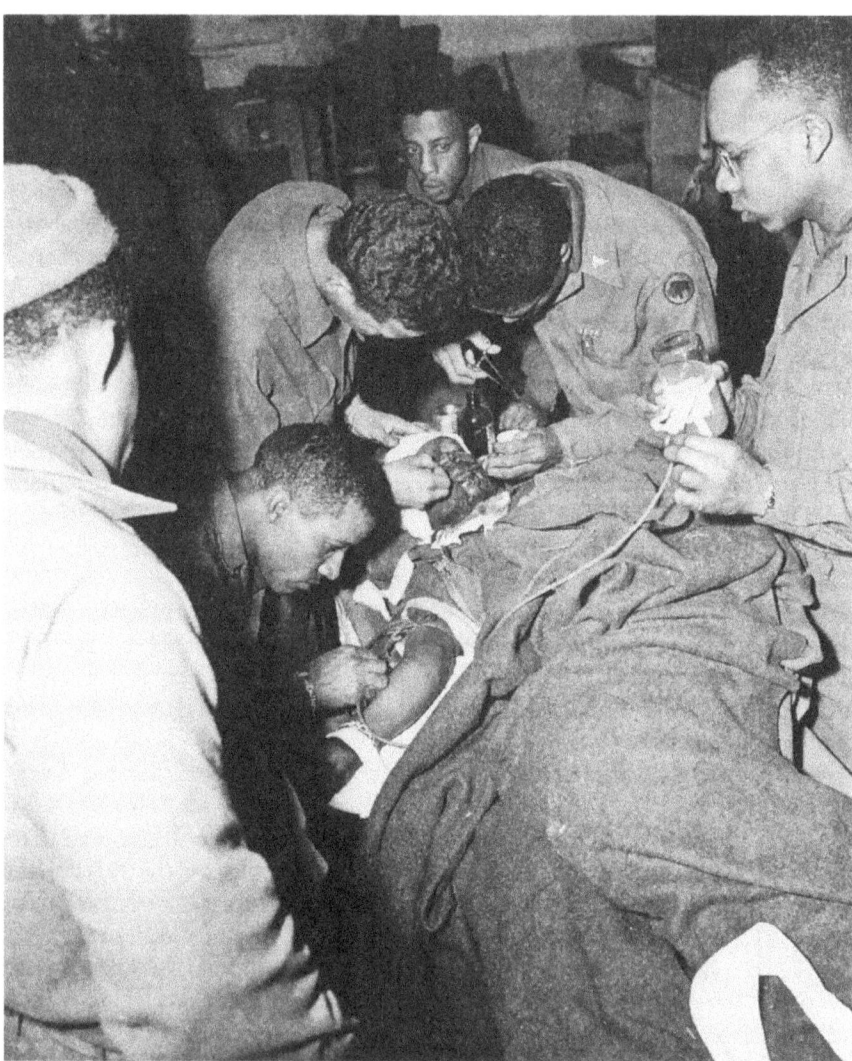

A wounded soldier receiving blood plasma and medical attention from 92nd Infantry Division doctors, somewhere in Italy, 1945. U.S. Army Photograph, National Archives and Records Administration, courtesy Lt. Col. Major Clark, U.S. Army (Retired).

African-American soldier who was an exception to the general rule. Runyon also wrote that when two of the white officers in C Company's advance group were wounded, their "platoons went to pieces," that the noncommissioned officers "had no control over the men," and that few soldiers were willing to help the wounded. Additionally, Runyon recounted that men from the mortar section, under fire from a machine gun that was not, however, pinning them down, "were on bended knee, praying." The next day, when the Company had been reorganized to resume the attack, Runyon noted that only 20 (Lieutenant Baker among them) of the remaining 70 members of the Company (16 had been killed, 50 wounded) followed Runyon back into battle even after they had been threatened with court-martial.[120]

Runyon closed his report with a number of "lessons" he had learned about his troops and combat generally. One was that "rapid disintegration takes place" among black troops when the leader becomes a casualty. Another was that the average black soldier "loses all control of his mind when subjected to overhead mortar and artillery fire" and is "terrified to fight at night." It is "a foolish officer," concluded Runyon, "who leads colored soldiers because invariably he loses half of his men."[121] Runyon included only one positive generalization: black soldiers were good shots and, after indoctrination, were aggressive in small-arms engagements. The overall portrait, however, was damning and strongly supported the 92nd's top commanders' assessment of black soldiers.[122]

In *Fragment of Victory*, a 1952 study of the Division, Paul Goodman, the 92nd's assistant S-2 (Intelligence), quoted extended passages from Captain Runyon's original 1 July report. These excerpts demonstrated that some of what Runyon said had undermined the Division's thesis regarding black soldiers; for that reason, these passages were omitted from the 12 April version of Runyon's report.[123] In the original account, Runyon attributed the lack of discipline of the advance group of Company C (when the men had failed to remain in their position near the castle and bunched up under fire) not to supposedly inherent deficiencies in black soldiers but "to the fact that many of these boys were strangers to one another and had never served together before in active combat." He offered a similar explanation for the failure of the balance of the men in C Company to go forward as the advance group had: "There are few men in active combat who do not know the meaning of fear. The poorer trained the troops and the less experience they have had in fighting together, the greater degree of fear they realize."[124] Runyon's implied criticism of the Division's training and the wholesale troop reshuffling that had taken place in the 370th during March suggested additional reasons, other than characteristics peculiar to race, for the poor performance of the Division's black soldiers—reasons that also put the senior white leadership in a less favorable light. That was undoubtedly the reason those passages were left out of the edited report.

Also omitted from the edited report were some of Runyon's descriptions of Baker's heroism. Lieutenant Baker, wrote Runyon, "broke into tears" when ordered to withdraw: "'Captain,' he said 'we can't withdraw. We must stay here and fight it out.' I knew Lieutenant Baker desperately wanted these men of 'C' Company to hold their ground and that he was willing to sacrifice his own life in an effort to win our battle."[125] Runyon's conviction that Baker would have given his life to achieve the Company's objective was not hyperbole but was consistent with the lieutenant's actions before and during the withdrawal. His heroism was such that some at the time believed (and some today) believe that he merited the Medal of Honor.

In the summer of 1945, an article appeared in the *Baltimore Afro-American*, a leading black newspaper, alleging that awards for heroism were "stepped down a notch wherever colored" were concerned. Its author, a black war correspondent, compared Lieutenant Baker's Distinguished Service Cross citation to the citation for Private James R. Hendrix, who earned a Medal of Honor during the Battle of the Bulge in December 1944. In the journalist's view, the heroic acts described in both citations were quite similar.[126]

Attempts to compare valorous acts performed in different contexts are subject to obvious difficulties. Yet in the case of Lieutenant Baker's Distinguished Service Cross, just such a comparison is possible. After General Almond left the 92nd in mid–August 1945, General Wood, who assumed command of the Division, recommended Captain Runyon for the Medal of Honor. The proposed decoration, ultimately disapproved by the War Department in favor of a Distinguished Service Cross, was based on Runyon's actions during Company C's attack on the morning of 5 April.[127]

A comparison of Lieutenant Baker's and Captain Runyon's award citations shows that both officers had indisputably demonstrated great courage under fire. Both had also shown superior leadership in combat—Runyon as a company commander, Baker as a platoon leader. The principal and telling difference between the two, however, was that Lieutenant Baker had repeatedly engaged in close combat with the enemy, whereas Runyon had not.[128] Although only one eyewitness has testified that Lieutenant Baker's award recommendation was downgraded from a Medal of Honor to a Distinguished Service Cross, it is clear that Baker had met a higher standard of merit for his Distinguished Service Cross than Runyon had met for his Medal of Honor recommendation.

The disparity may simply reflect the natural differences in award standards between two commanders—Almond and Wood—or may reflect Wood's personal relationship with Runyon. On the other hand, it may also indicate the existence in the Division of a double standard for the highest valor awards no matter who was in command. General Almond had not recommended any black infantryman for a Distinguished Service Cross in the wake of the failed February offensive, though he had recommended that two white infantry officers receive the award. Up to that point, Almond had always tied individual heroism to unit or group success on the battlefield when it came to the highest valor awards for infantry. He returned again to that standard with Baker's Distinguished Service Cross recommendation. For his part, Wood was certainly very familiar with the obvious contrast between what Baker and Runyon had accomplished personally on 5 April, yet he went ahead with a Medal of Honor recommendation for Runyon.

The focus, thus far, has appropriately been on the 92nd's infantry.[129] Others of the Division's organic elements—the artillery and combat engineers and two African-American units attached to the Division, the 758th Tank Battalion and the 679th Tank Destroyer Battalion—were also engaged in combat. Many men assigned to these units fought heroically and earned valor awards.

The Headquarters Battery and twenty total batteries, of the 597th, 598th, 599th, and 600th Field Artillery Battalions, provided fire support for the 92nd Infantry Division's operations. The 597th and 600th were completely African-American; the 598th and 599th had both black and white officers. The 598th entered combat with the 370th Regiment at the end of August 1944, and the three other battalions were committed during the first two weeks of November.[130]

Performing effectively throughout the war, the artillery units drew praise from many, including their commander, Brigadier General William H. Colbern, and from General Almond. Writing to Lieutenant General Truscott after the February offensive, Almond said that the artillery support had been "excellent" and "all that could be desired." After the War ended, the Division Board, assessing the 92nd's black soldiers, concluded that black artillerymen, when compared with black infantrymen, had more pride, were better disciplined, and took better care of their equipment. Unable to evaluate black soldiers without injecting a heavy dose of racism, however, the Board members explained that the artillerymen were better than the infantrymen in part because they were more closely supervised and free from "arduous, dangerous tasks."[131]

Certainly most artillerymen were out of harm's way, but many were not. During the night of 4-5 February, Private First Class Herman E. Rochelle, a member of a 597th forward observer party, laid a wire communications line over almost a half-mile of difficult terrain through a minefield and under mortar fire. When the line was cut in several places by enemy shell fire, Private First Class Rochelle not only repaired it under fire but also laid a second line. After completing this task, he noticed a house being used by the enemy as an observation post. Grabbing a bazooka and covered by another soldier in the forward observer party, Rochelle advanced over 100 yards in the face of small arms fire. About 75 yards from the house, Rochelle fired the bazooka, forcing the house's occupants to surrender and capturing their communications equipment.[132]

Private First Class Rochelle continued to repair breaks in the line while under fire until he was killed in action on 17 February. For his extraordinary heroism, the Division recommended Rochelle for the Distinguished Service Cross. The Fifth Army, however, disapproved the award, and Rochelle received a Silver Star—one of the 11 Silver Stars and over 100 Bronze Stars awarded to the 92nd Division's artillerymen.[133]

Lt. Spencer C. Moore, Company D, 365th Infantry Regiment, 92nd Infantry Division, with German prisoners in the background, May 1945, Modena, Italy. Courtesy Spencer C. Moore.

Despite their unit's early turmoil, men of the 317th Engineer Combat Battalion supported the Division's operations by clearing minefields and constructing river, stream, and canal crossings, often under fire. In this battalion, 24 were killed and 96 wounded in action with 20 of these casualties taken during the Division's unsuccessful effort to secure a foothold across the Cinquale Canal in February. In all, the 317th's combat engineers were awarded 9 Silver Stars and 34 Bronze Stars.[134]

Except for the flat terrain near the coast, most of the 92nd's sector on the northern Italian front was not well suited for armor operations. Nevertheless, and in spite of the fact that neither the 758th Tank Battalion nor the 679th Tank Destroyer Battalion was attached to the Division until 1945, both made significant contributions to combat operations. Attached to the 92nd on about 1 January 1945, the 758th, with both black and white officers, fought not as a battalion but in detachments supporting other units. Three of its tanks "drowned" in an attempt to cross the mouth of the Cinquale Canal in February and had to be destroyed. Early in the 92nd's April offensive, tanks from the 758th entered the city of Massa, long a Division objective. As the 92nd pursued retreating German and Italian Fascist forces, the 758th was given responsibility for the Division's coastal sector. Three of the 758th's officers won Silver Stars, and the unit totaled 44 Bronze Stars. Its casualties were relatively light: 4 killed and 16 wounded in action.[135]

The 679th Tank Destroyer Battalion, with only white officers, entered combat attached to the 92nd in mid–March 1945. Although in action for only about six weeks, the 679th enjoyed the distinction of silencing the coastal guns at Punta Bianca, which had survived repeated Allied naval shelling and air bombardment and had caused so many casualties in the 92nd. Between 14 and 19 April, the 679th employed as many as 36 of its 76-mm guns in coordinated, indirect, and rapid fire that hurled more than 11,000 rounds against the guns emplaced in concrete. The 679th's history stated the result very succinctly: "Punta Bianca guns did not fire after 0200, 19 April 1945." In all, the 679th fired over 47,000 rounds while supporting the 92nd. Two if its officers received Silver Stars, and five of its men were awarded Bronze Stars, all but one of them going to officers.[136]

## Other Ground Combat and Combat Support Units

Several African-American antiaircraft artillery units operated in the Mediterranean Theater during 1943–44. Among them, only the 450th Anti-Aircraft Artillery Battalion, after arriving in Italy, saw much action. No one in any of the units received awards for valor.

The 90th Coast Artillery Regiment followed the 450th into North Africa. Along with the 450th, it defended North African ports and airfields. Only infrequently were hostile aircraft either observed or fired on. One unit, for example, engaged enemy aircraft on but two occasions. In March 1944, the 90th Coast Artillery Regiment was redesignated the 90th Anti-Aircraft Artillery Group, the 897th Anti-Aircraft Artillery Battalion, and the 334th Searchlight Battalion.[137] The 334th Searchlight Battalion went to Corsica in May 1944 and to southern France in October, where, by December, it had been reorganized into several truck companies. The 897th met a similar fate after its arrival in southern France from North Africa.[138]

The 450th, however, deployed to Italy in November 1943 and defended a variety of Allied facilities. Its arrival was auspicious. Some of its personnel, on board two ships in Naples harbor with the organization's equipment, engaged attacking enemy aircraft. But neither the 450th's gunners nor its guns went into action. Instead, on one ship, some of the 450th's truckers manned two Bofors guns that had been hastily rigged by the ship's captain. On the other ship, another 450th support soldier fired at an attacking plane with a .50-caliber machine gun from the cab of one of the unit's trucks. From November 1943 through September 1944, the 450th Anti-Aircraft Artillery Battalion routinely fired on enemy aircraft, claiming several victims with some probably destroyed or damaged.[139]

The African-American 24th Chemical Company (Decontamination) landed at Salerno on 11 September 1943, two days after the Fifth Army's invasion had begun. The unit generated smoke over the harbor for several weeks, with its men often subject to bombing and strafing from enemy aircraft. The 24th continued its smoke-generating mission, along with other chemical activities, at different locations in Italy through February 1944, sustaining a few light casualties from hostile actions. None of its soldiers received any of the higher valor awards.[140]

## The 332nd Fighter Group

The black airmen of the 99th Pursuit Squadron arrived in North Africa in April 1943, entered combat in June, and moved, in turn, to bases in Sicily and Italy to support Allied landings. Near Anzio on 27 January 1944, one of the 99th's patrols spotted more than a dozen FW 190 German fighters dive-bombing and strafing Allied shipping near the shore. The P-40s attacked and quickly destroyed eight enemy aircraft.[141]

In June 1944, after a year of combat, the 99th joined the 332nd Fighter Group, which had been deployed to Italy in February. Commanded by Lieutenant Colonel Benjamin O. Davis, Jr., who had also commanded the 99th for four months in North Africa, the 332nd Fighter Group also included the 100th, 301st, and 302nd fighter squadrons. That summer, the 332nd was transferred to the 15th Air Force with the new mission of bomber escort, although it could still be used for ground support and other missions as the need arose.[142]

Lieutenant General Ira Eaker, Mediterranean Allied Air Force Commander, was enthusiastic about the 332nd's new role: "These colored pilots have very high morale and are eager to get started on their new strategic task of accompanying long range heavy bombers.... [T]heir Wing Commander ... has watched them closely in their indoctrination phase and he feels as I do, that they will give a good account of themselves."[143] General Eaker's expectations were soon fulfilled. On the third mission from their new base at Ramitelli, Italy, the 332nd's flyers destroyed five enemy aircraft that attempted to intercept a flight of B-24 Liberator bombers that the 332nd was escorting.[144]

Ranging the skies over the Mediterranean and into the heart of Germany after acquiring the long-range P-51, the 332nd flew over 1,500 missions (15,000 individual sorties). In all, the Tuskegee airmen destroyed 108 enemy planes in aerial combat and 150 on the ground. As escort fighters, the 332nd never lost a bomber to an enemy fighter. Two pilots even received Distinguished Flying Crosses for sinking a German destroyer off the Italian coastline in June 1944.[145]

A crew chief and his pilot (SSgt. Conige C. Mormon and Lt. "Lucky" Lester) on their P-51, 332nd Fighter Group, 15th Air Force, in Italy, mid-1944 or after. The three swastikas below the windshield signify that Lt. Lester had already shot down three German aircraft. U.S. Air Force Photograph, National Air and Space Museum, Smithsonian Institution.

Among their many awards, the 332nd's pilots counted 1 Silver Star, 95 Distinguished Flying Crosses, 744 Air Medals, and 5 Distinguished Unit Citations (2 earned by the 99th before it became a part of the 332nd).[146] Now retired, Lieutenant General Benjamin O. Davis, Jr., has recently verified that he did not submit any of his pilots for either a Distinguished Service Cross or a Medal of Honor.[147]

## Conclusion

Aside from the pilots of the 332nd Fighter Group, the African Americans in the Mediterranean Theater who saw significant combat and had the most opportunity to earn the highest valor awards served with the 92nd Infantry Division in northern Italy. Two obstacles make an analysis of the Division's awards policies and practices difficult. The first is the absence of the bulk of the 92nd's awards case files. Availability of these records would help in determining, for example, the number of award recommendations that were either elevated or downgraded from the original by any of several command echelons in the Division.[148] The second, and more formidable, barrier is the tendency for discrimination to be manifested in quiet and subtle ways, leaving few traces.

Sufficient evidence is available, however, to offer some conclusions. General Almond used valor awards only partially to recognize heroism. He also believed them valuable as means to inspire other soldiers in the Division. Furthermore, he apparently reserved Distinguished Service Cross recommendations for heroism that occurred in conjunction with battlefield success. This linkage was illustrated in the three Distinguished Service Cross recommendations for black infantrymen in September and early October 1944, when the Division performed well in the field. Almond's policy also probably explains why Lieutenant Fox's Distinguished Service Cross recommendation was not forwarded to the Fifth Army and why no black infantrymen were recommended by the Division for the award following the February offensive. In April, Lieutenant Baker performed heroically far out in front of his regiment, the 370th Infantry, which did not follow suit, even though the Japanese-American 442nd Infantry and the white 473rd Infantry were, at the same time, making substantial and rapid gains.

General Almond did not, however, apply his criterion consistently. Two of the Division's white infantry officers received Distinguished Service Cross recommendations amid the failure of the February offensive. The assistant adjutant's testimony that Lieutenant Baker had been recommended for the Medal of Honor, and General Wood's nomination of Captain Runyon for the Medal, further indicate that there were two different standards of merit for the highest valor awards in the Division.

There is no denying that the Division's senior white officers held deeply prejudiced, even racist, views of African-American soldiers. Initially, the degree of prejudice no doubt varied by individual and reflected prevailing attitudes in American society. When the Division did not produce results on the battlefield, however, the white officers' views led to an overarching and explicitly racist thesis about black infantry. Moreover, whether intended or not, this thesis provided the commanders a rationale for avoiding any personal responsibility for the Division's performance.

To be sure, a component of their thesis conceded that a few African-American soldiers could exhibit skill and heroism that merited valor awards. Still, the evidence suggests limits to that recognition, and the views these commanders expressed about the abilities of African Americans to fight as infantrymen in general could not help but prejudice their judgment and objectivity about the heroism of individual black soldiers in specific situations.

# Notes

1. Headquarters, Mediterranean Theater of Operations Report, "Participation of Negro Troops in the Post-War Establishment," 13 August 1945, folder "Army Ground Forces Report on Negro Troops," Box 183, Decimal 291.2, Army Ground Forces General Correspondence, 1942–48, Record Group (RG) 337, National Archives (NA), Washington, D.C.; [Morris J. MacGregor, Jr., et al.], *American Military History [Army Historical Series]* (Washington, D.C.: U.S. Government Printing Office, 1989), p. 473.
2. Headquarters, Mediterranean Theater of Operations Report, "Participation of Negro Troops in the Post-War Military Establishment," 13 August 1945.
3. Thomas St. John Arnold, *Buffalo Soldiers: The 92nd Infantry Division and Reinforcements in World War II, 1942–1945* (Manhattan, Kans.: Sunflower University Press, 1990), p. 7.
4. Major General Daniel Noce memorandum for Commanding General, Mediterranean Theater of Operations, "Participation of Negro Combat Troops in the North African Campaign," 23 April 1945, folder, "Negro Combat Units—Staff Study," Box 110, Allied Force Headquarters, Command Group, SAC Secretariat, Historical Section, Subject Files, 1943–45, RG 331, Washington National Records Center (WNRC), Suitland, Md.; Lieutenant General Mark W. Clark commendation letter to Commanding Officer, 450th AAA (AW) Bn, 29 November 1943, folder "CABN-450-0.3 (1376), Historical Record, 450th AAA (AW) Bn, Dec 43," Box 17171, 450th AAA (AW) Battalion, Coast Artillery, World War II Operations Reports, 1940–48, RG 407, WNRC.
5. Stanley Sandler, *Segregated Skies: All-Black Combat Squadrons of WWII* (Washington, D.C.: Smithsonian Institution Press, 1992), pp. 43–46.
6. Folder "QMCO-3404-0.3 (31926), Overseas Record, 3404th QM Truck Co, 22 May 43–22 Sep 45," Box 22673, 3404th Quartermaster Truck Company, Quartermaster, World War II Operations Reports, 1940–48, RG 407, WNRC; War Department Press Release, 27 July 1944, folder "Releases—Negro, 1943–1944," Box 243, Subject File, 1940–47, Civilian Aide to the Secretary, Office, Assistant Secretary of War, RG 107, NA.
7. Fifth Army General Order 63, 15 April 1944, Box 2077, Fifth Army, World War II Operations Reports, 1940–48, RG 407, WNRC; folder "ENBN-387-0.1 (21545), History, 387th Engr Bn (Sep), May 42–Nov 44," Box 18850, 387th Engineer Battalion (Sep), Engineers, World War II Operations Reports, 1940–48, RG 407, WNRC.
8. Determining the exact number of Silver Stars awarded to African Americans in the Mediterranean Theater is difficult for the same reasons that a precise calculation was not possible for the European Theater. The estimate for the Mediterranean Theater, based on extensive research in Army records, is about 100.
9. Hondon B. Hargrove, *Buffalo Soldiers in Italy: Black Americans in World War II* (Jefferson, N.C.: McFarland & Company, 1985), pp. 4–6, 15, 30–32; Ulysses Lee, *The Employment of Negro Troops [United States Army in World War II]* (Washington, D.C.: U.S. Government Printing Office, 1966), p. 556.
10. Arnold, *Buffalo Soldiers*, p. 216.
11. "Brief Outline of 92nd Infantry Division, 15 October 1942 to 6 September 1944," 19 October 1944, folder "Resume of Operations—92nd Inf Div," Box 13260A, 92nd Infantry Division, World War II Operations Reports, 1940–48, RG 407, WNRC.
12. Arnold, *Buffalo Soldiers*, pp. 7, 216–18.
13. Lee, *Employment of Negro Troops*, pp. 557, 567, 572–75, 580.

14. Major General Edward M. Almond "Approving Action of Commanding General 92d Infantry Division of Proceedings of Board of Review Appointed by Letter Orders Dated 23 June 1945 to Consider the Combat Effectiveness of Negro Officers and Enlisted Men," 2 July 1945, folder "Top Secret 92nd Infantry Division Combat Efficiency Analysis and Supplementary Report," Box 5869 (new Box 6), Far East Command, Chief of Staff General Records, 1945–50, RG 338, WNRC. The Fifth Army and the Headquarters, Mediterranean Theater of Operations, the command echelons immediately above the 92nd, similarly concluded that the Division's combat performance had been "unsatisfactory." See Lieutenant General Lucian K. Truscott, Report of Commanding General, Mediterranean Theater of Operations, "Participation of Negro Troops in the Post-War Military Establishment," 30 July 1945, folder "General Truscott's Letter File, Dec 1944–Aug 1945," Box 1, Fifth Army Secretary General Staff Correspondence, 1943–45, RG 338, WNRC; Headquarters, Mediterranean Theater of Operations Report, "Participation of Negro Troops in the Post-War Military Establishment," 13 August 1945.

15. Almond, "Approving Action," 2 July 1945.

16. Truman K. Gibson letter to Major General O. L. Nelson, Deputy Commander, Mediterranean Theater of Operations, "Report on Visit to 92nd Division," 12 March 1945, Papers of Edward M. Almond, U.S. Army Military History Institute, Carlisle Barracks, Penn.

17. Lee, *Employment of Negro Troops*, pp. 577–78.

18. Quoted in *ibid.*, p. 579.

19. Two exceptions are Paul Goodman, *A Fragment of Victory in Italy during World War II* (Carlisle Barracks, Penn.: Army War College, 1952), and Arnold's *Buffalo Soldiers*. Goodman, Assistant G-2 (Intelligence) in the 92nd Division, recognized that the "psychological and sociological factors" had some impact but avoided discussing them in his work because "every attempt to branch off in pursuit of psychological and sociological tangents clouded the picture of the military performance of the division" (preface, vii). Arnold, the Division's G-3 (Operations), did not even go that far, never once using the words "race," "segregation," "racial prejudice," or "discrimination."

20. Lee, *Employment of Negro Troops*, pp. 549–50.

21. Ernest F. Fisher, Jr., *Cassino to the Alps [United States Army in World War II]* (Washington, D.C.: U.S. Government Printing Office, 1977), p. 391.

22. Bernard C. Nalty, *Strength for the Fight: A History of Black Americans in the Military* (New York: Free Press, 1986), pp. 172–73.

23. Morris J. MacGregor, Jr., *Integration of the Armed Forces, 1940–1965 [Defense Studies Series]* (Washington, D.C.: U.S. Government Printing Office, 1981), pp. 136–37.

24. Hargrove, *Buffalo Soldiers in Italy*.

25. Almond "Approving Action," 2 July 1945; Lee, *Employment of Negro Troops*, pp. 495–96.

26. Interview of Truman K. Gibson by John A. Cash and Daniel K. Gibran, 12 March 1994, Chicago, Ill.

27. Interview of Parren J. Mitchell by John A. Cash, 1 March 1994, Washington, D.C.

28. Interview of Vernon J. Baker by John A. Cash and Daniel K. Gibran, 15 March 1994, Spokane, Wash.

30. Lee, *Employment of Negro Troops*, p. 334.

30. *Ibid.*, p. 295.

31. Interview of David Cason, Jr., in Mary Penick Motley, comp. and ed., *The Invisible Soldier: The Experience of the Black Soldier in World War II* (Detroit, Mich.: Wayne State University Press, 1975), p. 266.

32. Goodman, *Fragment of Victory*, p. 13; Lee, *Employment of Negro Troops*, p. 553. Historian Dale E. Wilson stated that, due principally to General Almond's racist attitudes, the 92nd Infantry Division was unprepared for combat. See "Recipe for Failure: Major General Edward M. Almond and Preparation of the U.S. 92d Infantry Division for Combat in World War II," *Journal of Military History* 56 (July 1992), pp. 473–88.

33. Lee, *Employment of Negro Troops*, pp. 553–54.

34. Anonymous letter to Lieutenant Bert Cumby, 23 February 1945, folder "Correspondence Regarding Personnel and Sundry Papers, April 1943–June 1945," Box 13620B, 92nd Infantry Division, World War II Operations Reports, 1940–48, RG 407, WNRC.

35. Quoted in Lee, *Employment of Negro Troops*, p. 334.

36. Gibson letter to Nelson, "Report on Visit to 92nd Division," 12 March 1945.

37. Lee, *Employment of Negro Troops*, pp. 538–53.

38. Brigadier General John E. Wood letters to Major General Edward M. Almond, 8, 15, 20, and 22 September 1944, all in folder "Correspondence Regarding Personnel and Sundry Papers, April 1943–June 1945," Box 13620B, 92nd Infantry Division, World War II Operations Reports, 1940–48, RG 407, WNRC.

39. Lieutenant Colonel John J. Phelan letter to Commanding General, 92nd Infantry Division, "Notes on the Actions of the 370th Infantry Regiment, Period of 7–12 October 1944," 13 October 1944, folder "Combat Report, 370th Inf Regt, 1944–45," Box 13620B, 92nd Infantry Division, World War II Operations Reports, 1940–48, RG 407, WNRC.

40. Notes of Colonel Raymond G. Sherman Remarks to Col. Semmes, G-1, IV Corps, 20 October 1944, folder "Correspondence Regarding Personnel and Sundry Papers, April 1943–45," Box 13620B, 92nd Infantry Division, World War II Operations Reports, 1940–48, RG 407, WNRC. A month later, Sherman submitted a formal, but abbreviated, version of the notes to General Almond. The formal report contained one important modification. Still saying that it was too early to be definite, Sherman added that the "tendencies" he observed in the majority of his solders indicated that "the process of making a good soldier would be much longer with the negro than with the white." See Colonel Raymond G. Sherman letter to Commanding General, 92nd Infantry Division, "The Negro Soldier in Combat," 26 November 1944, folder "Combat Report, 370th Inf Regt, 1944–45," Box 13620B, 92nd Infantry Division, World War II Operations Reports, 1940–48, RG 407, WNRC.

41. Days later, more than 25 men were found hiding in houses well away from the front, 4 in a home for the aged run by nuns. See the IV Corps report "Loss of Combat Efficiency of the 2d Battalion, 370th Infantry Regiment," 6 January 1945, folder "AG 333 Report of Investigation, Operations of 2nd Bn, 370th Inf Regt, 24–25 November 1944," Box 67, Decimal 333, Fifth Army Adjutant General, General Correspondence, RG 338, WNRC.

42. Brigadier General John E. Wood letter to Commanding General, 92nd Infantry Division, "Demonstrated Capability of Negro Troops," 25 November 1944, folder "Correspondence Regarding Personnel and Sundry Papers, April 1943–June 1945," Box 13620B, 92nd Infantry Division, World War II Operations Reports, 1940–48, RG 407, WNRC.

43. Major General Edward M. Almond letter to Lieutenant General Mark W. Clark, 27 November 1944, folder "Top Secret 92nd Infantry Division Combat Efficiency Analysis," Box 5869 (new Box 6), Far East Command, Chief of Staff General Records, 1945–50, RG 338, WNRC.

44. Lee, *Employment of Negro Troops*, pp. 562–67.

128  The Exclusion of Black Soldiers from the Medal of Honor

45. Major General Edward M. Almond letter to Lieutenant General Lucian K. Truscott, 11 February 1945, folder "Top Secret 92nd Infantry Division Combat Efficiency Analysis"; Lee, *Employment of Negro Troops*, pp. 568–72.

46. Colonel Raymond G. Sherman letter for Commanding General, 92nd Infantry Division, "The Negro Soldier in Combat," 8 March 1945; Colonel James Notestein letter for Commanding General, 92nd Infantry Division, "Tactical Notes," 15 January 1945; Colonel James Notestein letter for the Commanding General, 92nd Infantry Division, "Revised Tactical Notes," 23 February 1945; all in folder "Top Secret 92nd Infantry Division Combat Efficiency Analysis,"; copies of the investigations are in folder "Secret and Confidential Reports on the 366th Infantry during Its Period of Attachment to the 92nd Inf Div in Italy," Box 13620B, 92nd Infantry Division, World War II Operations Reports, 1940–48, RG 407, WNRC. A supplement to the investigation of the 366th's Second Battalion, involving the interrogation of several of the Division's General Staff section heads, is in folder "Top Secret 92nd Infantry Division Combat Efficiency Analysis."

47. Colonel J. D. Armstrong letter for Commanding General, 92nd Infantry Division, 21 February 1945, folder "Top Secret 92nd Infantry Division Combat Efficiency Analysis."

48. Lieutenant Colonel Alonzo G. Ferguson letter for Commanding General, 92nd Infantry Division, 13 February 1945, folder "Report on the Operations of the 366th Inf Regiment, Dec 1944–Sept 1945," Box 13620A, 92nd Infantry Division, World War II Operations Reports, 1940–48, RG 407, WNRC.

49. Major C. F. Mock, Jr., Notes on Gibson's Report, 27 March 1945, folder "Correspondence Regarding Personnel and Sundry Papers, April 1943–June 1945," Box 13620B, 92nd Infantry Division, World War II Operations Reports, 1940–48, RG 407, WNRC; Lee, *Employment of Negro Troops*, pp. 572–75.

50. *Ibid.*, pp. 582–84.

51. Colonel Raymond G. Sherman, "Narrative of Attack by 370th Infantry, April 5–8th (1945)," 8 May 1945, folder "Combat Report, 370th Inf Regt, 1944–45," Box 13620B, 92nd Infantry Division, World War II Operations Reports, 1940–48, RG 407, WNRC.

52. Colonel J. D. Armstrong letter for Commanding General, 92nd Infantry Division, "Efficiency of Colored Officers and Enlisted Men," 20 June 1945; Colonel James Notestein letter for Commanding General, 92nd Infantry Division, "Summation of Tactical Notes," 21 June 1945; all in folder "Top Secret 92nd Infantry Division Combat Efficiency Analysis," Brigadier General J. E. Wood letter for Commanding General, 92nd Infantry Division, "Estimate of Our Personnel," 21 June 1945, folder "Correspondence Regarding Personnel and Sundry Papers, April 1943–June 1945," Box 13620B, 92nd Infantry Division, World War II Operations Reports, 1940–48, RG 407, WNRC.

53. Colonel J. D. Armstrong letter for Commanding General, 92nd Infantry Division, "Efficiency of Colored Officers and Enlisted Men," 20 June 1945, folder "Top Secret 92nd Infantry Division Combat Efficiency Analysis."

54. *Ibid.*

55. *Ibid.*

56. See table "Battle Casualties 365th Infantry," 5 September 1945, folder "392 INF (365)-0.3 (45746), Opn Rpt—365th Inf Regt, 92nd Inf Div," Box 13673, 92nd Infantry Division, World War II Operations Reports, 1940–48, RG 407, WNRC.

57. General Joseph T. McNarney letter for Major General E. M. Almond, 16 June 1945; Major General E. M. Almond letter orders, 23 June 1945; "Proceedings of a Board of Review Appointed by Commanding General, 92nd Infantry Division on

the Subject, Combat Effectiveness of Negro Officers and Enlisted Men," 24–25 June 1945; Almond, "Approving Action," 2 July 1945; Major General E. M. Almond letter through Commanding General Fifth Army to Commanding General, Mediterranean Theater of Operations, 2 July 1945; all in folder "Top Secret 92nd Infantry Division Combat Efficiency Analysis." Apparently, no historian has ever cited the Board's report or General Almond's approving letter. In *Employment of Negro Troops*, Lee cited several of the 15 reference documents appended to the report but not the report itself or Almond's letter. Headquarters, Mediterranean Theater of Operations, attached the report, Almond's letter, and the reference documents as Exhibit F of its own study of the postwar use of African-American soldiers; General McNarney forwarded this to the Army chief of staff. See General Joseph T. McNarney letter to Chief of Staff, 13 August 1945, attaching Headquarters, Mediterranean Theater of Operations report, "Participation of Negro Troops in the Post-War Military Establishment," 13 August 1945, folder "Army Ground Forces Report on Negro Troops," Box 183, Decimal 291.1, Army Ground Forces General Correspondence, 1942–48, RG 337, NA.

58. Although Colonel McCaffrey's signature block appears at the end of the Board's report, he was the only Board member who did not sign it. Arnold states (*Buffalo Soldiers*, p. 206) that McCaffrey left the Division to return to the United States on 30 June 1945 and, therefore, may simply not have been present to sign. On the other hand, it is possible that the absence of his signature reflected McCaffrey's disagreement with some of the report's conclusions. In December 1944, Colonel McCaffrey had expressed his views on the 92nd's black soldiers to a visiting War Department staff officer. Colonel McCaffrey told the officer that there had been many examples of individual heroism. Yet he added: "the Negro generally could not overcome or escape his background of no property ownership, irresponsibility, and subservience. The Negro is panicky and his environment has not conditioned him to accept responsibilities." See Truman K. Gibson memorandum for Assistant Secretary of War John J. McCloy, 20 December 1944, folder "ASW 291.2 Negro Troops—F-Z," Box 37, Decimal 291.2, Assistant Secretary of War, General Correspondence of John J. McCloy, 1941–45, RG 107, NA.

59. "Proceedings of a Board of Review," 24–25 June 1945, paragraph (para) 6, folder "Top Secret 92nd Infantry Division Combat Efficiency Analysis."

60. *Ibid.*, para 7 ("They undoubtedly affected stability adversely but in degree rather than principle").

61. *Ibid.*, para 17.

62. *Ibid.*, para 10. Similarly, even though Colonel Sherman was a member of the Board, the report demeaned his 370th Infantry Regiment, enclosing the terms "battle-wise" and "battle-tested" in quotation marks preceding references to the 370th. See paras 12 and 20.

63. *Ibid.*, paras 24 and 38. White officers, said the Board, "have performed well and have been conspicuous in their steadfastness and cheerful acceptance of long hours and a disproportionate amount of responsibility made necessary by faults of the considerable majority of negro officers."

64. *Ibid.*, paras 27, 29, 30, 32. General McNarney, the Mediterranean Theater Commander, distanced himself to some extent from the 92nd's racist analysis. In his 13 August 1945 letter to the Army chief of staff, McNarney expressed his doubt that the difficulty in developing competent black junior officers and noncommissioned officers could be blamed "entirely upon inherent racial characteristics. The lack of initiative, the unwillingness to accept responsibility and the defensive attitude of negroes in general must be attributed in large part to the history of the race since its emancipation. They have had little opportunity for educational advancement, and few chances

to shoulder responsibility or to develop initiative." See McNarney letter to Chief of Staff, 13 August 1945, attaching Headquarters, Mediterranean Theater of Operations report.

65. Almond, "Approving Action," 2 July 1945; "Proceedings of Board of Review," 24–25 June 1945, paras 29 and 42. At the time the Board's report was prepared in late June, the Division had yet to award more than 120 of the approximately 260 Silver Stars it would bestow during the War.

66. In 1982, the Army awarded a Distinguished Service Cross (posthumous) to First Lieutenant John R. Fox of Cannon Company, 366th Infantry Regiment, for extraordinary heroism on 26 December 1944. See Department of the Army General Order 9, 15 April 1982, file in Military Awards Branch, Total Army Personnel Command, Alexandria, Va. While attached to the 92nd in the last month of the war, members of the 473rd Infantry Regiment earned three Distinguished Service Crosses, and the men of the Japanese-American Regimental Combat Team received five Distinguished Service Crosses and one Medal of Honor (Private First Class Sadao Munemori). Including the awards earned during service with the 92nd, the 442nd's soldiers received a total of 49 Distinguished Service Crosses while fighting in both Italy and northwestern Europe (more Distinguished Service Crosses than all but 11 of the Army's 89 divisions). See Albert F. Gleim and George B. Harris III, *Distinguished Service Cross Awards for World War II*, rev. 2d ed. (Fort Myer, Va.: Planchet Press, 1991).

67. The 92nd Infantry Division (along with Task Force 92, commanded by Brigadier General Wood and, for a time, by General Almond) awarded a total (including clusters, or second awards) of approximately 260 Silver Stars and 1,327 Bronze Stars (a large percentage for meritorious service rather than heroic achievement). These figures, like all award data on the 92nd in this chapter, are based on the following sources: General Orders of the 92nd Infantry Division, in Box 13633, 92nd Infantry Division, World War II Operations Reports, 1940–48, RG 407, WNRC; General Orders of the 92nd Infantry Division and Task Force 92, on microfiche in the Military Awards Branch, Total Army Personnel Command; and the Operations Reports for 3 August 1942–15 August 1945 and 15 August 1945–30 October 1945, prepared by the 92nd Division's Adjutant General Section, in Box 13660, 92nd Infantry Division, World War II Operations Reports, 1940–48, RG 407, WNRC. The General Orders on microfiche in the Military Awards Branch often identify the awardee's unit; the General Orders in the 92nd's World War II files at the Washington National Records Center usually do not. Additionally, the microfiche files contain some General Orders not found in the unit files. The Adjutant General Section reports identify the number of awards by type and military rank for each assigned unit and the major attached units.

68. Interview of Dennette A. Harrod by John A. Cash, 30 December 1993, Washington, D.C.; Interview of Mitchell, 1 March 1994; Interview of Hondon B. Hargrove by John A. Cash and Daniel K. Gibran, 13 March 1994, Lansing, Mich.

69. Interview of Harrod, 30 December 1993.

70. Adjutant General Section Operations Report, 3 August 1942–15 August 1945, Box 13660, 92nd Infantry Division, World War II Operations Reports, 1940–48, RG 407, WNRC. This report noted one of the Adjutant General's functions: "issuance from this headquarters of such directives as required from time to time to emphasize the Division Commander's policy of overlooking no deserving individual" (draft titled "Citations," folder "Combat Efficiency Analysis Incl-1 History," Box 13620, 92nd Infantry Division, World War II Operations Reports, RG 407, WNRC). Two days before leaving the 92nd, General Almond sent a letter to each of his commanders, requesting that he be informed if any of their officers or enlisted men deserved an award, since it "has always been my policy to insure appropriate awards to all of those who merit

same." See Major General Edward M. Almond letter [to each commander], "Awards and Decorations," 11 August 1945, folder "Resume of Operations—92nd Inf Div," Box 13620A, 92nd Infantry Division, World War II Operations Reports, 1940–48, RG 407, WNRC.

71. Final Report of Colonel Paul N. Starlings, Army Ground Forces Board, Mediterranean Theater of Operations, 7 May 1945, folder, "Negroes," Box 509, Chief of Military History, Records of the Historical Services Division, Publications, Unpublished Manuscripts, and Supporting Records, 1943–1977, 2-3.7 CJ5 Special Studies, The Utilization of Negro Manpower, RG 319, NA.

72. Adjutant General Section Operations Report, 3 August 1942–15 August 1945, Box 13660, 92nd Infantry Division, World War II Operations Reports, 1940–48, RG 407, WNRC. The Awards and Decorations Board members have not been identified. For an example of the 92nd Division form giving the Awards and Decorations Board recommendation with blocks for approval/disapproval by the G-1, chief of staff, and Division commander, see the Individual Personnel Record ("201 File") for Private First Class Walter A. Merritt, at the National Personnel Records Center, St. Louis, Mo.

73. The following 92nd Division General Orders could not be located: #36 from 1944; #31, 77, 99, 101–5 from 1945. Many General Orders did not contain award announcements.

74. Once the unit is known, the race of most individuals can be deduced from the following. Three units—the 597th and 600th Field Artillery Battalions and the attached 366th Infantry Regiment—had only African-American personnel. Only three of the 92nd's attached units were African-American (the 366th, the 758th Tank Battalion and the 679th Tank Destroyer Battalion). All of the enlisted men in the 92nd's assigned and attached African-American units were black. All of the officers in the 679th Tank Destroyer Battalion were white. Other ways to determine race are the Individual Personnel Records, at St. Louis, and the Army's World War II casualty data, maintained on microfiche by the Memorial Affairs Branch, Total Army Personnel Command. The latter source identifies the race of soldiers killed in action. The 92nd's General Orders indicate which of its awards were posthumous. Finally, Jehu C. Hunter, a veteran of the 365th Infantry Regiment (and author with Major Clark of the privately printed *The Buffalo Division in World War II*), assisted in identifying the race of several awardees.

75. 92nd Infantry Division Awards Case Files, Box 131, RG 338, WNRC.

76. Fifth Army Awards Case Files, Boxes 53–65, 314–24, RG 338, WNRC.

77. A search was conducted for the Individual Personnel Records of more than 150 men (excluding Japanese Americans) who were awarded Silver Stars by the 92nd Infantry Division. Only a few were located. Of these, the records of eight black soldiers contain the original award recommendation. In three cases, the original recommendation was for a decoration lower than the one finally awarded.

78. Derived from 92nd Infantry Division General Orders and Adjutant General Section Operations Reports.

79. *Ibid.* Of the approximately 100 Silver Stars the Division awarded to soldiers from its assigned (i.e., organic) units, blacks received 73 and white officers 24 (the race of 3 has not been identified).

80. The Division approved the 473rd Infantry Regiment's recommendation that Lieutenant Colonel John J. Phelan, formerly the 370th Infantry Regiment's executive officer, be posthumously awarded the Distinguished Service Cross. Lieutenant Colonel Phelan was killed in action two days after assuming command of the 473rd's First Battalion in the second week of April 1945. See a copy of the award recommendation, disapproved by Fifth Army, in Box 131, 92nd Infantry Division Awards Case Files, RG 338, WNRC.

81. More then 35 years after the war, through the efforts of Hondon Hargrove,

First Lieutenant John R. Fox became the second African American who served with the 92nd Infantry Division to receive a Distinguished Service Cross.

82. Staff Sergeant Fred D. Rhodes Decoration Case File, Binder 32, Box 62; Private Henry D. Roberts Decoration Case File, Box 317; Private Jake McInnis Decoration Case File, Binder 32, Box 62; Private First Class Herman E. Rochelle Decoration Case File, Binder 41, Box 62; all in Fifth Army Awards Case Files, RG 338, WNRC. Each was subsequently awarded a Silver Star. Because of the small quantity of 92nd Infantry Division awards case files that have been preserved, it has not been possible to determine, except in the cases of Lieutenant Fox and perhaps Lieutenant Baker, whether any other officers or enlisted men were recommended by one of the Division's lower echelons (regiment, battalion, or company) for a Distinguished Service Cross or Medal of Honor or whether the Division failed to forward recommendations that it had disapproved to the Fifth Army.

83. Staff Sergeant Rhodes Decoration Case File; 92nd Infantry Division General Order 42, 22 December 1944, General Orders, Box 13633, 92nd Infantry Division, World War II Operations Reports, 1940–48, RG 407, WNRC.

84. Private Roberts Decoration Case File; Fifth Army General Order 181, 4 December 1944, Box 2077, General Orders, Fifth Army, World War II Operations Reports. 1940–48, RG 407, WNRC. Private Roberts was reported missing in action on 31 October 1944.

85. Arnold, *Buffalo Soldiers*, pp. 35, 37.

86. Private McInnis Decoration Case File; 92nd Infantry Division General Order 40, 28 November 1944, General Orders, Box 13633, 92nd Infantry Division, World War II Operations Reports, 1940–48, RG 407, WNRC.

87. *Ibid.*

88. Hargrove, *Buffalo Soldiers in Italy*, pp. 47–48.

89. Lee, *Employment of Negro Troops*, pp. 558–59.

90. Hargrove, *Buffalo Soldiers in Italy*, pp. 53–54. According to Hargrove, Captain Dabney was the first member of the 366th to win a Silver Star. Actually, it appears that Dabney did not receive the award. See Colonel W. J. McCaffrey statement, 19 June 1945, folder "Report on the Operations of the 366th Inf Regiment, Dec 1944–Sept 1945," Box 13620A, 92nd Infantry Division, World War II Operations Reports, 1940–48, RG 407, WNRC.

91. Major General E. M. Almond letter for Commanding Officer, 371st Infantry, "Deficiency in Combat Performance of Individuals and Units, 366th Infantry," 7 December 1944, folder "Report on the Operations of the 366th Inf Regiment, Dec 1944–Sept 1945," Box 13620A, 92nd Infantry Division, World War II Operations Reports, 1940–48, RG 407, WNRC.

92. Colonel James Notestein first endorsement, 12 December 1944, to Major General E. M. Almond letter, 7 December 1944, *ibid.*

93. Major General E. M. Almond second endorsement, 14 December 1944, to Major General E. M. Almond letter, 7 December 1944, *ibid.*

94. Captain C. H. Welch letter for Commanding General, 92nd Infantry Division, "Report of Investigation of Deficiency in Combat Performance of Officers and EM of Co "B", 366th Infantry Regiment," 23 December 1944, folder "Secret and Confidential Reports on the 366th Infantry during its Period of Attachment to the 92nd Inf Div in Italy," Box 13620B, 92nd Infantry Division, World War II Operations Reports, 1940–48, RG 407, WNRC.

95. Colonel W. J. McCaffrey statement, 19 June 1945, folder "Report of the Operations of the 366th Inf Regiment, Dec 1944–Sept 1945," Box 13620A, 92nd Infantry Division, World War II Operations Reports, 1940–48, RG 407, WNRC.

96. 370th Infantry S-3 Journal, 2200 25 December 1944–2200 26 December 1944, folder "392 INF (370)-3.2 (45647), S-3 Jnl-370th CT, 92nd Inf Div, Dec 44," Box 13684, 92nd Infantry Division, World War II Operations Reports, 1940–48, RG 407, WNRC; Major Stephen O. Rossetti, "Account of Battle of Sommocolonia as Related by Partisans," no date, attached to Colonel W. J. McCaffrey memorandum for Commanding General, 92nd Infantry Division, 31 December 1944, in first but unmarked folder, Box 13620, 92nd Infantry Division, World War II Operations Reports, 1940–48, RG 407, WNRC; Hargrove, *Buffalo Soldiers in Italy*, pp. 62–63.

97. 598th Field Artillery Battalion Journal, 0001 26 Dec 44–2400 26 Dec 44, folder "392 FA (598)-0.2 (45584) Histl Rcd-598th FA Bn, 92nd Inf Div, Nov-Dec 44," Box 13669, 92nd Infantry Division, World War II Operations Reports, 1940–48, RG 407, WNRC; 370th S-3 Journal, 2200 25 December 1944–2200 26 December 1944, folder "392 INF (370)-3.2 (45647) S-3 Jnl-370th CT, 92nd Div, Dec 44," Box 13684, 92nd Infantry Division, World War II Operations Reports, 1940–48, RG 407, WNRC; 370th Infantry Regiment, "Events of December 26th–27th, Serchio Valley Sector," 22 February 1945, attached to Captain John J. Kelly letter of transmittal to Commanding General, 92nd Infantry Division, 4 March 1945, folder "392 INF (370)-0.3.0 (45653), Resume of Events (Serchio Valley Sector), 370th Inf Regt (CT), 92nd Inf Div, 26-27 Dec 44," Box 13681, 92nd Infantry Division, World War II Operations Reports, 1940–48, RG 407, WNRC; Interview of Otis Zachary by John A. Cash, 10 July 1994; Interview of Harrod, 30 December 1993; Interview of Wade H. McCree, Jr., in Motley, *Invisible Soldier*, p. 302; Edward A. Raymond, "Black Buffalo," *Field Artillery Journal*, January 1946, pp. 14–16; Hargrove, *Buffalo Soldiers in Italy*, pp. 64–65.

98. Interview of Brigadier General William H. Colbern by Major Bell I. Wiley, 2 July 1945, Almond Papers, U.S. Army Military History Institute; Colonel Edward A. Raymond letter for Major Robert H. Roush (Military Awards Branch, U.S. Army Personnel Center), 18 September 1980, in First Lieutenant John R. Fox Individual Personnel Record, National Personnel Records Center.

99. See Staff Summary, "Positive Findings," attached to Lieutenant Colonel James L. Hickman memorandum for President, Senior Army Decorations Board, "Recommendation for Award—Former First Lieutenant John R. Fox—Decision Memorandum," date illegible (but late 1981 or early 1982), in First Lieutenant Fox Individual Personnel Record; Interview of Harrod, 30 December 1993; Interview of Jefferson L. Jordan, in Motley, *Invisible Soldier*, pp. 279–94. The bodies of Fox and the other men killed in Sommocolonia were not found until the village was retaken from the Germans several days later. In an interview some 30 years later, Jefferson Jordan, graves registration officer for the 371st Infantry, who was in the party that found the bodies, said that a IV Corps officer told him that his party's mission was "secret" and that he should "check the bodies in the village, look for possible bullet holes at the base of the officers' skulls, and draw a conclusion as to whether or not they had been killed by American artillery, American aircraft, or German artillery." Jordan claimed that Fox's body was in a group of bodies, not anywhere near a house. Moreover, said Jordan, he could tell by the way the bodies were mutilated and stacked that death had occurred by aerial bombardment rather than artillery shelling (bombs, in his opinion, threw bodies straight up, artillery shells blew them backward). Though it is true that Allied aircraft attacked German forces near Sommocolonia on 26 December 1944 and, in fact, bombed the village on 27 December 1944 (after it had been taken by the Germans), a cover-up is not likely, even if an accidental bombing had occurred on 26 December. During World War II, the Army was not at all reluctant to protest errant strikes by the Army Air Forces. Indeed, General Almond complained to the Fifth Army about bombs dropped by friendly aircraft in the Division's rear area in mid–January 1945. In

any event, Lieutenant Fox indisputably called for artillery fire on his own position and would doubtless have welcomed bombs as well. See G-2 Periodic Report 1200 25 Dec 44–1200 26 Dec 44, folder "392-2.1 (18292) G-2 Periodic Report—92nd Inf Div, Dec 44," Box 16635; 370th Infantry Regiment Historical Narrative, December 1944, folder "392-0.3 (45414), Hist, 92nd Inf Div," Box 13621; and General Edward M. Almond letter for Commanding General, Fifth Army, folder "392-3.17, Operation Instructions, 92nd Inf Div, 24 Jan 44–12 Apr 45," Box 13656; all in 92nd Infantry Division, World War II Operations Reports, 1940–48, RG 407, WNRC.

100. Colonel McCaffrey memorandum for Commanding General, 31 December 1944.

101. Rossetti, "Account of Battle of Sommocolonia as Related by Partisans."

102. 370th Infantry Regiment, "Events of December 26th–27th, Serchio Valley Sector," 22 February 1945.

103. General Almond did approve a Silver Star (posthumous) for First Lieutenant Graham Jenkins, who was also killed in or near Sommocolonia on 26 December 1944 (92nd Division General Order 18, 6 May 1945). The citation, however, does not mention Jenkins being in or near the village. Some have claimed Jenkins was also recommended for a Distinguished Service Cross. (See Hondon B. Hargrove letter for Major Roush, 15 September 1980, First Lieutenant John R. Fox Individual Personnel Record, National Personnel Records Center.) If General Almond did not forward a Distinguished Service Cross recommendation for either Fox or Jenkins to the Fifth Army, then he exceeded his authority. Fifth Army policy, in effect since March 1944, was clear: "When a commander is not authorized to make an award, he will forward the recommendation through command channels stating his views, either favorable or unfavorable." See chapter 3.

104. Adjutant General Section Operations Report, 3 August 1942–15 August 1945, folder "392-13 (45540) Opn Rpt-Adjutant General Sec, 92nd Inf Div, 3 August 1942–15 Aug 1945," Box 13660, 92nd Infantry Division, World War II Operations Reports, 1940–48, RG 407, WNRC; Hargrove, *Buffalo Soldiers in Italy*, pp. 132–33.

105. Captain Gilbert S. Holbrook Decoration Case File, folder "AG 200.6-Special Binder, GO #49, 1945," Box 319; Captain Philip Thayer Decoration Case File, Box 59; Private First Class Herman E. Rochelle Decoration Case File, Binder 41, Box 62; all in Fifth Army Awards Case Files, RG 338, WNRC. The Fifth Army approved only Captain Holbrook's Distinguished Service Cross recommendation. See Fifth Army General Order 49, 5 May 1945, Box 2077, General Orders, Fifth Army, World War II Operations Reports, 1940–48, RG 407, WNRC.

106. Figures were derived from 92nd Infantry Division General Orders and from Adjutant General Section Operations Reports, 3 August 1942–15 August 1945 and 15 August 1945–30 October 1945.

107. First Lieutenant Vernon J. Baker report for Commanding General, 92nd Infantry Division, "Narrative of Action, 5 April 1945," 12 June 1945, folder "Top Secret 92nd Infantry Division Combat Efficiency Analysis," and Captain John F. Runyon, "Report on Company 'C', 370th Infantry, Combat Operations, 5–6 April 1945," 12 April 1945, folder "Top Secret 92nd Infantry Division Combat Efficiency Analysis"; Interview of Baker, 15 March 1994.

108. First Lieutenant Baker report for Commanding General, "Narrative of Action, 5 April 1945.

109. *Ibid.*

110. *Ibid*; Captain Runyon, "Report on Company 'C,' 370th Infantry, Combat Operations, 5–6 April 1945.

111. Fifth Army General Order 70, 10 June 1945, Box 2077, General Orders, Fifth Army, World War II Operations Reports, 1940–48, RG 407, WNRC; War Department

General Order 16, 8 February 1946 (on microfiche in file maintained by Military Awards Branch, Total Army Personnel Command); Lee, *Employment of Negro Troops*, pp. 583–84.

112. Interview of Robert Millender, in Motley, *Invisible Soldier*, p. 317.

113. Telephone conversation, John F. Runyon with Elliott V. Converse III, 26 September 1994.

114. Three searches of the Fifth Army awards case files failed to find Lieutenant Baker's decoration case file. Baker's Individual Personnel Record at the National Personnel Records Center contains a copy of his Form 66-4 ("Officer's and Warrant Officer's Qualification Card"), which notes the award of a Distinguished Service Cross but does not indicate whether the original recommendation differed from the final award.

115. Fifth Army General Order 70, 10 June 1945, Box 2077, General Orders, Fifth Army, World War II Operations Reports, 1940–48, RG 407, WNRC.

116. Commanding General, 92nd Infantry Division, message to Commanding Officer, 370th Infantry Regiment, 1500 12 June 1945, folder "392-0.12 (45671) Messages, 92nd Inf Div, 2 Feb–30 Aug 45," Box 13630, 92nd Infantry Division, World War II Operations Reports, 1940–48, RG 407, WNRC.

117. Almond note to C/S, 16 June 1945, folder "Top Secret 92nd Infantry Division Combat Efficiency Analysis."

118. Goodman, *Fragment of Victory* (pp. 130–33), quotes at length from Runyon's report and gives its date, in a footnote, as 1 July 1945.

119. There is additional evidence that Runyon's report was prepared on 1 July 1945 rather than 12 April 1945. Both Almond's "Approving" letter and the Division Board's report refer to the 15 appended reference documents by number. The 12 April 1945 version of Captain Runyon's report is identified as #11 in the listing of reference documents at the end of the Board's report. In the text of its report, the Board employed parenthetical citations to refer to the 15 appended supporting documents. In every instance that the Division Board cited Runyon's report, the numerical citation was enclosed in separate parentheses placed next to the parentheses used to enclose the numbers of the other reference documents—indicating that the citations to Runyon's report were added after the Board report had been completed. Furthermore, the entries citing Runyon's report were made with a different typewriter, both in the Board's report and Almond's "Approving" letter (the ribbon was evidently worn; the impression left by the keystrokes is lighter than the rest of the text).

120. Captain Runyon, "Report on Company 'C', 370th Infantry, Combat Operations, 5–6 April 1945.

121. *Ibid.*

122. *Ibid.*

123. Goodman, *Fragment of Victory*, pp. 130–33.

124. *Ibid.*, pp. 132–33.

125. *Ibid.*, p 132.

126. Report of Trends in the Negro Press, 23 August 1945, Analysis Branch, News Division, U.S. Army Bureau of Public Relations, folder "Negro Press," Box 223, Subject File, 1940–47, Civilian Aide to the Secretary, Office, Assistant Secretary of War, RG 107, NA. Private Hendrix's citation states:

> On the night of 26 December 1944, near Assenois, Belgium, he was with the leading element engaged in the final thrust to break through to the besieged garrison at Bastogne when halted by a fierce combination of artillery and small-arms fire. He dismounted from his halftrack and advanced against two 88-mm. guns, and, by the ferocity of his rifle fire, compelled the gun crews to take cover and then to surrender. Later in the attack he again left his vehicle, voluntarily, to aid 2 wounded soldiers, helpless and exposed to intense

machine-gun fire. Effectively silencing 2 hostile machine-guns, he held off the enemy by his own fire until the wounded men were evacuated. Pvt. Hendrix again distinguished himself when he hastened to the aid of still another soldier who was trapped in a burning half-track. Braving enemy sniper fire and exploding mines and ammunition in the vehicle, he extricated the wounded man and extinguished his flaming clothing, thereby saving the life of his fellow soldier. Private Hendrix, by his superb courage and heroism, exemplified the highest traditions of the military service.

See Committee on Veterans' Affairs, U.S. Congress, Senate, Senate Committee Print No. 3, *Medal of Honor Recipients, 1863–1978*, 90th Cong.,1st sess. (Washington, D.C.: U.S. Government Printing Office, 1979), p. 576.

127. Index Card, Captain John F. Runyon, Box 1645, Index Cards for Awards and Decorations, Awards and Decorations Branch, MTO Adjutant General, RG 492, WNRC. The index card shows that General Wood's recommendation was received at Mediterranean Theater Headquarters on 30 November 1945, disapproved by that headquarters, and forwarded to the War Department on 22 December 1945. No decoration case file for Captain Runyon has been found. Captain Runyon mentioned in a telephone conversation with Elliott V. Converse III, on 26 September 1994, that he had been General Wood's aide before becoming Company C's Commander. As the 92nd Division drew closer to inactivation in the fall of 1945, Captain Runyon was assigned as the Division's assistant chief of staff and, for a short while, its chief of staff.

128. Fifth Army General Order 70, 10 June 1945, and War Department General Order 16, 8 February 1946 (on microfiche in file maintained by Military Awards Branch, Total Army Personnel Command). Lieutenant Baker's citation states:

> For extraordinary heroism in action, on 5 and 6 April 1945, near Viareggio, Italy. Second Lieutenant Baker demonstrated outstanding courage and leadership in destroying enemy installations, personnel and equipment during his company's attack against a strongly entrenched enemy in mountainous terrain. When his company was stopped by the concentrated fire from several machine gun emplacements, he crawled to one position and destroyed it, killing three Germans. Continuing forward, he attacked an enemy observation post and killed its two occupants. With the aid of one of his men, Second Lieutenant Baker attacked two more machine gun nests, killing or wounding the four enemy soldiers occupying these positions. He then covered the evacuation of the wounded personnel of his company by occupying an exposed position and drawing the enemy's fire. On the following night, Second Lieutenant Baker voluntarily led a battalion advance through enemy minefields and heavy fire toward the division objective. Second Lieutenant Baker's fighting spirit and daring leadership were an inspiration to his men and exemplify the highest traditions of the Armed Forces.

Captain Runyon's citation states:

> Captain John F. Runyon heroically led Company C, 370th Infantry Regiment, in an assault on the German's Gothic Line near Montignosa, Italy, on 5 April 1945. While other elements of the attacking force were able to make only limited gains, he accomplished an advance of nearly two miles against strong enemy forces advantageously placed on high ground. Forced to withdraw when support of the deep penetration failed, he returned with the remnants of his company, leaving behind 16 enemy dead, uncounted wounded, and a trail of havoc, which included the destruction of six machine guns, four dugouts, and two observation posts. Captain Runyon's fearless conduct, soldierly skill, and great determination inspired his company in an exploit which opened the way for a successful onslaught by a fresh regiment.

129. The Division awarded personnel of the 365th Infantry Regiment 15 Silver Stars; the 370th, 35 Silver Stars; the 371st, 19 Silver Stars; and the 366th, 11 Silver Stars.

130. Brigadier General William H. Colbern letter for Commanding General, 92nd Infantry Division, "Combat Efficiency of Personnel," 11 March 1945, folder "Top Secret 92nd Infantry Division Combat Efficiency Analysis."

131. *Ibid.*; Interview of Brigadier General William H. Colbern by Major Bell I. Wiley, 2 July 1945, Almond Papers, U.S. Army Military History Institute; Major General E. M. Almond letter for Lieutenant General Lucian K. Truscott, 11 February 1945, folder "Top Secret 92nd Infantry Disivion Combat Efficiency Analysis"; "Proceedings of a Board of Review," 24–25 June 1945, para 27, folder "Top Secret 92nd Infantry Division Combat Efficiency Analysis."

132. Private First Class Herman E. Rochelle Decoration Case File, Binder 41, Box 62, Fifth Army Awards Case Files, RG 338, WNRC; 92nd Infantry Division General Order 28, 21 May 1945, Box 13660, 92nd Infantry Division, World War II Operations Reports, 1940–48, RG 407, WNRC.

133. Adjutant General Section Operations Reports, 3 August 1942–15 August 1945 and 15 August 1945–30 October 1945, Box 13660, 92nd Infantry Division, World War II Operations Reports, 1940–48, RG 407, WNRC.

134. 317th Combat Engineer Battalion History, folder "392 ENG-0.3 (45572) Hist-317th Engr C Bn, 92nd Inf Div, 15 Oct 42–1 Sept 45," Box 13667; Adjutant General Section Operations Reports, 3 August 1942–15 August 1945 and 15 August 1945-30 October 1945, Box 13660; both in *ibid*. Two of the 317th's white officers received four of the nine Silver Stars.

135. Reports of action for January, February, April, and May 1945, folders "ARBN-758-0.3 (18344) Report of Action, 758th Light Tank Bn," Boxes 16778 and 16779, 758th Tank Battalion, Armored, World War II Operations Reports, 1940–48, RG 407, WNRC; Adjutant General Section Operations Reports, 3 August 1942–15 August 1945 and 15 August 1945–30 October 1945, Box 13660, 92nd Infantry Division, World War II Operations Reports, 1940–48, RG 407, WNRC; Lee, *Employment of Negro Troops*, pp. 570–71, 584–85.

136. Folder "TDBN-679-0.1, History 679th Tank Destroyer Bn, 7 Nov 44–27 Oct 45," Box 23685, 679th Tank Destroyer Battalion, World War II Operations Reports, 1940–48, RG 407, WNRC; Adjutant General Section Operations Reports, 3 August 1942–15 August 1945 and 15 August 1945–30 October 1945, Box 13660, 92nd Infantry Division World War II Operations Reports, 1940–48, RG 407, WNRC; Lee, *Employment of Negro Troops*, p. 586.

137. Major General Daniel Noce memorandum for Commanding General, Mediterranean Theater of Operations, "Participation of Negro Combat Troops in the North African Campaign," 23 April 1945, folder "Negro Combat Units—Staff Study," Box 110, Allied Force Headquarters, Command Group, SAC Secretariat, Historical Section, Subject Files, 1943–45, RG 331, WNRC; Historical Record, 7 October 1944, folder "CABN-897-0.1, History, 897th AAA (AW) Bn, 15 Mar–15 Sep 44," Box 17458, 897th AAA (AW) Battalion, Coast Artillery, World War II Operations Reports, 1940-48, RG 407, WNRC; Unit History, folder "CABN 334-0.1, Unit History, 334th AAA S/L Bn, 1 May 42–31 Dec 44," Box 17063, 334th AAA Searchlight Battalion, Coast Artillery, World War II Operations Reports, 1940–48, RG 407, WNRC.

138. Unit History, folder "CABN 334-0.1, Unit History, 334th AAA S/L Bn, 1 May 42–31 Dec 44," Box 17063, 334th AAA Searchlight Battalion; Historical Record, 7 October 1944, folder "CABN-897-0.1, History 897th AAA (AW) Bn, 15 Mar–15 Sep 44," Box 17458, 897th AAA (AW) Battalion; both in *ibid.*

139. Historical Record, Nov-Dec 43–Jan, Apr, Sep 44, folder "CABN-450-0.3 (1376) Historical Record-450th AAA (AW) Bn," Box 17171, 450th Anti-Aircraft Artillery Battalion, *ibid.*

140. Historical Record, Sep-Dec 43, Feb-Dec 44, folder "CWCO-24-0.3 (1365) 24th Cml Co (Decon)-Historical Records," Box 18536, 24th Chemical Company (Decontamination), Chemical, World War II Operations Reports, 1940–48, RG 407, WNRC.
141. Sandler, *Segregated Skies*, pp. 56–57.
142. *Ibid.*, pp. 92–95.
143. Quoted in *ibid.*, p. 95.
144. *Ibid.*
145. Nalty, *Strength for the Fight*, p. 153; Sandler, *Segregated Skies*, p. vii; Interview of Walter Downs in Motley, *Invisible Soldier*, p. 195.
146. Nalty, *Strength for the Fight*, p. 153; Interview of Downs, in Motley, *Invisible Soldier*, p. 196.
147. Telephone Conversation, Lieutenant General Benjamin O. Davis, Jr., with Elliott V. Converse III, 19 October 1994.
148. In addition to the Bronze Star elevated to a Distinguished Service Cross for Private McInnis, two other examples of upgraded recommendations have been found, both from Bronze to Silver Star. See the Individual Personnel Records of First Lieutenant Melvin W. Walker and Private First Class Walter A. Merritt, National Personnel Records Center.

*Chapter 6*

# Valor Awards to Black Soldiers in the Pacific and in the China-Burma-India Theater

## Introduction

On 8 March 1943, Private George Watson of the 29th Quartermaster Regiment was on board a troop ship that was attacked by enemy bombers near Porloch Harbor, New Guinea. After abandoning the ship, Private Watson remained in the water and assisted others who could not swim to reach a life raft. After saving several lives, Private Watson drowned when the suction of the sinking ship dragged him beneath the surface. For his extraordinary heroism, Private Watson was awarded the Distinguished Service Cross—the first black soldier in World War II to receive the Army's second-highest decoration for valor.[1] His was one of the 3 Distinguished Service Crosses and an estimated 20–30 Silver Stars earned by black soldiers in the Pacific. None, however, were awarded the Medal of Honor. Nor has any evidence been found to indicate that an African American was recommended for the Medal either in the Pacific, where over 100,000 black soldiers were in uniform, or in the China-Burma-India Theater, where more than 20,000 served.[2]

Even though black combat units—the 93rd Infantry Division, the 24th Infantry Regiment, and more than 15 antiaircraft artillery battalions—were deployed to the Pacific, the overwhelming majority of the higher valor awards here went to black soldiers assigned to service units. Black soldiers in Pacific combat units, in contrast to those in the European and Mediterranean Theaters, were given little opportunity to engage the enemy and were often employed as service troops on work details. Even when they did go into action, African-American infantry, artillery, and antiaircraft artillery units were involved largely in mop-up operations far from the forward battle areas of the two-pronged Allied advance toward Japan across the Central and Southwest Pacific, that began in the spring of 1942.[3]

Above, soldiers unloading cases of 90-mm shells on Kwajalein, Marshall Islands, 17 February 1944. U.S. Air Force Photograph, National Air and Space Museum, Smithsonian Institution. Below, a soldier of the 811th Engineer Aviation Battalion rolling a barrel of asphalt to the dump for use as runway surface at No. 3 Field, Iwo Jima, 1945. U.S. Air Force Photograph, National Air and Space Museum, Smithsonian Institution. The overwhelming majority of black soldiers in World War II were assigned to service units.

## The 24th Infantry Regiment and the 93rd Infantry Division

The 24th Infantry Regiment, with about 125 white officers and nearly 3,300 black enlisted men, was among the first African-American units deployed to the Pacific. On 4 May 1942, it debarked on Efate in the South Pacific's New Hebrides Islands, more than 1,000 miles east of Australia. Until early 1944, the Regiment provided perimeter defense, loaded and unloaded ships, built roads and airfields, and performed a variety of other work details on Efate and in the Solomon Islands. During this period, the only hostile action the men of the 24th Infantry encountered was occasional bombardment by enemy aircraft. At the end of January 1944, the 24th's First Battalion left Guadalcanal at the southern end of the Solomons for Bougainville at the northwestern tip of the island chain. On Bougainville, the battalion was assigned to XIV Corps reserve and given a variety of support tasks but no active combat role initially, even though the Americal (Americans in Caledonia) Division and the 37th Infantry Division were fighting Japanese forces on the island.[4] Because of developments in Washington, however, the battalion's status would soon change.

Until March 1944, the War Department and the Army's Pacific commanders apparently did not contemplate using black infantry except as garrison troops to relieve first-line white divisions. Indeed, field commanders were never enthusiastic about receiving black soldiers of any kind. But on 6 March 1944, the War Department, under pressure from both within and outside the African-American community, decided to assign large black units into combat as soon as possible. Washington radioed the Army commander in the South Pacific Area, Lieutenant General Millard F. Harmon, whose forces were engaged on Bougainville, to commit to battle a regimental combat team from the 93rd Infantry Division, then only recently arrived on Guadalcanal.[5]

Activated at Fort Huachuca in May 1942, the 13,000-man 93rd Infantry Division was trained at the Arizona post, in Louisiana, and in California's Mohave Desert prior to deploying to the Pacific in January 1944 under the command of Major General Raymond G. Lehman. The Division's principal organic units included the 25th, 368th, and 369th Infantry Regiments; a Division Artillery Headquarters Battery and the 593rd, 594th, 595th, and 596th Field Artillery Battalions; the 93rd Cavalry Reconnaissance Troop; and the 318th Engineer Battalion. All of the Division's enlisted men were black, as were 65 percent of its officers.[6]

After arrival at Guadalcanal, the Division was split up. Some elements stayed on Guadalcanal while the remainder were shipped to other nearby islands, where they began garrison duty. Moving from island to island in the South and Southwest Pacific for over a year, the fragmented 93rd would not assemble as a division again until April 1945 on Morotai, the northernmost of the Moluccas Islands about 300 miles south of Philippines. In the meantime, at the end of March 1944 in response to the War Department's orders, the 25th Infantry Regiment, accompanied by the 593rd Field Artillery Battalion, the 93rd Cavalry Reconnaissance Troop, a company of the 318th Engineer Battalion, and other small supporting units from the 93rd (together designated the 25th Regimental Combat Team) left Guadalcanal for Bougainville. There they joined the 24th Infantry Regiment's First Battalion, which had been committed to combat within days of the War Department's policy decision.[7]

Over 20,000 Japanese soldiers occupied Bougainville when the Third Marine Division, backed up by the Army's 37th Infantry Division, assaulted the island on 1 November 1943. By the beginning of March 1944, American forces (with the Army's Americal Division having replaced the Third Marine Division) established a ten-mile perimeter surrounding their beachhead and two captured airfields. In March, the Japanese attacked the perimeter but were thrown back after sustaining heavy casualties.[8]

The 24th Infantry Regiment's First Battalion, which initially engaged the enemy on 12 March 1944, and each of the 25th Regimental Combat Team's battalions, with some elements first in action on 30 March, were attached to regiments of the Americal and 37th Infantry Divisions. The black infantry units, however, saw only limited combat on Bougainville. The sector of the defensive perimeter held by the 24th's First Battalion was not attacked during the heavy fighting in March, and by mid-June, when the regiments were withdrawn, the black soldiers' battle experience consisted largely of small-unit combat patrols; only rarely were they engaged in company- or battalion-size operations.[9] On one of these latter occasions, the poor performance of one company from the 25th Infantry influenced the 93rd Infantry Division's future role in the Pacific war out of all proportion to the significance of the action.

On 6 April 1944, Company K, Third Battalion, 25th Infantry Regiment, was assigned to block a trail about a mile and a half beyond the American perimeter. As the company neared its objective, one of its platoons reported seeing a few Japanese soldiers and began firing. Though only a squad of Japanese troops may have been involved, much of the rest of the company started firing wildly. When one platoon was ordered to withdraw and reorganize toward the rear, the other platoons began a disorganized retreat. After less than an hour of confused action and indiscriminate firing, 10 men from Company K had been killed and 20 wounded—most apparently by their comrades.[10] Occurring only a week after the 25th arrived on Bougainville, this incident gave rise to the long-lived rumor that the entire 93rd Infantry Division had broken and run.[11]

In truth, though not outstanding, the 24th and 25th Infantry Regiments had performed creditably, particularly for inexperienced troops, during their brief combat assignments on Bougainville. On 10 May 1944, Major General Oscar W. Griswold, the XIV Corps Commander, formally assessed the combat efficiency of both units. In his report to General Harmon, Griswold pointed

Infantry of the First Battalion, 25th Regimental Combat Team, en route to Hill 165, Bougainville, 15 April 1944. U.S. Army Photograph, National Archives and Records Administration, courtesy Col. William A. DeShields, U.S. Army (Retired).

out that in March the 24th's patrol work had been "inferior" and the unit's combat efficiency too low for its use in offensive operations; by early May, however, the First Battalion had improved so much that he was able to rate its combat efficiency as "good." Although General Griswold also judged the 25th Regimental Combat Team's artillery as "good," his assessment of its infantry was less favorable. When elements of the 25th Infantry had operated alone (i.e., not in conjunction with white units), their performance had been unsatisfactory: "Patrol work was poor, and night bivouacs frequently involved dangerous disorder." Griswold acknowledged that the 25th's soldiers had received little training in jungle operations, but neither did the men seem to learn very rapidly. He also found deficiencies in the initiative and sense of responsibility of both black junior officers and noncommissioned officers. The 25th's infantry, in Griswold's view, had not improved as much as the 24th's, and he rated the 25th's as only "fair."[12]

Unit evaluations aside, several black soldiers distinguished themselves in combat on Bougainville during the spring of 1944. Two earned Silver Stars. On 8 April, a 15-man patrol from the 25th's Company F was ambushed by an estimated 20 or more Japanese soldiers equipped with two light machine guns. Private Isaac Sermon, carrying a Browning Automatic Rifle, was hit in the neck during the initial burst of fire from the Japanese. Disregarding his wound, Sermon knelt down and opened fire, killing three of the Japanese. He was then hit three more times. As his patrol withdrew, Sermon managed to keep pace for more than 600 yards before dropping from loss of blood and exhaustion. He was then carried the rest of the way to safety by other members of the patrol. Private Sermon's courage and stamina, however, had enabled his unit to reorganize, break through the ambush, and return to friendly lines.[13]

Another Silver Star for gallantry in action went to Staff Sergeant Rothchild Webb of the 93rd Cavalry Reconnaissance Troop. On 17 May 1944, one of the Reconnaissance Troop's patrols ran into enemy forces, and a bitter firefight ensued. Caught in a Japanese cross fire, three men were killed and four wounded, including the patrol's commanding officer, Second Lieutenant Charles R. Collins, who nonetheless was able to direct an orderly withdrawal. Both the lieutenant, who had been partially blinded, and another soldier were so badly injured, however, that they could not withdraw with the others. Three soldiers, Staff Sergeant Webb included, remained with the two wounded men to aid and protect them. For three days, the five men evaded capture in enemy-held territory before reaching safety.[14]

Although the 93rd Cavalry Reconnaissance Troop remained in combat on Bougainville until October 1944, the balance of the 25th Regimental Combat Team and the 24th Infantry's First Battalion left the island in June. In December 1944, the entire 24th Infantry Regiment was shipped 1,500 miles north to Saipan and Tinian in the Marianas Islands, which had been seized six months earlier. On Saipan and Tinian, the 24th's principal garrison mission was to kill or capture Japanese soldiers who had not yet surrendered. The Regiment's work was so effective that it drew praise from two flag officers heading a survey group from the Army inspector general's office. In the last month of the war, the 24th performed the same function on the Kerama Islands in the Ryukyu chain, southeast of Japan, and received the formal surrender of the Japanese forces there. During its wartime service, the Regiment received only one Silver Star (awarded to a white medical officer for gallantry in action on Bougainville).[15]

After Bougainville, the 93rd Infantry Division continued to provide security, serve as a labor force, and train on a series of South Pacific islands. In August 1944, Major General Harry H. Johnson assumed command of the Division, relieving Major General Lehman, who had returned to the United States for medical reasons. At the same time, General Douglas MacArthur radioed the War Department that the 93rd was "not a good Division" but that efforts were under way "to develop it so that it can be used in combat with distinction." Coming under the control of MacArthur's Eighth Army in October 1944, the 93rd carried out garrison duties, including labor details, at bases on New Guinea and other islands in the Southwest Pacific Area.[16]

PFC Sam Montana of Rockford, Illinois, and PFC Joe Medunc, of Dickinson, North Dakota, both of the 25th Regimental Combat Team, manning their machine gun on Hill 250, Bougainville, 8 April 1944. U.S. Army Photograph, National Archives and Records Administration, courtesy Lt. Col. Major Clark, U.S. Army (Retired).

Early in 1945, Walter White, Executive Director of the National Association for the Advancement of Colored People and accredited as a war correspondent, visited the 93rd on New Guinea. He submitted a lengthy report on the Division to the President and the War Department in mid–February. In the report, White refuted rumors about the Division's behavior in combat. Although White noted some discriminatory practices in the Division (particularly with respect to officer promotion and assignment), he praised the measures that General Johnson had taken to correct them. White's main point, however, was to urge that the 93rd be prepared for, and given, a full-fledged combat assignment.[17]

On 1 March 1945, White met with General MacArthur at his headquarters in the Philippines. During an apparently cordial visit in which White pressed for the 93rd Division's employment as a combat force, MacArthur left White with the impression that the 93rd would be brought together as a unit and, if circumstances warranted, employed in combat. A week later, White followed up on the meeting with a letter to MacArthur repeating his requests regarding the 93rd and with another report to the President and the War Department summarizing his discussion with the general.[18]

The day after his meeting with White, MacArthur received a message from Army Chief of Staff General George C. Marshall informing the Pacific commander of the contents of White's first report. Responding to Marshall's message, General MacArthur denied that the 93rd had been subject to any discrimination and defended its employment under his command. Clearly resentful of the black leader's involvement, MacArthur asserted, "The violent opinions and unfounded statements of Mister White would seem to mark him as a troublemaker and menace to the war effort."[19]

President Franklin Roosevelt responded to White in mid–March. In a letter that was probably drafted in the War Department and that reflected several of the points MacArthur had made to Marshall, the President told White that the discriminatory practices alleged by the black leader were without factual basis, that General MacArthur held no racial prejudice toward the 93rd, and that the Division was being readied for combat. "Long periods of garrison duty, and the employment of divisions over widespread areas," wrote the President, "are characteristic conditions of the Southwest Pacific Area.... Few divisions have been assembled for final training in one area prior to combat."[20]

What impact White's intervention had on the 93rd Division is uncertain. Though the full Division did assemble on Morotai, elements of two of its regiments had already left for the island the day before White met with MacArthur and two days before the general found out, from Marshall, about the contents of White's first report.[21] In any case, the 93rd did not receive, either then or later, the significant combat role White had advocated.

Morotai Island, about equidistant from both New Guinea and the Philippines, was invaded by the 31st Infantry Division on 15 September 1944. By April 1945, when the 93rd relieved the 31st and occupied Morotai, approximately 500 Japanese scattered in small groups remained on the island. In addition to operating the port, the 93rd's mission was to prevent these forces from consolidating and to kill or capture as many as possible. On 2 August 1945, a small patrol captured the colonel who commanded the Japanese forces on the island. Four men received Silver Stars for gallantry during this operation, including Sergeant Alfonzia Dillon, an African American and member of the 93rd Cavalry Reconnaissance Troop. Dillon distinguished himself during the patrol's assault when he placed "accurate and deadly fire" on the enemy position and during its withdrawal when he courageously acted as rear guard.[22]

At the end of June 1945, a combat team from the 93rd, composed of the bulk of the 368th Infantry Regiment, the 594th Field Artillery Battalion, and several smaller supporting units, departed Morotai for Zamboanga on the southwestern end of Mindanao Island in the southern Philippines and for Jolo Island in the Sulu Archipelago (an island chain halfway between the Philippines and Borneo to the southwest). Relieving elements of the 41st Infantry Division at both locations, the 368th Regimental Combat Team was charged with ferreting out remaining Japanese forces.[23]

General MacArthur and American forces returned to the Philippines at

Leyte on 20 October 1944. In January 1945, the northern island of Luzon was invaded. Here intensive fighting, involving ten American divisions, lasted through June 1945. In the southern Philippines, a force less than half this size ended significant, organized Japanese resistance by May.[24] Thus, as had become typical for 93rd Division units, the 368th Regimental Combat Team would be engaged solely in mop-up operations near Zamboanga and on Jolo.

Nonetheless, in July and August 1945, the 368th reported killing over 1,000 Japanese soldiers and capturing almost 100. Its losses totaled 6 killed and 14 wounded. Sometimes the Americans were involved in fierce firefights. For example, on Jolo on 17 July, a patrol from Company I, led by First Lieutenant Ricardo Santiago, encountered a force of approximately 100 Japanese—almost three times the size of the patrol. Though subjected to heavy machine-gun and rifle fire, the patrol defeated the numerically superior Japanese, inflicting an estimated 50 casualties while suffering 6 of its own killed and 12 wounded.[25] When the fighting broke out, Staff Sergeant Leonard E. Dowden moved his squad to within 30 yards of the Japanese force. He then crawled forward alone to assault a machine-gun position. As Dowden advanced, he was hit in the chest but heroically continued ahead, ordering one of his fellow soldiers who had started out to help him to remain under cover. Ten yards from the machine gun and still exposed to enemy fire (and despite his wound), Dowden raised himself to throw a hand grenade. Before he could release it, however, he was hit in the neck and killed. For the extraordinary heroism that cost him his life, Staff Sergeant Dowden received the Distinguished Service Cross—the only such award earned by a 93rd Infantry Division soldier in World War II.[26]

For the entire war, in addition to Staff Sergeant Dowden's Distinguished Service Cross, men from the 93rd earned a total of eight Silver Stars. Three went to African-American enlisted men, one to a Japanese-American enlisted man, three to white officers, and one to another officer whose race has not been identified.[27] No soldier from the Division was awarded a Medal of Honor.

The small number of higher valor awards reflected the Division's relative lack of combat. So did its casualty figures. Though the 93rd's 25th Regimental Combat Team had gone into action in the South Pacific five months before the 92nd's 370th Regimental Combat Team entered combat in Italy, the 93rd suffered fewer than 150 casualties during the war while the 92nd took approximately 2,800.[28] Moreover, after October 1944, the 93rd was governed by Eighth Army awards policy, which emphasized the relationship between combat service and the number of valor awards that were to be approved: "Higher commanders will balance approval of recommended awards among units to insure that they are generally proportional to the relative combat service performed by the various units of the entire command."[29] Although no statement of the 93rd Division's awards policy has been found, it is likely that Major General Johnson, the Division's commander, was aware of and followed Eighth Army policy.

## Antiaircraft Artillery Units

About 12,000 black soldiers in more than 15 antiaircraft artillery units served in the Pacific during World War II.[30] They were deployed from the Friendly Islands (in the South Pacific, just west of the international date line and 2,000 miles from Australia), through the Southwest Pacific, to Okinawa in the Ryukyu Islands near Japan. Only one unit, the 49th Coast Artillery Battalion, experienced extensive combat. Several others were subjected to hostile fire, and a few engaged enemy aircraft. As the War progressed and the need for antiaircraft defenses declined, many of these units lost their tactical mission and were assigned service duties. A few black air-defense gunners received Bronze Stars or were awarded Purple Hearts. Research indicates that only one—First Lieutenant Robert J. Peagler, an African-American officer assigned to the 870th Anti-Aircraft Artillery Battalion—earned one of the three highest valor awards. Ironically, Lieutenant Peagler's Distinguished Service Cross resulted from the extraordinary heroism he displayed as an infantryman.

Although the 77th Coast Artillery Regiment, which arrived at Tongatapu in the Tonga Islands in mid–May 1944, was the first African American air-defense unit to reach the Pacific combat zone, the first to come under fire and to engage enemy forces were probably the two battalions of the 76th Coast Artillery Regiment, stationed on Espíritu Santo in the New Hebrides Islands.[31] In October 1942, they were shelled by Japanese submarines, and during the first nine months of 1943, they were bombed several times by aircraft.[32] After the War, the 14th Anti-Aircraft Artillery Command reported that on each occasion, the black soldiers had behaved with professional calm and efficiency:

> Many shells [from the submarines] fell in the areas of Batteries C, G, and F on one occasion, and in every battery, the men went promptly to their guns, prepared to fire, and awaited orders calmly. At the Battery C area, shells were actually bursting in the area as the men crossed an open space to reach their gun pits, but there was no evidence of panic. In sporadic air raids on the same island, troops of this organization manned their equipment and carried out their orders to fire or withhold fire, as the case might be. During one raid, Japanese aircraft ... dropped bombs ... wounding two members of an automatic weapons battery, one of them seriously. The wounding of these men had no apparent adverse effect on the behavior of the other men at the gun positions.[33]

Other antiaircraft artillery units also experienced some aerial bombing and returned fire, occasionally damaging or destroying Japanese aircraft. On Okinawa on 6 August 1945, for example, gunners of the 503rd Anti-Aircraft Artillery Battalion shot down the last two Japanese planes destroyed by land-based antiaircraft artillery in World War II.[34]

Among the African-American air-defense units, the 49th Coast Artillery Battalion was involved in the most combat. Stationed on Espíritu Santo in the New Hebrides from October 1942 through the end of 1943, the battalion

Soldiers of Section 2, Battery B, 49th Coast Artillery Battalion, preparing to reload their 155-mm "Long Tom" during action against Japanese positions on Bougainville, 16 April 1944. U.S. Army Photograph, National Archives and Records Administration, courtesy Col. William A. DeShields, U.S. Army (Retired).

trained with a variety of weapons, including 155-mm guns in a field artillery role. Sent to Bougainville in January 1944, it performed in this capacity with distinction for much of 1944, particularly during the Japanese attack on the American perimeter in March. According to the 14th Anti-Aircraft Artillery Command, the 49th "made an excellent record in combat firing. Counter battery fire was not allowed to interfere with its firing mission; combat morale was good, in spite of some personnel losses at gun positions." On Bougainville, two men from the 49th were killed and three wounded in action; six soldiers received Bronze Stars, and the unit was awarded a commendation from the XIV Corps artillery commander.[35]

The 49th Coast Artillery Battalion's combat opportunity was the exception rather than the rule for African-American antiaircraft artillery units. Like the black infantry units, most of the air-defense battalions reached locations that were generally secure by the time they arrived. Many did not experience combat or hostile fire at all, and some were eventually given service missions.[36] In his meeting with General MacArthur, Walter White raised the issue of the use of black antiaircraft artillerymen as labor troops but was told (according to White) that it was the result of the reduced air threat and the shortage of service units in the Pacific.[37]

The Tenth Army, two divisions of which, along with the Marines, invaded Okinawa on 1 April 1945 under Admiral Chester Nimitz's command, found a different mission for one African-American antiaircraft artillery battalion that was not needed for air defense. The 870th Anti-Aircraft Artillery Battalion had been stationed in the Hawaiian Islands since June 1942 as part of the 369th Coast Artillery Regiment. Ordered to Okinawa, the 870th arrived on 10 May 1945. Within a week, the Tenth Army converted the unit, with its black officers and enlisted men, to infantry and assigned it to relieve a battalion garrison force from the 77th Infantry Division on Kerama Island, also part of the Ryukyu chain.[38] Equipped with appropriate weapons and trained in infantry tactics for a few days by one officer and 25 enlisted men from the 27th Infantry Division, the 870th left Okinawa and arrived at Kerama on 22 May 1945. It sent out its first combat patrol the next day. Before the end of the war on 14 August 1945, the 870th's men killed some 70 Japanese soldiers and captured or received the surrender of more than 850 people, including Japanese and Korean civilians.[39]

At 8:00 A.M. on 24 June 1945, three platoons from the 870th—supported by fire from a Navy gunboat, a white field artillery battalion, and a black antiaircraft artillery battalion (the 466th—using its 40-mm guns as field weapons)—launched an assault on the high ground held by the Japanese about 300 yards from a village occupied by American forces. First Lieutenant Robert J. Peagler, advancing up a hill at the head of the lead platoon, was the first to draw fire after reaching its crest. From there he directed machine-gun and Browning Automatic Rifle (BAR) fire on two Japanese pillboxes and other defensive emplacements. When the BAR jammed, Lieutenant Peagler charged forward alone through heavy machine-gun fire, throwing hand grenades and firing his M-1 rifle at the nearest Japanese pillbox. Peagler killed six enemy soldiers and captured a grenade launcher before he was struck and killed by Japanese sniper fire. The black lieutenant's extraordinary heroism inspired other members of his platoon to continue advancing. Besides Lieutenant Peagler, 2 black enlisted men were killed and 9 wounded during the engagement. Japanese losses were 20 dead and 10 wounded. On 17 December 1945, General Headquarters, United States Army Forces Pacific, announced the posthumous award of the Distinguished Service Cross to Lieutenant Peagler.[40]

## Amphibian Truck Companies

Hundreds of African-American service units were deployed to the Pacific. The first to arrive were the 810th and 811th Engineer Aviation Battalions, which had left New York at the end of January 1942, stopped briefly in Australia at the end of February, and reached Nouméa, New Caledonia, in the South Pacific in early March.[41] The first black soldiers to come under fire in the Pacific were men from the 96th Engineer General Service Regiment who were caught in an unexpected air raid at Port Moresby, New Guinea, on 28 April 1942.[42] Sometimes service troops had to become front-line soldiers. When Japanese forces launched a surprise parachute assault behind the American perimeter on Leyte in early December 1944, black soldiers from the 839th Engineer Aviation Battalion took up weapons, formed defensive perimeters around their company areas, and drove out the attacking Japanese.[43] Yet direct contact with the enemy, or even exposure to hostile fire, was the exception for the vast majority of service troops—black or white. For any soldier among them to win one of the higher valor awards, like the Distinguished Service Cross earned by Private George Watson in the waters off New Guinea in March 1943, was an extraordinary event. Such generalizations, however, were not entirely applicable to men in one type of service unit: the soldiers in the amphibian truck companies that directly supported combat forces going ashore on island beaches throughout the Pacific.

More than 25 African-American amphibian truck companies, numbering over 4,500 men, operated in the Pacific.[44] Many came under fire; about half were part of the D-Day assault waves on Biak, Leyte, Iwo Jima, and Okinawa. Several participated in more than one operation. The 477th Amphibian Truck Company, for example, went ashore with the first wave of infantry on Saipan (16 June 1944) and Tinian (24 July 1944) and was also part of the follow-on forces landing on Leyte and Okinawa after the initial invasion.[45] In all, 17 black soldiers from four companies earned Silver Stars, and many others were awarded Bronze Stars.[46]

The amphibian truck, or "duck" (from the acronym, DUKW) as it was called, had been developed in 1942. The vehicle was a truck, two and one-half tons, made buoyant by sealed, empty tanks that were part of its body. It could travel 45 miles per hour on land and 5 knots on water.[47] Normally, each company had 48 DUKWs and about 180 soldiers (5 officers and 175 enlisted men).[48]

Made to order for the Pacific islands, where there were few ports or other docking facilities, the DUKW unloaded cargo from ships standing offshore and transported it to a dump on the beach or to an inland dispersal point. During initial beach assaults, the DUKWs usually carried artillery pieces and ammunition ashore.[49] They often returned filled with casualties. Sometimes DUKWs performed as seagoing ambulances over extended periods. For more than two months following the Okinawa invasion, for example, the African-American 472nd Amphibian Truck Company carried over 12,000 casualties to offshore vessels.[50]

The 810th Amphibian Truck Company was the first African-American DUKW unit to operate in the Southwest Pacific area, arriving at Milne Bay, New Guinea, in November 1943.[51] On 27 May 1944, a platoon (16 DUKWs) from the 812th Amphibian Truck Company landed with the assault force invading Biak, an island off New Guinea's northwestern coast. Two days later, four men from the platoon (Lieutenant Robert Vogt, Private First Class Joseph Nesmith, Private Ralph A. Nicholas, and Technician Fifth Grade Marcus P. Sanchez) each earned a Silver Star for gallantry in action. After evacuating casualties from a beach, they voluntarily returned to ensure that no one had been left behind. Finding a platoon of 40 men in a dangerously exposed position, the four soldiers from the 812th, continuously exposed to enemy mortar and small-arms fire, successfully evacuated the platoon in two trips to the beach.[52]

Eleven African-American amphibian truck companies participated in the Leyte operation from October 1944 through February 1945. Four companies—the 472nd, 823rd, 827th, and 828th—landed on D-Day, 20 October 1944.[53] Although none of these soldiers received any of the higher valor awards, some came under fire, either from air attacks or from Japanese snipers as the truckers transported supplies to units inland. The commanding officer of the 823rd Amphibian Truck Company, which came ashore on Leyte two hours after the first forces, described his unit's participation in the operation:

> Our separate platoons went in about H plus two hours, carrying a maximum load of one 105mm Howitzer, plus ammunition and equipment and personnel. Only one "DUKW" of the forty-eight failed, and it was repaired in the water and arrived at the Battery area one hour late. After getting the guns in place, the "DUKWs" commenced unloading 18,000 odd rounds of 105mm ammunition out of each of the three L.S.T.'s that carried the Artillery [units], and they didn't stop until all were unloaded—about seventy-two hours later. Many of the men and officers were under severe enemy fire, but no casualties resulted, and the manner of their performance under their baptism of enemy fire was exemplary. We were orally commended by the Commanding General of the 96th Division Artillery.[54]

Although the 823rd suffered no casualties, men from other DUKW units were less fortunate; seven black soldiers from the 827th were awarded Purple Hearts.[55]

At Leyte, the Japanese had chosen to oppose the American invaders largely inland rather than on the beaches. The Japanese response on tiny, 11-square-mile Iwo Jima, located in the Central Pacific about halfway between Japan and the Mariana Islands 1,500 miles to the southeast, was much different.[56] At Iwo Jima, two African-American DUKW companies, the 471st and the 473rd, went ashore on D-Day, 19 February 1945, and a third, the 476th, on D-Day plus one. All were attached to Marine divisions during the invasion.[57] For four days, the black soldiers encountered heavy fire from the well-entrenched Japanese defenders. Private Maurice A. Paris, one of the amphibian truckers, described what it was like as he headed his DUKW toward shore shortly after nightfall on the second day:

Getting on the beach was far from easy. I circled a couple of times, then started in, gritting my teeth. A string of mortar shells increased my temperature when they landed about 20 feet in front of my Duck. I kept going. All during the time I was working, the Japs kept dropping mortar and machine-gun fire all around. I figured the sands of time had just about run out for me. Sure enough, just as soon as I got the last 105mm gun unloaded, a mortar shell scored a direct hit at the stern, and knocked out my Duck. The next day found me dodging shells in another Duck. You see the stuff had to be landed.[58]

In the four days from 19 to 22 February 1945, the courageous soldiers from the 471st, 473rd, and 476th Amphibian Truck Companies won 19 Silver Stars (14 to black enlisted men, some posthumously) at Iwo Jima.[59]

Among the Silver Star awards to African-American DUKW drivers, the one given for the gallantry in action exhibited by Technician Fifth Grade Tommie L. Holloway, 471st Amphibian Truck Company, was typical. On 19 February 1945, Holloway landed his DUKW, under heavy mortar fire and loaded with a howitzer, gun crew, and ammunition, on one of the Iwo Jima beaches. While he was driving his vehicle to an artillery battery to be unloaded, sniper fire pierced his windshield. After delivering the cargo, he found the road back to the beach jammed; he and his assistant driver had to dig in. When an officer asked Holloway to carry small-arms ammunition to some Marine infantry, he responded immediately. As Holloway attempted to reach their position, the driver's compartment of his truck was hit several times by machine-gun fire from an enemy pillbox, and he was forced to take cover again. Holloway waited for dark, delivered the ammunition to the Marines, and returned to the beach. At dawn, he attempted to get back out to the ammunition ship, but his DUKW was in such bad shape that he had to return to shore. There he patched the bullet holes with sticks and rags. The repair job worked, and for two more days, Technician Fifth Grade Holloway made many trips back and forth until the ammunition ship was unloaded. All the while, he ignored both enemy fire and the fact that his DUKW was becoming less seaworthy with each successive trip.[60]

Following the Iwo Jima landings, African-American DUKW companies played a key role in the invasion of Okinawa on 1 April 1945. Indeed, six of the nine amphibian truck companies involved in the assault were black.[61] Okinawa, however, was more like Leyte than Iwo Jima; except for the air attacks, the Japanese chose to defend inland and put up only scattered, light resistance on the beaches.[62] Still, even though they did not receive any of the higher valor awards, black soldiers suffered some casualties during the operation, including at least two killed in action, before organized Japanese resistance ended on 21 June 1945.[63]

In evaluating the DUKW's performance at Okinawa, the commander of the 474th Amphibian Truck Company wrote that it was "the most important single piece of equipment used on the beach" and that if "used properly and with care it will be the most outstanding single innovation of the war."⁶⁴ But if the DUKWs had proved their worth, so too had the courageous and skilled black soldiers who operated them—on Okinawa and many other Pacific islands.

## The China-Burma-India Theater

By the end of World War II, over 21,000 soldiers in more than 100 black units were serving in the China and Burma-India Theaters (CBI). With the exception of a few hundred black soldiers assigned to the 484th Anti-Aircraft Artillery Battalion, all were in service units, mostly truck companies and engineer outfits.⁶⁵

Though rarely getting close to enemy forces or encountering hostile fire, the African-American troops made a major contribution to the war effort through their work on construction of the Ledo Road, connecting the ports of India to the interior of China. The task of carving out the 270-mile route, which traversed jungle rain forests and rugged mountains, began in mid-December 1942 and was finally completed in January 1945. Of the 15,000 American soldiers who built the road, 60 percent were black. As the road advanced, so did the many African-American quartermaster truck companies that carried supplies over it.⁶⁶

Until the overland route to China was completed, support for American and Chinese forces had to be provided by air "over the Hump" from airfields in northern India. African-American engineer troops built and maintained many of these fields. Black quartermaster troops also developed techniques for packing and loading air-dropped food and other supplies. Some were assigned to forward areas to receive and issue the air-dropped material.⁶⁷

Although service troops in the CBI faced only a low threat of attack from enemy forces, the scarcely imagined sometimes occurred. On 25 October 1942, at an airfield near Assam, India, Private Mack B. Anderson, of the African-American 823rd Engineer Aviation Battalion, single-handedly manned a .30-caliber machine gun during a strafing attack by 18 Japanese Zero fighters. Several of the aircraft, in an attempt to silence the machine gun, made repeated passes over Anderson's exposed position. Nonetheless, he fired the automatic weapon until it jammed. With complete disregard for his own safety, Private Anderson then took out his .45-caliber pistol and continued firing at the attacking aircraft. For his gallantry in action, Private Anderson was awarded the Silver Star by the Tenth Air Force.⁶⁸

## Conclusion

The relative lack of awards-related records such as decoration case files and individual personnel ("201") files hampers investigation of possible Medal

Men of Company B, 445th Signal Heavy Construction Battalion, eating lunch from the chow truck on the line between Kanjikoah and Tinsukia in India, 16 March 1945. Overseas for 21 months at the time of this photograph, they had strung 52 miles of wire for the British in 16 days. U.S. Army photograph, National Archives and Records Administration, courtesy Col. William A. DeShields, U.S. Army (Retired).

of Honor recommendations for black soldiers who served in the Pacific during World War II. The collection of decoration case files preserved from the China-Burma-India Theater is extensive, but among the Pacific records, only those of the Sixth Army (where few blacks served) are comparable. Eighth and Tenth Army records contain few decoration case files. None of these crucial records for the three African-American Distinguished Service Cross winners—Staff Sergeant Dowden, Lieutenant Peagler, and Private Watson—have been found. Moreover, their individual personnel files could not be located at the National Personnel Records Center in St. Louis and have probably been destroyed.

In one respect, however, the paucity of awards records is not crucial to this study, for with the exception of some African-American amphibian truck companies, most black units, the infantry and artillery units in particular, had little opportunity to engage in combat. Despite its good performance on Bougainville in 1944, the 24th Infantry Regiment spent the rest of the war as a garrison unit, providing security, conducting mop-up operations, and serving as a labor force. The same was true for the 13,000-man 93rd Infantry Division after the mostly negative assessment that the XIV Corps commander gave the 25th Regimental Combat Team, even though his conclusion was based largely on one company's failure. As a consequence of the decisions made by some commanders to deny African-American combat units a significant and sustained opportunity to fight, black service troops earned a disproportionate share of the higher valor awards won by black soldiers in the Pacific.[69]

## Notes

1. United States Army Forces Far East General Order 32, 15 June 1943, Box T512, USAFFE Adjutant General, Record Group (RG) 338, Washington National Records Center (WNRC), Suitland, Md.

2. General Headquarters, United States Army Forces Pacific Study, "Participation of Negro Troops in the Post War Establishment," 2 September 1945; and Major General Frank D. Merrill, Tenth Army Chief of Staff, letter to Commander in Chief, United States Army Forces Pacific, "Participation of Negro Troops in the Post War Military Establishment," 15 August 1945; both in folder "291.2, #1," Box 1552, GHQ AFPAC, Adjutant General, General Correspondence, 1945, RG 338, WNRC; War Department Press Release, 8 October 1945, folder "Sep-Oct 45," Box 107, Press and Radio News Releases, 1921–47, News Branch, Public Relations Division, RG 165, National Archives (NA). One black veteran, assigned to a service unit in the Pacific in World War II, reflected a view held by many African-American veterans when he explained, many years after the War, why he believed no black soldier had received a Medal of Honor: "The reason for this 'oversight' is quite easy to understand if you know the military. Most of your military officers come from the south and this is particularly true of the army. In black divisions few blacks reached the level of captain, and it is officers who put a name in for a medal. The recommendation to receive any medal can be stopped all the way up the line of command. The Medal of Honor was beyond us as soon as the recommendation reached the level of major. I think you know there were no helluva lot of Distinguished Service Crosses awarded to our men, less than eight received it. The cracker officers thought they were doing you a damned favor when they 'gave' you the Bronze Star. Notice I said 'gave.' We Negroes never earn anything; they 'give' us medals out of the 'kindness' of their hearts." Interview of Bill Stevens, in Mary Penick Motley, comp. and ed., *The Invisible Soldier: The Experience of the Black Soldier in World War II* (Detroit, Mich.: Wayne State University Press, 1975), p. 78.

3. The Pacific was not a "theater of operations" with Allied forces under the direction of a single commander, as in Europe or the Mediterranean. In the spring of 1942, the U.S. Joint Chiefs of Staff divided the Pacific's vast expanse into two theaters: the Southwest Pacific Area, commanded by General MacArthur (at first from Australia and later the Philippines), and the Pacific Ocean Areas (POA), commanded by Admiral Chester W. Nimitz in Hawaii. The POA was subdivided into the North, Central, and South Pacific Areas. Nimitz directly controlled the first two, and Admiral William F. Halsey, Jr., his deputy, oversaw the South Pacific. Each of the POA "areas" had a senior Army commander. The China-Burma-India Theater was also created in 1942 and included Army and Army Air Forces personnel in those locations. See Morris J. MacGregor, Jr., et al., *American Military History [Army Historical Series]* (Washington, D.C.: U.S. Government Printing Office, 1989), pp. 428, 503, and map #42. The bulk of Army

forces (including most black soldiers) were under General MacArthur's command. Between April 1945, when General Headquarters Army Forces Pacific was created, and the end of July 1945, he assumed control of those forces under Admiral Nimitz's command. Similarly, during this period, naval forces under MacArthur were released to Nimitz. See Joseph Bykofsky and Harold Larson, *The Transportation Corps: Operations Overseas [United States Army in World War II]* (Washington, D.C.: U.S. Government Printing Office, 1957), p. 544.

4. Historical Record and History of the 24th United States Infantry, 1 July 1943, 1 October 1943, and 1 January 1944, folder "INRG-24-0.1 (3959) Historical Record and History of the 24th United States Infantry, Apr 42-Dec 43"; Historical Record and History of the 24th United States Infantry, 31 March 1944, folder "INRG-24-0.1 (3959) Historical Record and History of the 24th United States Infantry, 1 Jun-30 Sep 44"; both in Box 21132, 24th Infantry Regiment, World War II Operations Reports, 1940-48, RG 407, WNRC; Ulysses Lee, *The Employment of Negro Troops [United States Army in World War II]* (Washington, D.C.: U.S. Government Printing Office, 1966), pp. 497-98.

5. Lee, *Employment of Negro Troops*, pp. 432, 436, 471-85; Bernard C. Nalty, *Strength for the Fight: A History of Black Americans in the Military* (New York: Free Press, 1986), pp. 166-69.

6. 93rd Infantry Division Summary of Operations in World War II, March 1946, folder "393-0.3 (21723) 93rd Inf Div, Summary of Opns in WW II, 15 May 42-3 Feb 46," Box 13696, 93rd Infantry Division, World War II Operations Reports, 1940-48, RG 407, WNRC; Interview of Major General R. G. Lehman by Major Bell I. Wiley, 26-27 October 1944, Fort Sam Houston, Tex., folder "Negroes," Box 509, Chief of Military History, Records of the Historical Services Division, Publications, Unpublished Manuscripts, and Supporting Records, 1943-47, 2-3.7 CJ5 Special Studies, The Utilization of Negro Manpower, RG 319, NA.

7. Lee, *Employment of Negro Troops*, pp. 500-501.

8. Ronald H. Spector, *Eagle against the Sun: The American War with Japan* (New York: Free Press, 1985), pp. 243-46, 283-84.

9. Historical Record and History of the 24th United States Infantry, 30 June 1944, folder "INRG-24-0.1 (3959) Historical Record and History of the 24th United States Infantry, 1 Jun-30 Sep 44," Box 21132, 24th Infantry Regiment, World War II Operations Reports, 1940-48, RG 407, WNRC; 25th Infantry Regiment Unit History, folder "393 INF (25)-0 (21717) 25th Inf Unit Hist, Jan 44-Feb 46," Box 13712, 93rd Infantry Division, World War II Operations Reports, 1940-48, RG 407, WNRC; Lee, *Employment of Negro Troops*, pp. 498, 500-514.

10. Lee, *Employment of Negro Troops*, pp. 506-9.

11. *Ibid.*, pp. 511-12.

12. Major General O. W. Griswold letter to Commanding General, United States Army Forces in the South Pacific Area (USAFISPA), "Report on the 1st Bn, 24th Inf Regt and 25th RCT," 10 May 1944, folder "214-3.0, Rpt 1st Bn, 24th Inf Regt and 25 RCT, Hq XIV Corps, 10 May 44," Box 4639, XIV Corps, World War II Operations Reports, RG 407, WNRC. Brigadier General Leonard R. Boyd, the 93rd's assistant division commander, reacted strongly but privately to the rating Griswold had given the 25th Infantry. Boyd had been sent to Bougainville from the 93rd's Headquarters on Guadalcanal to take charge of the 25th Regimental Combat Team's overall operations as a provisional brigade commander. In a letter to Major General J. E. Hull, assigned to the important War Department General Staff Operations Division (OPD), Boyd wrote:

> Dame Rumor has it that we (the division) have been unwelcome even before our arrival here in the Solomons. At Guadalcanal we found a frankly skeptical attitude

as to our ability as an administrative as well as a combat unit. Secondly, this same rumor had it that ours was a shotgun marriage to the XIV Corps and it was apparent that we had two strikes against us and no balls. One high-ranking USAFISPA officer and the C.G. XIV Corps were insistent on as early test as possible to determine our combat ability. My plea for a gradual entry into combat was met with the statement that other green units had gone into heavy action without their men being better seasoned and that we would have to prove our value at once. As a result, the battalions of the 25th Infantry were split up among regiments of the Americal Division.... In one of [our] attacks, ordered by the foster parent, and not especially well planned, one company out beyond the perimeter ran into a Jap force and later broke and pulled out to the rear in confusion. It was bad, but the incident immediately was used to characterize the division and negro troops. (Last week a similar action took place in the Americal Division, which was considered regrettable but not important.) ... Informal conversation with Division (Americal) and Corps officials leaves no doubt in my mind that most of them have a basic distrust of the negro officer and his ability to lead negro soldiers in combat.... I feel that the higher officers in XIV Corps are perfectly willing to see this division relegated to service troop status and that they do not want relatively untried colored troops, with their racial problems, under their command. Nor are they anxious to give these negro troops an impartial opportunity to demonstrate their worth. (This is outspoken, but my firm belief.) The foregoing is my explanation of the "Fair" report recently made on our combat efficiency.

Boyd Letter to Hull, 17 May 1944, folder "Bougainville," Box 2, Papers of Leonard R. Boyd, Hoover Institution Archives, Stanford, Calif.

13. 25th RCT S-3 Journal Sheet, 9 April 1944, with Lieutenant Strong patrol report attached, folder "393 INF(25)-3.4 (6650) 25th RCT (93rd Inf Prov Bde)Messages, 2–29 Apr 1944," Box 13717, 93rd Infantry Division, World War II Operations Reports, 1940-48, RG 407, WNRC; 25th Infantry Regiment History, folder "393 INF (25)-0 (21717) 25th Inf-Unit Hist, Jan 44–Feb 46," Box 13712, 93rd Infantry Division, World War II Operations Reports, 1940–48, RG 407, WNRC; XIV Corps General Order 131, 31 October 1944, Box 4630, XIV Corps, World War II Operations Reports, 1940–48, RG 407, WNRC.

14. 93rd Cavalry Reconnaissance Troop History, folder "393 CAV-0.3 (21709) 93rd Cav Rcn Troop (Mecz) Unit Opns Hist, 23 Jan 44–14 Aug 45;" Extract of USAFISPA General Order 1097, 20 July 1944, in 93rd Cavalry Reconnaissance Troop History, folder "393 CAV-0.1 (6364) Hist 93d Cav Rcn Tp, Yr 44"; both in Box 13705, 93rd Infantry Division, World War II Operations Reports, 1940–48, RG 407, WNRC.

15. Major General Virgil L. Peterson letter for the Deputy Chief of Staff, "Exemplary Conduct of the 24th Infantry Regiment at Saipan," 14 May 1945, folder "291.2 Sec II Cases 83-144," Box 189, Decimal 291.2, 1944–45, Chief of Staff Security Classified General Correspondence, 1942–47, RG 165, NA; Colonel Julian G. Hearne, Jr., letter to Commanding General Army Service Command I, "Battle Participation Credit," 1 September 1945, folder "200.6, #10," Box 3330, Decimal 200.6, GHQ SWPA/AFPAC Adjutant General, General Correspondence, 1944–46, RG 338, WNRC; Extract of USAFISPA General Order 1077, 17 July 1944, in Historical Record and History of the 24th United States Infantry, 30 September 1944, folder "INRG-24-0.1 (3959) Historical Record and History of the 24th United States Infantry, 1 Jan–30 Sep 44," Box 21132, 24th Infantry Regiment, World War II Operations Reports, 1940–48, RG 407, WNRC; Lee, *Employment of Negro Troops*, pp. 515, 533–35.

16. 93rd Infantry Division Summary of Operations in World War II, March 1946,

folder "393-0.3 (21723) 93d Inf Div Summary of Operations in World War II, 15 May 42–3 Feb 46," Box 13696, 93rd Infantry Division, World War II Operations Reports, 1940–48, RG 407, WNRC; Extract of Message from MacArthur, 9 August 1944, folder "ASW 291.2 Negro Troops—Civilian Aide," Box 15, Decimal 291.2, Assistant Secretary of War, Formerly Security Classified Correspondence of John J. McCloy, 1941–45, RG 107, NA; Lee, *Employment of Negro Troops*, pp. 516, 523–25.

17. Walter White memorandum to the President (copies to the Under Secretary and Assistant Secretary of War), 12 February 1945, folder "93rd Division," Box 259, Office, Assistant Secretary of War, Civilian Aide to the Secretary, Subject File, 1940–47, RG 165, NA.

18. Walter White letter to General MacArthur, 8 March 1945, and Walter White memorandum to the President (copies to the Under Secretary and Assistant Secretary of War), 8 March 1945; both in folder "291.1 Sec II Cases 83-144," Box 189, Decimal 291.2, 1944–45, Chief of Staff Security Classified General Correspondence, 1942–47, RG 165, NA.

19. Marshall Message to GHQ SWPA (Personal for MacArthur), 2 March 1945, folder "291.2, 3/42 through 6/45," Box 2785, Decimal 291.2, GHQ SWPA Adjutant General, General Correspondence, 1942–45, RG 338, WNRC; MacArthur message (Personal for Marshall), 4 March 1945, folder "291.2," Box 4622, GHQ SWPA, Office of the Commanding General, Advance Echelon, Adjutant General, Top Secret General Correspondence, 1944–45, RG 338, WNRC.

20. Franklin D. Roosevelt letter to Walter White, 19 March 1945, Papers of the National Association for the Advancement of Colored People, Manuscript Division, Library of Congress, Washington, D.C. Roosevelt's letter apparently responded only to White's first report. See Colonel Harrison A. Gerhardt memorandum for General Henry I. Hodes, 26 March 1945, folder "291.2 Sec II Cases 83-144," Box 189, Decimal 291.2, 1944–45, Chief of Staff Security Classified General Correspondence, 1942–47, RG 165, NA.

21. 93rd Infantry Division Summary of Operations in World War II, March 1946, folder "393-0.3 (21723) 93d Inf Div Summary of Operations in WW II, 15 May 42–3 Feb 46," Box 13696; and Overseas Operations of 369th Infantry Regiment, 19 September 1945, folder "393 INF (369)-0.3 (21715) 369th Inf Regt Overseas Opns, 28 Jan 44–22 Sep 45," Box 13720; both in 93rd Infantry Division, World War II Operations Reports, 1940–48, RG 407, WNRC. In *Employment of Negro Troops* (pp. 529–31), Lee implied that the 93rd's move to Morotai may have resulted from White's activities. Lee did not mention MacArthur's name-calling or cite Roosevelt's letter.

22. Lee, *Employment of Negro Troops*, pp. 525–27; 93rd Infantry Division General Order, 13 August 1945, Box 13699, 93rd Infantry Division, World War II Operations Reports, 1940–48, RG 407, WNRC. The other Silver Star winners were two white officers—Lieutenant Colonel Jack McKenzie (the 93rd Division's G-3) and Major Peveril O. Settle, Jr.—and one of the Division's Japanese-American interpreters, Technician Third Grade Stanley J. Nakanishi.

23. 93rd Infantry Division Summary of Operations in World War II, March 1946, folder "393-0.3 (21723) 93d Inf Div Summary of Operations in WW II, 15 May 42–3 Feb 46," Box 13696, 93rd Infantry Division, World War II Operations Reports, 1940–48, RG 407, WNRC.

24. MacGregor et al., *American Military History*, pp. 516–20.

25. 368th 3rd Battalion Journal Entry, 19 July 1945, folder "393 INF (368) 70.7 Journal 3d Bn, 368th Inf Regt, 93d Inf Div, 20 Jan–9 Sep 45"; and 368th RCT Operations History, 2 October 1945, folder "393 INF (368)-0.3 (21716) 368th RCT-Hist of Opns, 5 Jan 44–1 Sep 45"; both in Box 13719, 93rd Infantry Division, World War II Operations Reports, 1940–48, RG 407, WNRC; Headquarters 368th RCT letter to

Commanding General, United States Army Forces Pacific, "Battle Participation Credit," 19 September 1945, folder "200.6, #11," Box 3330, Decimal 200.6, GHQ SWPA/AFPAC Adjutant General, General Correspondence, 1944–46, RG 338, WNRC; War Department Press Release, 17 September 1945, folder "Aug–Sep 45," Box 106, Press and Radio News Releases, 1921–47, News Branch, Public Relations Division, RG 165, NA.

26. General Headquarters, United States Army Forces Pacific General Order 408, 20 December 1945, Box T1309, General Orders 1945, AFPAC Adjutant General, RG 338, WNRC. Lieutenant Santiago, who was wounded in the encounter, received a Silver Star (X Corps General Order 113, 22 August 1945, Microfiche # 270, Military Awards Branch, Total Army Personnel Command).

27. In addition to the seven previously identified, Captain Wesley F. Thompson, Jr., a white officer, was awarded a Silver Star for gallantry in action at Toem, Dutch New Guinea, on 25 May 1945 (93rd Infantry Division General Order 67, 26 June 1945). Lieutenant Santiago's race has not been determined.

28. The 93rd Infantry Division casualty figure was derived from the (undated and unsigned) statistical breakdown through 5 July 1945 in Section 5, "Colored Troops, Vol I," Box 1549, Decimal 322.999, AFPAC Pacific Warfare Board, RG 338, WNRC. To this figure (114 killed and wounded in action) were added the 6 killed and 14 wounded in action reported by the 368th RCT during its operations in the southern Philippines in July and August 1945, in Headquarters 368th RCT letter to Commanding General, United States Army Forces Pacific, "Battle Participation Credit," 19 September 1945. The casualty figure for the 92nd Infantry Division came from Adjutant General Section Operations Report, 3 August 1942–15 August 1945, Box 13660, 92nd Infantry Division, World War II Operations Reports, 1940–48, RG 407, WNRC.

29. Eighth Army Circular 4, "Decorations," 30 September 1944, folder "200.6, 1942-Jul/Dec 45," Box 100, Eighth Army Awards Case Files, RG 338, WNRC.

30. The units included the 76th Coast Artillery Regiment (later 76th Anti-Aircraft Artillery [AAA] Group), 77th Coast Artillery Regiment (later 77th AAA Group), 49th Coast Artillery Battalion (Bn) (originally Second Bn, 54th Coast Artillery Regiment), 76th AAA Gun Bn, 77th AAA Gun Bn, 100th AAA Gun Bn, 207th AAA Automatic Weapons (AW) Bn, 208th AAA (AW) Bn, 234th AAA (AW) Bn, 369th AAA Gun Bn, 374th AAA Searchlight Bn, 466th AAA (AW) Bn, 477th AAA (AW) Bn, 503rd AAA Gun Bn, 741st AAA Gun Bn, 742nd AAA Gun Bn, 870th AAA (AW) Bn, 933rd AAA (AW) Bn, and the 938th AAA (AW) Bn. The units have been identified as African American from several sources, principally T/O Colored Units, Continental and Foreign, 7 July 1945, Box 443, Decimal 291.2, G-1 Decimal File, 1942–June 1946, RG 165, WNRC; War Department Press Release, 25 June 1945, folder "Jun 1945," Box 103, Press and Radio News Releases, 192147, News Branch, Public Relations Division, RG 165, NA; and Lee, *Employment of Negro Troops*. Battalion sizes varied (and fluctuated) but generally numbered about 700 officers and enlisted men.

31. 77th AAA Group Training and Equipment Status Report (undated), folder "CAGP-77-0.1 Hist 77th AAA Gp, 1 Nov 43–15 Aug 45," Box 17668, 77th Anti-Aircraft Artillery Group; and 76th AAA Group History, folder "CAGP-76-0.1 Hist 76th AAA GP, 10 Aug 42–15 Aug 45," Box 17667, 76th Anti-Aircraft Artillery Group; both in Coast Artillery, World War II Operations Reports, 1940–48, RG 407, WNRC.

32. 76th AAA Group History, folder "CAGP-76-0.1 Hist 76th AAA Gp, 10 Aug 42–15 Aug 45," Box 17667, 76th Anti-Aircraft Artillery Group, Coast Artillery, World War II Operations Reports, 1940–48, RG 407, WNRC.

33. 14th Anti-Aircraft Command Report to Pacific Warfare Board, "Negro Questionnaire," 15 July 1945, Section 15, folder "Colored Troops, Vol II," Box 1549, Decimal 322.999, AFPAC Pacific Warfare Board, RG 338, WNRC.

34. 53rd AAA Brigade History, folder "CABR 53-0.1, Hist 53d AAA Bde, 1941–45," Box 17529, 53rd Anti-Aircraft Artillery Brigade, Coast Artillery, World War II Operations Reports, 1940–48, RG 407, WNRC; War Department Press Release, 19 November 1945, folder "Oct-Nov 45," Box 108, Press and Radio News Releases, 1921–47, News Branch, Public Relations Division, RG 165, NA. Other units credited with destroying, probably destroying, or damaging enemy aircraft were the 741st AAA Gun Bn and the 938th AAA (AW) Bn. See 741st AAA Gun Bn History, 1 September 1945, folder "CABN 741-0.1 (30505) Unit Hist-741st AAA Gun Bn, 7 Sep 43–15 Aug 45," Box 17391, 741st Anti-Aircraft Artillery Battalion; and 938th AAA (AW) Bn History, 1 January 1945, folder "CABN 938-0.1, Hist 938th AAA (AW) Bn, 10 Feb 41–15 Feb 45," Box 17471, 938th Anti-Aircraft Artillery (AW) Battalion; both in Coast Artillery, World War II Operations Reports, 1940–48, RG 407, WNRC.

35. 49th Coast Artillery Bn History, folder "CABN 49-0.1 (47781) Unit Hist—49th CA Bn, 15 Feb 41–27 Aug 45," Box 16892, 49th Coast Artillery Battalion, Coast Artillery, World War II Operations Reports, 1940–48, RG 407, WNRC; 14th Anti-Aircraft Command Report to Pacific Warfare Board, "Negro Questionnaire," 15 July 1945, Section 15, folder "Colored Troops, Vol II," Box 1549, Decimal 322.999, AFPAC Pacific Warfare Board, RG 338, WNRC; Lee, *Employment of Negro Troops*, pp. 501–2, 515.

36. Among the antiaircraft artillery units not coming under fire were the 207th, 208th, 234th, 369th, 477th, and 742nd. Distance from hostile fire, however, did not mean the absence of risk. When the 466th AAA (AW) Battalion arrived at Espíritu Santo in the New Hebrides in October 1943, the islands were no longer under much threat. The men trained at a Navy automatic weapons school on a small island near Espíritu Santo. During one voyage to the island, the boat carrying soldiers from the 466th capsized and 45 enlisted men drowned. See folder "CABN 466-0.1 Hist 466th AAA (AW) Bn, 15 Oct 42–Aug 45," Box 17201, 466th Anti-Aircraft Artillery (AW) Battalion, Coast Artillery, World War II Operations Reports, RG 407, WNRC.

37. Walter White memorandum to the President (copies to the Under Secretary and Assistant Secretary of War), 8 March 1945, folder "291.2 Sec II Cases 83-144," Box 189, Decimal 291.2, 1944–45, Chief of Staff Security Classified General Correspondence, 1942–47, RG 165, NA. For the impact on morale caused by relieving one of these units of its tactical mission and assigning it labor details, see 477th AAA (AW) Bn History, folder "CABN 477-0.1 (11315) Hist 477th AAA (AW) Bn, 7 Sep 43–15 Aug 45," Box 17219, 477th Anti-Aircraft Artillery (AW) Battalion, Coast Artillery, World War II Operations Reports, 1940–48, RG 407, WNRC.

38. 870th AAA (AW) Battalion History, folder "CABN 870-0.1 (13214) Hist 870th AAA (AW) Bn, 1 Jan–31 Dec 44," and folder "CABN 870-0.1 (13214) Unit Hist, 870th AAA (AW) Bn, 10 May–30 Sep 45," both in Box 17451, 870th Anti-Aircraft Artillery (AW) Battalion, Coast Artillery, World War II Operations Reports, 1940–48, RG 407, WNRC; Lee, *Employment of Negro Troops*, pp. 121–22; MacGregor et al., *American Military History*, p. 521. Prior to the war, the 369th had been a New York National Guard infantry regiment. Following the Army's August 1940 expansion, the 369th was converted into an antiaircraft artillery unit and inducted into federal service in January 1941.

39. 870th AAA (AW) Battalion History, folder "CABN 870-0.1 (13214) Unit Hist, 870th AAA (AW) Bn, 10 May–30 Sep 45," Box 17451, 870th Anti-Aircraft Artillery (AW) Battalion, Coast Artillery, World War II Operations Reports, 1940–48, RG 407, WNRC; Tenth Army Action Report, Ryukyus, folder "110-0.3, Action Report, Ryukyus, Vol 1 of 3, Tenth Army, 20 Mar–30 Jun 45," Box 2940, Tenth Army, World War II Operations Reports, 1940–48, RG 407, WNRC; Lieutenant Colonel Wilmer F. Lucas letter to Commanding General, United States Army Forces Middle Pacific,

"Combat Infantryman Badge," 10 August 1945, folder "200.6, #7," Box 3329, Decimal 200.6, GHQ SWPA/AFPAC Adjutant General, General Correspondence, 1944–46, RG 338, WNRC.

40. General Headquarters, United States Army Forces Pacific General Order 401, 17 December 1945, Box T1309, General Orders, 1945, AFPAC Adjutant General, RG 338, WNRC; Lieutenant Colonel Wilmer F. Lucas letter to Commanding Officer, Army Garrison Force, Kerama Retto, "Narrative of Operations by Elements of the 870th AAA (AW) Bn," 24 June 1945, folder "CABN 870-0.1 (13214) Unit Hist— 870th AAA (AW) Bn, 10 May–30 Sep 45," Box 17451, 870th Anti-Aircraft Artillery (AW) Battalion, Coast Artillery, World War II Operations Reports, 1940–48, RG 407, WNRC. The award citation described a much more significant role in the engagement for Lieutenant Peagler than the following account written by Lieutenant Colonel Lucas, who commanded the 870th:

> It seems that Lt. Peagler may have been a little in advance of the 1st Plat of Btry B because, after proceeding for a distance of 120 to 125 yards of what was now a gentle slope of the ridge, he was the first to draw fire. His location at that time was on the crest of the ridge.... Sniper fire was the first fire to be encountered. Lt. Thomas cleaned out several snipers on the slope of the ridge to his left. At this time the 3d Plat of Btry B, located the first machine gun nest to the right front. Lt. Peagler was the first to observe the machine gun nest. The machine gun nest was over the ridge, in a gully set to cover any approach over the ridge. In order to fire on the nest, it was necessary to stand, and in doing so become a perfect target. Lt. Peagler called a bazooka man, Pfc Dabney, and as he raised to point out the machine gun nest to this bazooka man, he was drilled through the temple by a sniper on his right.

Lucas, however, wrote his account the evening of the action, when the roles played by particular individuals may not yet have been sorted out. Lucas noted in his report, "Individual actions of a specific meritorious nature and worthy of further consideration are being thoroughly screened for subsequent appropriate recommendations." Though neither Lieutenant Peagler's Decoration Case File nor his Individual Personnel Record has been located, a letter from Headquarters, Okinawa Base Command to the commanding general, Army Forces, Western Pacific, requesting the status of a number of award recommendations, indicates that the award originally recommended for Lieutenant Peagler may have been a Silver Star. See Major C. F. Test letter to Commanding General, Army Forces, Western Pacific, "Awards and Decorations," 15 November 1945, folder "200.6, Awards and Decorations, Okinawa Base Command, 1945," Box 3, Pacific Awards Case Files, National Personnel Records Center (NPRC), St. Louis, Mo. The small collection of World War II awards case files currently housed at the NPRC is scheduled to be transferred to the National Archives.

41. Lee, *Employment of Negro Troops*, pp. 594–95.

42. *Ibid.*, p. 600.

43. Captain Jonathan B. Turner, 839th Engineer Aviation Battalion, memorandum for Colonel Curtis, "Replies to AG291.2 (23 May 1945)," undated (but after 23 May 45), Section 10, folder "Colored Troops, Vol II," Box 1549, Decimal 322.999, AFPAC Pacific Warfare Board, RG 338, WNRC.

44. The units were identified as African-American from T/O Colored Units, Continental and Foreign, 7 July 1945, Box 443, Decimal 291.2, G-1 Decimal File, 1942–June 1946, RG 165, WNRC. They included the 471–477, 488, 490–494, 808–814, 820, and 823–828 Amphibian Truck Companies.

45. 477th Amphibian Truck Company History, folder "TCCO 477-0.1 Hist 477th Amph Truck Co, TC, 16 Dec 43–30 Nov 45," Box 23384, 477th Amphibian Truck

Company, Transportation, World War II Operations Reports, 1940–48, RG 407, WNRC. Three of the 477th's soldiers were wounded in action.

46. The four were the 471st (8 Silver Stars, Iwo Jima), the 473rd (3 Silver Stars, Iwo Jima), the 476th (3 Silver Stars, Iwo Jima), and the 812th (3 Silver Stars, Biak Island). If the Silver Stars awarded to white officers are included, the total is 23.

47. Geoffrey Perret, *There's a War to Be Won: The United States Army in World War II* (New York: Ballantine Books, 1991), pp. 104–5. Unlike the most acronyms, only one letter in DUKW bore any resemblance to the characteristic or function it represented. "D" meant the year 1942, "U"—utility vehicle, "K"—four-wheel drive, and "W"—two rear-driving axles.

48. Apparently, the African-American amphibian truck companies were all commanded and staffed by white officers. The records researched for this study gave no indication that any were black. The assumption that they were white, however, may be erroneous. After October 1943, the only amphibian truck companies activated by the Army were African-American. See Lee, *Employment of Negro Troops*, p. 420.

49. See, for example, the 810th Amphibian Truck Company's mission statement in its Initial Historical Summary, 19 June 1944, folder "TCCO 810.0.1 (46367) Histl Summary, 810th Amph Truck Co, TC, 10 Jul 43–23 Apr 44," Box 23404, 810th Amphibian Truck Company, Transportation, World War II Operations Reports, 1940–48, RG 407, WNRC.

50. See folder "TCCO 472-0.1 Hist 472d Amph Truck Co, TC Oct 43–31 Dec 45," and folder "TCCO 472-0.3 A/A Rpt 472d Amph Truck Co, TC, 25 Apr–30 Jun 45"; both in Box 23383, 472nd Amphibian Truck Company, Transportation, World War II Operations Reports, 1940–48, RG 407, WNRC.

51. Initial Historical Summary, 19 June 1944, folder "TCCO 810-0.1 (46367) Histl Summary 810th Amph Truck Co, TC, 10 Jul 43–23 Apr 44," Box 23404, 810th Amphibian Truck Company, Transportation, World War II Operations Reports, 1940–48, RG 407, WNRC.

52. Historical Record, 3rd Platoon, 812th Amphibian Truck Co, 2 September 1944, folder "TCCO 812-0.1 (30681) Hist 812th Amph Truck Co, TC, 27 May–20 Aug 44"; Extract of 41st Infantry Division General Order 29, 17 June 1944, and Extract of 41st Infantry Division General Order 30, 17 June 1944, folder "TCCO 812-0.1 Historical File, 812th Amph Truck Co, TC, 10/4–4/46"; both folders in Box 23404, 812th Amphibian Truck Company, Transportation, World War II Operations Reports, 1940–48, RG 407, WNRC.

53. Bykofsky and Larson, *Transportation Corps*, pp. 534–35. The authors of this volume in the Army's World War II "Green Series" histories were apparently unaware that these units were African-American. The index has a separate entry for "Negro" units, yet none of the African-American amphibian truck companies are listed under it; other black units, however, are identified as such, both in the index and in the text. The other companies (474th, 477th, 808th, 813th, 820th, 825th, and 826th) arrived in the days and weeks following the initial invasion.

54. 823rd Amphibian Truck Company History, 6 February 1945, folder "TCCO 823-0.1 (46375) Hist 823d Amph Truck Co, TC, 8 Jul 44–Sept 45, Nov-Dec 45," Box 23406, 823rd Amphibian Truck Company, Transportation, World War II Operations Reports, 1940–48, RG 407, WNRC.

55. 827th Amphibian Truck Company History, 30 January 1945, folder "TCCO 827-0.3 (20448) Hist 827th Amph Truck Co, TC, 20 Oct 44–30 Jan 45," Box 23407, 827th Amphibian Truck Company, Transportation, World War II Operations Reports, 1940–48, RG 407, WNRC.

56. Spector, *Eagle against the Sun*, pp. 422, 426–28, 494–503, 511–17.

164    The Exclusion of Black Soldiers from the Medal of Honor

57. Bykofsky and Larson, *Transportation Corps*, pp. 535–36 (but the units are not identified as African-American); Lee, *Employment of Negro Troops*, p. 637.
58. War Department Press Release, 28 May 1945, Box 102, Press and Radio News Releases, 1921–47, News Branch, Public Relations Division, RG 165, NA.
59. 471st Amphibian Truck Company History, 8 January 1946, folder "TCCO 470.0.1 (30360) Hist 471st Amph Truck Co, TC, 15 Oct 43–15 Jan 46"; Headquarters Island Command Iwo Jima General Order 69, 18 August 1945, in folder "TCCO 471-1.6 (30357) Dec & Awards, 471st Amph Truck Co, TC, Yr 44–45"; both folders in Box 23382, 471st Amphibian Truck Company, Transportation, World War II Operations Reports, 1940–48, RG 407, WNRC; 473rd Amphibian Truck Company History, attaching Headquarters Island Command, Iwo Jima, General Order 35, 4 June 1945, and Headquarters Island Command, Iwo Jima, General Order 108, 24 November 1945, folder "TCCO 473-0.1 (31710) Hist 473rd Amph Truck Co, TC, 15 Oct 43–Dec 45," Box 23383, 473rd Amphibian Truck Company, Transportation, World War II Operations Reports, 1940–48, RG 407, WNRC; 476th Amphibian Truck Company History, 1945, citing Headquarters Island Command Iwo Jima, General Order 93, 10 October 1945, General Order 95, 15 October 1945, and General Order 99, 22 October 1945, folder "TCCO 476-0.1 (30368) Hist 476th Amph Truck Co, TC, Yr 45," Box 23383, 476th Amphibian Truck Company, Transportation, World War II Operations Reports, 1940–48, RG 407, WNRC. In addition to 5 Silver Stars, the men of the 476th earned 17 Bronze Stars (including one to Private Maurice A. Paris). During the Iwo Jima invasion, two of the 476th's soldiers were killed, six wounded, and three injured. The unit also lost 29 of its 48 DUKWs to enemy fire and rough surf.
60. Headquarters Island Command, Iwo Jima, General Order 69, 18 August 1945, folder "TCCO 471-1.6 (30357) Dec & Awards, 471st Amph Truck Co, TC Yr 44–45," Box 23382, 471st Amphibian Truck Company, Transportation, World War II Operations Reports, 1940–48, RG 407, WNRC.
61. Bykofsky and Larson, *Transportation Corps*, pp. 539-41 (the six units—472nd, 474th, 477th, 814th, 827th, and 828th—are not identified as African American).
62. Spector, *Eagle against the Sun*, pp. 532–40.
63. 814th Amphibian Truck Company History, Box 23505, 814th Amphibian Truck Company; 827th Amphibian Truck Company History, 30 January 1945, folder "TCCO 827-0.3 (20448) Hist 827th Amph Truck Co, TC, 20 Oct 44–30 Jan 45," Box 23407, 827th Amphibian Truck Company; both in Transportation, World War II Operations Reports, 1940–48, RG 407, WNRC.
64. 474th Amphibian Truck Company, Report of Participation in Iceberg [Okinawa] Operation, undated, folder "TCCO 474-0.1 Hist 474th Amph Truck Co, TC, 15 Oct 43–30 Jan 46," Box 23383, 474th Amphibian Truck Company, Transportation, World War II Operations Reports, 1940–48, RG 407, WNRC.
65. War Department Press Release, 8 October 1945, folder "Sep-Oct 45," Box 107, Press and Radio News Releases, 1921–47, News Branch, Public Relations Division, RG 165, NA. In the fall of 1944, the China-Burma-India Theater was divided into two theaters: China and Burma-India. The only records of the 484th Anti-Aircraft Artillery Battalion to have been preserved are a few of its General Orders, which unfortunately do not provide much information about its activities.
66. Lee, *Employment of Negro Troops*, pp. 610–19.
67. *Ibid.*, pp. 615–16.
68. 823rd Engineer Aviation Battalion History, folder "ENBN 823-0.2 Hist 823d Engr Avn Bn, 15 Feb 42–22 Feb 44," Box 18908, 823rd Engineer Aviation Battalion, Engineers, World War II Operations Reports, 1940–48, RG 407, WNRC; Headquarters Tenth Air Force General Order 36, 8 December 1942, on microfilm (Tenth Air

Force General Orders File), Air Force History Support Office, Bolling AFB, Washington, D.C.

69. In the summer of 1945, General MacArthur's adjutant general reported total casualty figures through 31 July 1945 for forces under MacArthur's command. White casualties numbered 10,512 officers and 100,309 enlisted men. African-American casualties totaled 11 officers and 321 enlisted men. See Colonel C. E. Curtis memo for File, "Participation of Negro Troops in the Post War Establishment," 27 August 1945, Section 17, folder "Colored Troops, Vol II," Box 1549, Decimal 322.999, AFPAC Pacific Warfare Board, RG 338, WNRC.

*Chapter 7*

# Black Recipients of the Distinguished Service Cross in World War II

## Introduction

Considered the second highest Army award for valor in combat in the pyramid of honors, the Distinguished Service Cross was given for extraordinary heroism in connection with military operations against an armed enemy of the United States. Congress authorized the medal in July 1918 in legislation that also clarified questions relating to the Medal of Honor. An important reason for establishing the Distinguished Service Cross was to maintain the position of the Medal of Honor as the one award recognizing the few truly extraordinary acts of bravery in battle. The Committee on Military Affairs, which had prepared the bill, stated: "It is believed that if a secondary medal ... had been authorized in the past, the award of the ... Medal of Honor would have been more jealously guarded than it was for many years. And it is certain that the establishment of such a secondary medal now will go far toward removing the temptation to laxity with regards to future awards of the greater medal."[1]

The establishment of the Distinguished Service Cross in 1918 created, for the first time in American history, the notion of "degrees of service to the country, each worthy of recognition, but only *one* of which could be accorded supreme recognition."[2] The Distinguished Service Cross, therefore, was juxtaposed between the Medal of Honor and the Silver Star in order to protect the uniqueness of the Medal of Honor. But the Distinguished Service Cross was also perceived as an award of extremely high standing and in practice was given out in modest numbers in World War II. The report of the General Board on Awards and Decorations in the European Theater of Operations noted, for example: "Standards for this decoration have been held extremely high, in the opinion of many, excessively so. In the European Theater of Operations, awards fell far short of the maximum number indicated in the quota system devised by 12th Army Group. It is now realized that many Silver Stars should have been Distinguished Service Crosses."[3]

## List of Black Distinguished Service Cross Recipients

By mid–1947, the U.S. Army had awarded 4,750 Distinguished Service Crosses to its officers and enlisted men. Of that total, blacks accounted for 8, less than .2 percent.[4] Early in 1946, the Negro Interest Section in the Army's Bureau of Public Relations identified and published the names of five of the eight.[5] In 1982, when the Army awarded a posthumous Distinguished Service Cross to Lieutenant John Fox, the number of known black Distinguished Service Cross recipients stood at six. Research for this study has added another three names to the list, thus increasing to *nine* the total number of black soldiers known to have been awarded the Distinguished Service Cross in World War II."[6]

| Name/Service Number | Unit | General Order #, Date (Date of Action) |
|---|---|---|
| 1st Lt. Vernon J. Baker 01307638 | Co C, 370 IR, 92 ID | #70, 5th Army 10 Jun 1945 (5 Apr 1945) |
| S/Sgt. Edward A. Carter, Jr. 39164078 | 56 A I Bn, 12 AD, 7 Army Inf Co #1 (Prov) | #580, 7th Army 4 Oct 1945 (23 Mar 1945) |
| S/Sgt. Leonard E. Dowden# 38315204 | Co I, 368 IR, 93 ID | #408, AFPAC 20 Dec 1945 (17 Jul 1945) |
| 1st Lt. John R. Fox# 0387718 | Cannon Co, 366 IR, 92 ID | #9, DA, 15 Apr 1982 (26 Dec 1944) |
| PFC Willy F. James, Jr.# 37223753 | Co G, 413 IR, 104 ID | #512, 7th Army 14 Sep 1945 (7 Apr 1945) |
| 1st Lt. Robert J. Peagler# 01045552 | 870 AAA (AW) Bn | #401, AFPAC 17 Dec 1945 (24 Jun 1945) |
| 1st Lt. Charles L. Thomas 01824391 | Co C, 614 TD Bn, 103 ID | #58, 7th Army 20 Feb 1945 (14 Dec 1944) |
| PFC Jack Thomas 34743054 | Co E, 60 IR, 9 ID | #255, 3rd Army 18 Sep 1945 (9 Apr 1945) |

| Name/Service Number | Unit | General Order #, Date (Date of Action) |
|---|---|---|
| Private George Watson#<br>34229603 | 29 QM Regiment | #32, FE, 15 Jun 1943<br>(8 Mar 1943) |

#Awarded posthumously.

## Individual Summaries

**First Lieutenant Vernon J. Baker.** Born in Cheyenne, Wyoming, Vernon J. Baker worked as a railroad porter before enlisting in the Army in June 1941. He graduated from Officer Candidate School in January 1943 and deployed to Italy in the summer of 1944 with the 92nd Infantry Division as a platoon leader in Company C, 370th Infantry Regiment. In October 1944, Lieutenant Baker was wounded in action, hospitalized for six weeks, and awarded the Purple Heart.

At 5:00 A.M. on 5 April 1945, Lieutenant Baker advanced at the head of his weapons platoon and, along with Company C's three rifle platoons, moved toward their objective, Castle Aghinolfi—a German mountain strongpoint on the high ground just east of the coastal highway and about two miles from the 370th Infantry Regiment's line of departure.

Moving more rapidly than the rest of the Company, Lieutenant Baker and about 25 men reached the south side of a draw some 250 yards from the castle within two hours. In reconnoitering for a suitable position to set up a machine gun, Lieutenant Baker observed two cylindrical objects pointing out of a slit in a mount at the edge of a hill. Crawling up and under the opening, he stuck his M-1 into the slit and emptied his clip, killing the observation post's two occupants. Moving to another position in the same area, Baker stumbled upon a well-camouflaged machine-gun nest, the crew of which was eating breakfast. He shot and killed both enemy soldiers.

After Captain John F. Runyon, Company C's commander, joined the group, a German soldier appeared from the draw and hurled a grenade, which failed to explode. Lieutenant Baker shot the enemy soldier twice as he tried to flee. Baker then went down into the draw alone. There he blasted open the concealed entrance of another dugout with a hand grenade, shot one German soldier who emerged after the explosion, tossed another grenade into the dugout, and entered, firing his submachine gun and killing two more Germans.

As Lieutenant Baker climbed back out of the draw, enemy machine-gun and mortar fire began to inflict heavy casualties among the group of 25 soldiers, killing or wounding about two-thirds of them. When expected reinforcements did not arrive, Captain Runyon ordered a withdrawal in two groups. Breaking into tears, Lieutenant Baker protested: "Captain, we can't withdraw. We must stay here and fight it out." Despite these strong feelings, Lieutenant Baker volunteered to cover the withdrawal of the first group of mostly walking wounded and to remain to assist in the evacuation of the more seriously wounded. During the second group's withdrawal, Lieutenant Baker, supported by covering fire from one of his platoon members, destroyed two machine-gun positions (previously bypassed during the assault) with hand grenades.

In all, the men of Company C had killed 26 Germans, wounded many others, and destroyed 6 machine-gun positions, 2 observer posts, and 4 dugouts. Baker himself had accounted for 9 of the dead enemy soldiers, 3 of the machine guns, an observer post, and a dugout.

For showing extraordinary heroism and leadership on 5 April 1945 and for leading a battalion advance through enemy minefields and heavy fire the next day, Captain Runyon recommended Lieutenant Baker for the Distinguished Service Cross. The Fifth Army approved and announced the award in General Orders on 10 June 1945. Lieutenant Baker received the decoration at a ceremony in Italy on 4 July 1945.

**Staff Sergeant Edward A. Carter, Jr.**  Staff Sergeant Edward A. Carter, Jr., who had entered the Army from Los Angeles, California, had very little time to adjust to his role as a volunteer infantryman assigned to the Seventh Army's Infantry Company No. 1 (Provisional). Less than two weeks after the Company had been organized, one of its detachments, including Carter, was in combat with the 12th Armored Division's 56th Armored Infantry Battalion, and Staff Sergeant Carter had earned a Distinguished Service Cross for extraordinary heroism.

At about 8:30 A.M. on 23 March 1945, Carter and his fellow rifle-squad members were riding on a tank advancing toward Speyer, Germany. Suddenly the tank began taking bazooka and small-arms fire from a large warehouse to its left front. After dismounting from the tank and taking cover, Staff Sergeant Carter volunteered to lead a three-man patrol across 150 yards of open field to reconnoiter the warehouse. When one man in the patrol was killed by intense small-arms fire, Staff Sergeant Carter ordered the other two back to a protected position from which they could provide covering fire for him as he advanced alone. Though one of the men was killed and the other wounded before reaching cover, Staff Sergeant Carter continued on through enemy fire. As he moved forward, Carter was first wounded three times in his left leg, then in an arm, and finally, a hand.

Despite his five wounds, Staff Sergeant Carter, now crawling, kept moving under heavy enemy fire toward the objective. Within 30 yards of the warehouse, he took cover behind an earthen bank. After he had remained for about two hours behind the protective cover, eight German riflemen approached his position. Staff Sergeant Carter killed six and captured the other two. Using

Second Lieutenant Vernon J. Baker at Fort Rucker, Alabama, 1943, soon after graduating from Officer Candidate School. U.S. Army Photograph, National Archives and Records Administration, courtesy Lt. Col. Major Clark, U.S. Army (Retired).

the two prisoners as a shield, Carter withdrew across the open field. Even after reaching safety, Staff Sergeant Carter would not let himself be evacuated until he had relayed full information about the enemy's position.

Staff Sergeant Carter's company commander recommended him for the Distinguished Service Cross on 10 July 1945. After approval by Headquarters, 56th Armored Infantry Battalion, and the 12th Armored Division's Combat Command "B" Headquarters, Major General Roderick R. Allen, Commanding General of the 12th Armored Division, approved the recommendation on 25 July 1945. Late in August, the Seventh Army's decorations board unanimously endorsed the award, and it was announced on 4 October 1945 in Seventh Army General Order 580.

**Staff Sergeant Leonard E. Dowden.** Originally from New Orleans, Louisiana, Staff Sergeant Leonard E. Dowden was the only member of the 93rd Infantry Division to receive a Distinguished Service Cross for gallantry in action of World War II.

In July 1945, the Division's 368th Infantry Regiment was charged with the responsibility for clearing remaining Japanese forces from Jolo Island, located in the Sulu Archipelago halfway between the Philippines and Borneo. On 17 July, an I Company patrol that included Staff Sergeant Dowden encountered

Staff Sergeant Edward A. Carter, Jr. Courtesy Mr. Edward A. Carter III.

a force of approximately 100 Japanese—almost three times the numerical size of the American unit. When fighting broke out, Dowden moved his squad to within 30 yards of the Japanese. He then crawled forward alone to assault a machine-gun position. While advancing, Dowden was hit in the chest but heroically continued ahead, ordering one of his fellow soldiers, who had started out to help him, to remain under cover. Ten yards from the machine gun and still exposed to enemy fire (and despite his wound), Dowden raised himself to throw a hand grenade. But before he could release it, he was hit in the neck and killed.

For the extraordinary heroism that cost him his life, Staff Sergeant Dowden received the Distinguished Service Cross posthumously. Headquarters, United States Army Forces Pacific announced the award in General Order 408 on 20 December 1945.

**First Lieutenant John R. Fox.** Born in Cincinnati, Ohio, and educated at Wilberforce University, John R. Fox joined the Army in February 1941. In December 1944, Fox's regiment, the 366th Infantry, entered combat in Italy attached to the 92nd Infantry Division.

**First Lieutenant John R. Fox. Courtesy Lt. Col. Major Clark, U.S. Army (Retired).**

During the night of 25–26 December 1944, enemy soldiers dressed as civilians infiltrated the village of Sommocolonia in the Serchio Valley. Occupied by two platoons of the 366th Infantry and by Italian partisans, the village was attacked between 5:00 A.M. and 7:00 A.M. by uniformed German and Italian Fascist forces after a mortar and artillery barrage. Several hours of street fighting followed.

Lieutenant Fox, assigned to the 366th's Cannon Company and acting as a forward observer for the 598th Field Artillery Battalion, took a position, along with the other members of his observer party, on the second floor of a house in the village from where he could best observe the enemy forces and direct friendly artillery fire. At about 8:00 A.M., Fox began to call for artillery support. Soon enemy troops reached his location; he could hear their efforts to enter the building. Fox continued to adjust close-in fire until the shells were landing very near the house. He then radioed the 598th's Fire Direction Center (FDC): "That [last] round is just where I want it—bring it in sixty more yards." The FDC duty officer called the 598th's commander to inform him of Fox's request; he, in turn, radioed Fox to verify that the request had been called correctly. Fox answered: "Fire it! There are more of them than there are of us. Put fire on my OP [Observation Post]." Thereupon the 598th fired a battery volley (12 rounds of 105-mm high explosive), destroying the building and killing Fox and the other men in the observer party as well as dozens of enemy soldiers.

For his extraordinary valor in Sommocolonia, Lieutenant Fox was recommended for the Distinguished Service Cross. Several witnesses, among them Brigadier General William H. Colbern, the 92nd Infantry Division's artillery commander, testified that they saw the recommendation. But either lost or destroyed, it was not acted on.

On 15 April 1982, based on evidence compiled and submitted by Dr. Hondon B. Hargrove, a veteran of the 92nd's service in Italy, the Department of the Army awarded the Distinguished Service Cross (posthumously) to First Lieutenant John R. Fox. The decoration was presented to Mrs. Arlene Fox, the lieutenant's widow, in a ceremony at Fort Devens, Massachusetts, on 15 May 1982.

**Private First Class Willy F. James, Jr.**  From Kansas City, Missouri, Private First Class Willy F. James, Jr., was one of the more than 2,800 African-American soldiers in the European Theater who volunteered and were selected as infantry replacements early in 1945. After training in France, James became a member of the black platoon assigned to Company G of the 413th Infantry Regiment, 104th Infantry Division.

On 7 April 1945, the 413th had established a bridgehead across the Weser River in the heart of Germany. To secure and expand the bridgehead, Company G was ordered to capture the town of Lippoldsberg. Private First Class James, first scout of the lead squad in the assault platoon attempting to seize some houses on the town's outskirts, was 150 yards out in front of his squad and the first to draw enemy fire. When joined by his platoon leader, James volunteered to advance farther to pinpoint enemy positions. Under fire, he made his way 200 yards across open terrain, observed the German positions for more than half an hour, and returned to his platoon with the vital information.

Based on the intelligence that Private First Class James had provided, the platoon launched its assault on the outlying buildings that were its original objective. James now volunteered again, this time to lead a squad in the attack. During the assault, Private First Class James's platoon leader was hit by enemy sniper fire. Immediately going to his aid, again across open ground, Willy F. James, Jr., was killed by machine-gun fire. His extraordinary heroism inspired his platoon to reach its objective and contributed to the 413th's ability to enlarge its bridgehead over the Weser.

Private First Class James' platoon leader recommended him for the Distinguished Service Cross on 26 May 1945. Within a month, the recommendation had been approved by the 413th's Second Battalion and Regimental commanders and the 104th Infantry Division and XXI Corps commanders. Early in July, the recommendation received the favorable endorsement of the Seventh Army's decorations board. Lieutenant General Geoffrey Keyes, Seventh Army Commander, awarded the Distinguished Service Cross (posthumously) to Private First Class James by General Order of 14 September 1945.

**First Lieutenant Robert J. Peagler.** In the closing months of the war in the Pacific, Lieutenant Peagler's unit, the 870th Anti-Aircraft Artillery Battalion, left the Hawaiian Islands, where it had been stationed for nearly three years, and arrived at Okinawa in the Ryukyu Islands on 10 May 1945. There the 870th's black soldiers found out that they would participate in the fighting not in an air-defense role but as infantry. After a few days of training in infantry tactics, the 870th was sent to Kerama Island to engage Japanese forces that were still putting up a stiff resistance.

At 8:00 A.M. on 24 June 1945, three platoons from the 870th assaulted the high ground held by the Japanese, situated about 300 yards from a village occupied by American forces. First Lieutenant Peagler was the first to draw enemy fire as he advanced up a hill at the head of his platoon. From the crest of the hill, he directed machine-gun and Browning Automatic Rifle (BAR) fire on two Japanese pillboxes and other defensive emplacements. When the BAR jammed, Peagler charged forward, throwing hand grenades and firing his M-1 rifle at the nearest Japanese pillbox. He killed six enemy soldiers and captured a grenade launcher before he was struck and killed by Japanese sniper fire.

The extraordinary heroism that inspired the other members of his platoon to continue advancing but resulted in the loss of his own life was recognized with the award of the Distinguished Service Cross by General Headquarters, United States Army Forces Pacific, on 17 December 1945.

**First Lieutenant Charles L. Thomas.** On 14 December 1944 near Climbach, France, First Lieutenant Charles L. Thomas, Commander of Company C, 614th Tank Destroyer Battalion, became the second African American to earn the Distinguished Service Cross in World War II. Before the war, Thomas had been a molder and metal pourer for the Ford Motor Company; he was a student at Wayne State University in Detroit, Michigan, when inducted into the Army as a private in January 1942. Assigned to the 614th, he was sent to Tank Destroyer Officer Candidate School at Camp Hood, Texas. In March 1943, he was commissioned a second lieutenant and deployed with the 614th to England and then to the Continent in November 1944.

On 14 December, a platoon from Thomas' company was the lead element in a task force that included a platoon of tanks from the 756th Tank Battalion and a reinforced rifle company from the 411th Infantry Regiment. The task force's objective was to take the town of Climbach, which was occupied by German forces and located five miles from the German border and the Siegfried Line. Lieutenant Thomas volunteered to lead the platoon from his company and act as point for the task force in an armored scout car. Around 2:00 P.M., about 700 yards from the town, the scout car was disabled by enemy artillery and small-arms fire, halting the task force advance. Though wounded, Thomas helped the other men out of the scout car. Once free of the wrecked vehicle, Thomas was several times wounded again in the chest, arms, and legs. Nevertheless, he began to direct the placement and firing of the platoon's antitank guns. Realizing that he would be unable to continue commanding the unit, Lieutenant Thomas still refused evacuation until he had prepared the platoon leader to take over.

The personal courage and leadership that Lieutenant Thomas displayed in getting the tank-destroyer platoon into action assisted other task force elements to flank the German positions in and around Climbach. By nightfall, German forces had withdrawn from the town.

Lieutenant Colonel John P. Blackshear, the task force commander and the 411th Infantry Regiment's executive officer, recommended Lieutenant Thomas for the Distinguished Service Cross on 21 December 1944. The 411th's commander approved the recommendations, as did the 103rd Infantry Division and XV Corps commanders. Lieutenant General Alexander M. Patch, the Seventh Army Commander, concurred, and orders announcing the award of the Distinguished Service Cross to Lieutenant Thomas were published on 20 February 1945.

**Private First Class Jack Thomas**  An orphan from Albany, Georgia, Private First Class Thomas entered the Army in March 1943 and arrived in the European Theater by the end of the year as a truck driver assigned to a service unit. Answering the call in December 1944 for volunteer infantry replacements, Private First Class Thomas was one of the approximately 40 African-American soldiers in the separate platoon assigned to Company E of the 60th Infantry Regiment, Ninth Infantry Division.

During April 1945, the 60th Infantry Regiment was engaged in operations to reduce the pockets of German resistance in the Ruhr Valley and the Harz Mountains in western Germany. On 9 April, Company E's black platoon, reinforced by a bazooka team for antitank defense, was directed to investigate a German roadblock defended by a tank near the town of Herzgerode. Private First Class Thomas' squad and the bazooka team, with Thomas out ahead in the lead, approached to the right of the enemy position to knock out the tank. Deploying into a skirmish line, Thomas and the other men opened fire on the tank to keep enemy soldiers from manning it. Thomas advanced beyond the skirmish line and threw two hand grenades, which wounded several of the enemy. When heavy German fire from automatic weapons and small arms wounded the two bazooka team members, Private First Class Thomas, while under fire, ran to the bazooka position and fired the weapon twice, keeping the Germans away from the tank. As enemy fire continued, Thomas then picked up one of the bazooka men and carried him to safety across a 100-yard clearing.

Company E's commander recommended Private First Class Thomas for a Distinguished Service Cross in early July 1945. The 60th Infantry Regiment's Second Battalion commander quickly approved it, as did Colonel William C. Westmoreland, the regimental commander. By late August, the recommendation had reached Lieutenant General George S. Patton's Third Army

**First Lieutenant Charles L. Thomas. Courtesy the Burton Historical Collection of the Detroit Public Library.**

Headquarters. There the Third Army's decorations board unanimously disapproved the proposed Distinguished Service Cross, recommending a Silver Star instead. General Patton did not agree. The handwritten letters "DSC" followed by the initial "P" appear at the bottom of the board's Silver Star recommendation. On 18 September 1945, a Third Army General Order announced the award of the Distinguished Service Cross to Private First Class Jack Thomas. Thomas received the Distinguished Service Cross during a ceremony at Kunzelsau, Germany, on 19 October 1945.

**Private George Watson.** The first African American to earn the Distinguished Service Cross in World War II, Private Watson was inducted into the Army from Birmingham, Alabama. Trained initially at Fort Benning, Georgia, he was assigned to the 29th Quartermaster Regiment.

On 8 March 1943, Private Watson was on board a ship that was attacked by enemy bombers near Porloch Harbor, New Guinea. When the ship was abandoned, Private Watson remained in the water and assisted other soldiers who could not swim to reach the safety of a life raft. This extraordinary heroism saved several lives but cost Private Watson his own life when the suction of the sinking ship dragged him beneath the surface.

United States Army Forces Far East General Order 32, 15 June 1943, awarded Private Watson the Distinguished Service Cross. On 4 July 1944, during a ceremony at Fort Benning, the George Watson Memorial Field on the grounds of the reception center for new inductees was dedicated to the heroic African-American soldier's memory and was marked with a granite rock bearing a bronze plaque.

## Notes

1. Quoted in U.S. Department of the Army, Public Information Division, *The Medal of Honor of the U.S. Army* (Washington, D.C.: U.S. Government Printing Office, 1948), p. 21.

2. *Ibid.*

3. Report of the General Board, United States Forces European Theater, "Awards and Decorations in a Theater of Operations," G-1 Section, Study Number 10, p. 8, Box 2, Reports of the General Board, USFET, Records of the U.S. Army, Dwight D. Eisenhower Library, Abilene, Kans.

4. The percentage is about the same for Silver Stars. By mid-1947, the Army had awarded approximately 75,000 Silver Stars. An estimated 200, or .3 percent of that total, had been won by African Americans (about 60 in Europe, close to 100 in the Mediterranean, and 20–30 in the Pacific and CBI).

5. The five were Baker, Carter, Charles L. Thomas, Jack Thomas, and Watson. See War Department Press Release, 18 February 1946, folder "Jan-Mar 46," Box 110, Press and Radio News Releases, 1921–47, News Branch, Public Relations Division, Record Group 165, National Archives, Washington, D.C.

6. Decoration Case Files have been located for Staff Sergeant Carter, Private First Class James, Lieutenant Thomas, and Private First Class Thomas. All of the World War II Individual Personnel Records ("201" files) for the black Distinguished Service Cross recipients, located at the National Personnel Records Center in St. Louis, appear to have been destroyed in the 1973 fire. Although the "201" files for Lieutenants Baker and Fox and Private First Class Thomas contain some records, these were apparently added after the fire.

## Chapter 8

# Conclusions and Recommendations

### The Medal of Honor

The Medal of Honor is the highest-ranking and best-known United States decoration for heroism in combat. Over the years, the Medal has come to symbolize the very highest measure of individual acts of gallantry in battle in the American military. Often mistakenly called the Congressional Medal of Honor, "it is in fact awarded in the name of the Congress of the United States and, whenever possible, the President of the United States personally makes its presentation."[1] For decades after its creation during the Civil War, there was no consistent policy or criterion for the Medal's award, nor were there clear rules or procedures for documenting and validating the acts of gallantry befitting the decoration. In 1916, Congress created a special board to investigate and report past awards of the Medal of Honor by the Army and struck 911 from the list of 2,625 that had been awarded. Wanting to reserve the Medal for those few acts of truly extraordinary heroism in battle, the Army bestowed only 95 during World War I. In July 1918, Congress finally redefined the criteria and set forth precise rules for the award, saying in legislation that the recipient must "distinguish himself conspicuously by gallantry and intrepidity at the risk of life above and beyond the call of duty."[2]

### The Medal of Honor and Black Soldiers in World War II

The Army was guided by this same policy of parsimony when it entered World War II, awarding only 294 Medals of Honor in that conflict. However, not one was awarded to an African American even though nearly a million blacks served as soldiers in the War. In fact, in all the major wars and campaigns since the inception of the Medal of Honor during the Civil War, only in World War II did no black soldier receive the nation's highest honor for heroism in battle.

This study found no official documentation for the nomination of a black soldier for the Medal of Honor during the entire period of the War and only four claims for an official submission: one for Staff Sergeant Ruben Rivers of A Company, 761st Tank Battalion, whose company commander remembers submitting a recommendation for the Medal of Honor in 1944 (the company clerk also remembers typing the paperwork); testimony by a warrant officer that he prepared the citation for a Medal of Honor for First Lieutenant Vernon J. Baker of the 370th Infantry Regiment, 92nd Infantry Division, for heroism in combat in Italy in 1945; statements in the press and in private correspondence that the Bronze Star of Corporal Waverly B. Woodson, a medic in the 320th Anti-Aircraft Barrage Balloon Battalion on Omaha Beach on 6–7 June 1944, may have been originally submitted as a higher award and perhaps considered by the European Theater for upgrade to a Medal of Honor; and a statement in an African-American newspaper that Staff Sergeant Edward A. Carter, Jr., of the Seventh Army's Infantry Company No. 1 (Provisional), who received a Distinguished Service Cross for heroism in battle in March 1945, had been originally recommended by his commanders for a Medal of Honor.[3] Therefore, the original approach of this study—to find every nomination of a black soldier for the Medal of Honor and to discover any irregularities in the processing of the nomination—proved incapable of fully explaining the lack of an award to a black soldier in the War.

However, research for this study did reveal irregularities in the processing of Medal of Honor recommendations. War Department policy directives contained ambiguities and inconsistencies in the criteria for distinguishing the Medal of Honor from the Distinguished Service Cross and the Silver Star and in the documentation required to support the recommendation for the awarding of the Medal of Honor. As a consequence, instructions issued by theater commanders for awards in general, and for the Medal of Honor in particular, differed, resulting in variations in procedures among the theaters. Moreover, for the Medal of Honor, War Department policy clearly stipulated that only the War Department could bestow the award; but at lower levels it was unclear that every nomination had to be forwarded to the War Department for determination no matter what intermediate echelons of command thought about the merit of the nomination. As a result, some commanders did not forward Medal of Honor nominations that they disapproved. Near the end of the War, the War Department clarified its policy about disapproval authority. Commanders complied and sent disapproved nominations forward. General Douglas MacArthur, Southwest Pacific Commander, who had pocketed many of the nominations he disapproved, acted reluctantly and only after considerable delay. In the Mediterranean, commanders apparently did not search their files for previous Medal recommendations that had been forwarded to Washington.

Research for this study uncovered no contemporary official documents that proved directly that there was bias against African Americans in the awarding of decorations. Nor do the relative numbers of Distinguished Service Crosses bestowed on whites and blacks by themselves demonstrate racial discrimination. However, this study found that the lack of an award of the Medal of Honor to a black soldier was most definitely, but indirectly, the result of racial bias. This lack of an award was rooted in the same racial assumptions and attitudes that characterized Army policy toward blacks and that pervaded the attitudes of more than a few of the key commanders of black combat units.

To begin with, black Americans in the Army served in units of their own, segregated by race and led overwhelmingly, especially above the company level, by white officers, most of whom shared the general views and assumptions prevalent in white American society at the time. The policy of segregation, which was inherently racist, hampered the training, undermined the morale, and reduced the efficiency and effectiveness of black units.

Furthermore, most of these units were service-oriented rather than combat units trained for or used in a direct combat role. Those few black units that were combatant were deployed relatively late in the War. A few, such as the 761st Tank Battalion and the 614th Tank Destroyer Battalion, experienced intense and sustained combat in the European Theater. The organic units of the 92nd Infantry Division (including the attached 366th Infantry Regiment) served an important combat role in Italy from August 1944 to May 1945 but fought mostly in a defensive role. The 93rd Infantry Division and the 24th Infantry Regiment served largely in garrison duties or in mopping-up operations in the Pacific. Thus even in combat units, most African Americans had more limited opportunities to distinguish themselves for awards of valor than did other soldiers.

Finally, it is clear that white division and regimental leaders of the 92nd Infantry Division, the black unit that logged the most combat man-hours for African Americans in the War, lacked confidence in the fighting abilities of their men. The 92nd fought for several months in northern Italy at the end of the War, but as a matter of policy its commanders linked the highest valor awards for black infantrymen to unit success in battle as well as to individual acts of heroism. At the end of the War, in a special assessment of black officers, the leaders of the Division attributed its poor performance *entirely* to what they described as the innate deficiencies of African Americans as infantrymen rather than to any of the myriad factors that were understood to affect combat effectiveness during that era, factors including leadership. Such attitudes had to prejudice the judgment and objectivity of the leadership about the heroism of individual black soldiers in specific situations and thus influence the awarding of decorations in the Division. Indeed, black officials and leaders, and black officers, noncommissioned officers, and enlisted men in the Division, during the War insisted, and still today insist, that there was an unwritten policy never to propose a black soldier for the Medal of Honor. The existence of a double standard in the Division is suggested by the fact that the only soldier in the

Division recommended for the Medal of Honor was a white company commander, whose heroism occurred in the same action in which one of his own black platoon leaders performed clearly more courageous acts that had greater impact on the enemy. Both, however, received the Distinguished Service Cross.

## Recommendations

The Army's policy of racial segregation, the impact of this policy on the efficiency and effectiveness of black units, the limited opportunities for black soldiers to serve in combat (also the product of racial assumptions), and the racial prejudice of some individuals in command of black troops together acted to prevent the award of a Medal of Honor to an African-American soldier during World War II. Alone, these circumstances justify a reconsideration by the Army of some of the most outstanding acts of gallantry by black soldiers, for bestowal of the Medal of Honor.

But it is also true that Army studies after the War conceded that the acts of heroism required for the Medal of Honor were extremely difficult to differentiate from those meriting the two next-highest awards and that the language describing the three contained overlapping terms and concepts. That was one reason the War Department reserved for itself final determination on the award and why the Army acted to clarify obfuscations and enforce its policy of requiring units to forward submissions for the Medal regardless of whether field commanders thought the nomination had merit. As one officer on the War Department Decorations Board in 1946 put it, "The personal equation enters."[4] After the War, Secretary of War Robert P. Patterson noted of the awards process: "There are cases that are reported inadequately. There are cases where human errors are made."[5] In a November 1946 letter to a U.S. Senator who complained about discrimination against National Guard and Reserve troops in the granting of awards (a charge that Patterson denied), the Secretary of War wrote: "Because of the large numbers of decorations already awarded, I am convinced that little can be done by retroactive action to correct any errors of the past without inducing greater errors and dissatisfaction. However, where corrective action is found possible and meritorious, you may be sure that it will be taken."[6]

If the Army decided to reconsider Distinguished Service Cross recipients for the Medal of Honor, such reconsideration would have more than one precedent. After World War I, General John J. Pershing ordered a review of Distinguished Service Cross recipients for consideration for upgrade because only four Medals of Honor had been awarded by the time of Armistice. As a result of this exercise, several dozen more Medals of Honor were bestowed. In 1943, North African Theater Commander General Dwight D. Eisenhower asked his Fifth Army commander to do the same because Eisenhower wanted to increase

Staff Sergeant Ruben Rivers. Courtesy David J. Williams.

the number of Medals of Honor awarded in the Theater; as a result, four Distinguished Service Crosses were upgraded to Medals of Honor.

Therefore, this study recommends that the Army evaluate, for elevation to the Medal of Honor, the Distinguished Service Crosses earned by black soldiers during World War II and, in addition, consider whether Staff Sergeant Ruben Rivers, who may have been officially recommended for the Medal for his heroic acts in battle in 1944 and who in any case died unrecognized for acts of valor that resulted in his death, also merits the award.

## Notes

1. Philip K. Robles, *United States Military Medals and Ribbons* (Rutland, Vt.: Charles Tuttle Company, 1971), p. 18.
2. United States Department of the Army, Public Information Division, *The Medal of Honor of the U.S. Army* (Washington, D.C.: U.S. Government Printing Office, 1948), p. 21.
3. See pages 71–75, 114–118, 79–80, and 84–85 above.
4. Colonel Guy M. Talcott letter to Major General J. E. Sloan, 17 May 1946, attached to Major General J. E. Sloan memorandum for the Deputy Chief of Staff, "War Department Decorations," 1 July 1946, folder "200.6, 1 July 46–15 July 46," Box 694, Decimal 200.6, G-1 Decimal File, June 1946–48,

Record Group (RG) 165, Washington National Records Center, Suitland, Md.

5. "Statement of the Honorable Robert P. Patterson, Reviewing the Report of the Doolittle Board," War Department Press Release, 25 June 1946, folder "RPP/Off. Enl. Men (Doolittle Board) SAFE," Box 5, Secretary of War Subject File (Safe File), 27 September 1945–24 July 1947, RG 107, National Archives (NA), Washington, D.C.

6. Robert P. Patterson letter to Senator Joseph F. Guffey, 29 November 1946, folder "200.6, Rewards, Badges, Decorations and Citations," Box 203, Decimal 200.6, Office, Administrative Assistant to the Secretary of War, Coordination and Records, Decimal File, Feb 1946–June 1947, RG 107, NA.

# Bibliography

## Archives and Manuscript Collections

**U.S. Army Center of Military History, Washington, D.C.**
Unit Histories and Other Records Related to Black Soldiers

**U.S. Army Military History Institute, Carlisle Barracks, Pennsylvania**
Papers of Edward M. Almond
Papers of Benjamin O. Davis, Sr.
Papers of James C. Evans
Unit Histories and Other Records Related to Black Soldiers

**Dwight D. Eisenhower Library, Abilene, Kansas**
Papers of Terry De La M. Allen
Papers of Harold R. Bull
Papers of Mark W. Clark (microfilm)
Papers of J. Lawton Collins
Papers of Jacob L. Devers (microfilm)
Papers of Dwight D. Eisenhower (Pre-Presidential)
Papers of Alvan C. Gillem, Jr.
Papers of Courtney H. Hodges
Papers of Willard S. Paul
Papers of Walter Bedell Smith
Records of the U.S. Army
Secretary General Staff Records (microfilm)
Supreme Headquarters Allied Expeditionary Force (microfilm)

**Hoover Institution Archives, Stanford, California**
Papers of Leonard R. Boyd

**Library of Congress, Washington, D.C.**
Papers of the National Association for the Advancement of Colored People

**Douglas MacArthur Memorial Library and Archives, Norfolk, Virginia**
Record Group 3 (Records of Headquarters, Southwest Pacific Area, 1942–1945)
Record Group 4 (Records of General Headquarters, U.S. Army Forces Pacific, 1942–1947)
Record Group 6 (Records of General Headquarters, Far East Command, 1947–1951)
Record Group 9 (Collection of Messages [Radiograms], 1945–1951)

Record Group 10 (General Douglas MacArthur's Private Correspondence, 1908–1964)
Record Group 29A (Selected Papers of Richard J. Marshall)
Record Group 30 (Papers of Richard K. Sutherland)

**George C. Marshall Research Library, Lexington, Virginia**
Papers of George C. Marshall

**National Archives, Washington, D.C. (and the Annex named the Washington National Records Center, Suitland, Maryland)**
Record Group 107 (Records of the Secretary of War)
Record Group 165 (Records of the War Department, General and Special Staffs)
Record Group 319 (Records of the Army Staff)
Record Group 330 (Records of the Secretary of Defense)
Record Group 331 (Records of Allied Operational and Occupation Headquarters, World War II)
Record Group 332/492 (Records of the U.S. Army Theaters of War, World War II)
Record Group 337 (Records of the Army Ground Forces)
Record Group 338 (Records of U.S. Army Commands, 1942–) Includes awards case files
Record Group 407 (Records of the Army Adjutant General) Includes World War II Operations Reports, 1940–48 (the Army's World War II Unit Historical Records)

**National Personnel Records Center, St. Louis, Missouri**
Individual Personnel Records ("201" Files)
Awards Case Files

**Franklin D. Roosevelt Library, Hyde Park, New York**
Papers of John J. McCloy
Papers of Eleanor Roosevelt
Papers of Franklin D. Roosevelt

**Harry S Truman Library, Independence, Missouri**
Papers of Clark M. Clifford
Papers of George M. Elsey
Papers of Charles Fahy
Papers of Phileo Nash
Papers of David K. Niles
Papers of Stephen J. Spingarn
Records of the President's Committee on Civil Rights
Records of the President's Committee on Equality of Treatment and Opportunity in the Armed Forces
Papers of Harry S Truman (Confidential File, Official File, President's Secretary's File)

## Private Sources

Affidavits (submitted to the Department of the Army)
Ashby, Charles P., 13 October 1993.
Bracey, Homer A., 25 June 1990.
Weston, Theodore., 22 June 1990.
Williams, David J., 30 June 1990.

## Interviews

| Name | Position | Date |
|---|---|---|
| Arnold, Thomas St. John | G-3, 92d Inf Div | 8 Apr 94 |
| Ashby, Charles P. | Co Clerk, 761st Tank Bn | 28 Mar 94 |
| Baker, Vernon J. | Plt Ldr 92d Inf Div | 15 Mar 94 |
| Bates, Paul L. | Bn Cmdr, 761st Tank Bn | 27 Jan 94 |
| Beasley, Louis J. | Chaplain, 92d Inf Div | 31 Mar 94 |
| Brennan, Daniel | Rifleman, 24th Inf Regt | 26 Mar 94 |
| Brewer, Jesse | Btry Officer, 92d Inf Div Arty | 28 Mar 94 |
| Clark, Major | Btry Officer, 92d Inf Div Arty | 25 Apr 94 |
| Crecy, Warren Jr. | (son of Plt Ldr, 761st Tank Bn) | 31 Mar 94 |
| Davis, B. O. Jr. | Cmdr, 332d Fighter Group | 26 Feb 94 |
| Day, Daniel | Staff Officer, Negro Interest Section, War Dept | 25 Apr 94 |
| Gibson, Truman K. | Civilian Aide, Sec of War | 12 Mar 94 |
| Gittens, Johnny | Rifleman, 93d Inf Div | 24 Apr 94 |
| Hamlet, James | Plt Ldr, 92d Inf Div | 27 May 94 |
| Hargrove, Hondon B. | Btry Officer, 92d Inf Div Arty | 13 Mar 94 |
| Harrod, Dennette A. | 366th Inf Regt | 30 Dec 93 |
| Hunter, Jehu | Signal Off, 92d Inf Div | 8 Mar 94 |
| Jackson, Jessie | Recon Sgt, 93d Inf Div | 21 Apr 94 |
| Jackson, Leonard | Btry Off, 92d Inf Div Arty | 25 Apr 94 |
| Lee, Samson | Chmn, Afri-Amer Vet Assoc | 7 Jun 94 |
| Long, Jerome | Historian, ETO "5th" Platoons | 25 Apr 94 |
| McCaffrey, William J. | Chief of Staff, 92d Inf Div | 8 Apr 94 |
| Martin, John T. | Trans Off, 92d Inf Div | 3 Apr 94 |
| Mitchell, Parren J. | Co Cmdr, 92d Inf Div | 1 Mar 94 |
| Pleasant, Sanford | Sqd Ldr, 93d Inf Div | 27 Apr 94 |
| Runyon, John F. | Co Cmdr, 92d Inf Div | 10 July 94 |
| Smith, Wilson | Chmn, Black Medal of Honor Assoc | 27 May 94 |
| Stokes, Russell | Plt Ldr, 92d Inf Div | 25 Apr 94 |
| Vanderhouef, Floyd | 56 Armored Inf Bn | 26 Apr 94 |
| Van Meter, Robert | Asst Adjutant, 92d Inf Div | 30 Mar 94 |
| Williams, David J. | Co Cmdr, 761st Tank Bn | 27 Jan 94 |
| Woodson, Waverly | Medic, 320th Barrage Balloon Bn | 18 Nov 93 |
| Zachary, Otis | Btry Off, 92d Inf Div | 10 July 94 |

## Public Documents

U.S. Congress. Senate. Committee on Veteran's Affairs. Senate Committee Print No. 3. *Medal of Honor Recipients, 1863–1978*. 90th Cong. 1st sess. Washington, D.C.: U.S. Government Printing Office, 1979.

U.S. Department of the Army. Public Information Division. *The Medal of Honor of the U.S. Army*. Washington, D.C.: U.S. Government Printing Office, 1948.

U.S. Department of Defense. American Forces Information Service. *Armed Forces Decorations and Awards*. 1992.

## Newspapers

*Pittsburgh Courier*. 1944–45.
*Stars and Stripes* (European ed.). 1944–45.

## Articles and Books

Ambrose, Stephen E. "Blacks in the Army in Two World Wars." In Stephen E. Ambrose and James A Barber, Jr., eds., *The Military in American Society*. New York: Free Press, 1972.
Anderson, Trezzvant W. *Come Out Fighting: The Epic Tale of the 761st Tank Battalion*. Germany: Salzburg Druckerei und Verlag, 1945.
Arnold, Thomas St. John. *Buffalo Soldiers: The 92nd Infantry Division and Reinforcements in World War II, 1942–45*. Manhattan, Kans.: Sunflower University Press, 1990.
Blake, Joseph A. "The Congressional Medal of Honor in Three Wars." *Pacific Sociological Review* 16 (April 1973): 166–76.
Bykofsky, Joseph and Harold Larson. *The Transportation Corps: Operations Overseas [United States Army in World War II]*. Washington D. C.: U.S. Government Printing Office, 1957.
Chwialkowski, Paul. *In Caesar's Shadow: The Life of General Robert Eichelberger*. Westport, Conn.: Greenwood Press, 1993.
Clark, Mark W. *Calculated Risk*. New York: Harper and Brothers Publishers, 1950.
Cornish, Dudley. *The Sable Arm: Negro Troops in the Union Army, 1861–1865*. New York: Longmans, Green and Company, 1956.
Dalfiume, Richard M. *Desegregation of the U.S. Armed Forces: Fighting on Two Fronts, 1939–1953*. Columbia: University of Missouri Press, 1969.
Davis, Benjamin O., Jr. *Benjamin O. Davis, Jr.: American*. Washington, D. C.: Smithsonian Institution Press, 1991.
Fisher, Ernest F., Jr. *Cassino to the Alps [United States Army in World War II]*. Washington, D. C.: U.S. Government Printing Office, 1977.
Foner, Jack D. *Blacks and the Military in American History: A New Perspective*. New York: Praeger Publishers, 1974.
Gleim, Albert F., and George B. Harris III. *Distinguished Service Cross Awards for World War II*. Rev. 2d ed. Fort Myer, Va.: Planchet Press, 1991.
Goodman, Paul. *A Fragment of Victory in Italy during World War II*. Carlisle Barracks, Penn.: Army War College, 1952.
Griffith, Robert K., Jr. *Men Wanted for the U.S. Army: America's Experience with an All-Volunteer Army between the World Wars, 1919–1941*. New Haven, Conn.: Greenwood Press, 1982.
Hargrove, Hondon B. *Buffalo Soldiers in Italy: Black Americans in World War II*. Jefferson, N.C.: McFarland & Company, 1985.
Hunter, Jehu C., and Major Clark. *The Buffalo Division in World War II*. N.P.: By the authors, 1985.
James, D. Clayton. *The Years of MacArthur, Volume II, 1941–1945*. Boston: Houghton Mifflin Company, 1975.
Kenworthy, E. W. "The Case Against Army Segregation." *Annals of the American Academy of Political Science* 275 (May 1952): 28–29.
Lee, Ulysses. *The Employment of Negro Troops [United States Army in World War II]*. Washington, D.C.: U.S. Government Printing Office, 1966.
MacGregor, Morris, J., Jr. *Integration of the Armed Forces, 1940–65 [Defense Studies Series]*. Washington, D.C.: U.S. Government Printing Office. 1981.
MacGregor, Morris J., Jr. et al. *American Military History [Army Historical Series]*. Washington, D.C.: U.S. Government Printing Office, 1989.
Motley, Mary Penick, comp. and ed. *The Invisible Soldier: The Experience of the Black Soldier in World War II*. Detroit, Mich.: Wayne State University Press, 1975.

Murphy, Edward F. *Heroes of WWII*. New York: Ballantine Books, 1991.
Nalty, Bernard C. *Strength for the Fight: A History of Black Americans in the Military*. New York: Free Press, 1986.
Osur, Alan M. *Blacks in the Army Air Forces during World War II: The Problem of Race Relations*. Washington, D.C.: U.S. Government Printing Office, 1977.
Perret, Geoffrey. *There's a War to be Won: The United States Army in World War II*. New York: Ballantine Books, 1991.
Pogue, Forrest C. *George C. Marshall: Organizer of Victory, 1943–1945*. New York: Viking Press, 1973.
Raymond, Edward A. "Black Buffalo." *Field Artillery Journal 36* (January 1946): 14–16.
Robles, Philip K. *United States Military Awards and Ribbons*. Rutland, Vt.: Charles Tuttle Company, 1971.
Sandler, Stanley. *Segregated Skies: All-Black Combat Squadrons of WWII*. Washington, D.C.: Smithsonian Institution Press, 1992.
Spector, Ronald H. *Eagle Against the Sun: The American War with Japan*. New York: Free Press, 1985.
Stillman, Richard J. "The Role of the Negro in the U.S. Armed Forces, 1939–1968," *Irish Defense Journal*, March 1969, 102–3.
Stimson, Henry L., and McGeorge Bundy. *On Active Service in Peace and War*. New York: Harper Brothers, 1947.
Truscott, Lucian K., Jr. *Command Missions*. New York: E. P. Dutton and Company, 1954.
Wilson, Dale E. "The Army's Black Tank Battalions." *Armor*, March-April 1982, 30–31.
———. "Recipe for Failure: Major General Edward M. Almond and Preparation of the U.S. 92d Infantry Division for Combat in World War II." *Journal of Military History* 56 (July 1992): 473–88.

# Index

Boldface indicates photograph.

Adams, Major General E. S. 44–45
Advisory Committee on Negro Troop Policies 15–16, 34, 35n
Airborne Division, 101st 77, 78
Air Medal: 332nd Fighter Group and 123
Allen, Major General Roderick R. 171
Allen, Major General Terry 82
Almond, Major General Edward M. 95–119, **107**, 126n, 127n, 130n, 134n
American Expeditionary Force (AEF) 24, 50
Amphibian truck companies 150–54, 162n, 163n, 164n; 471st Amphibian Truck Company 152, 153, 162n, 163n; 472nd Amphibian Truck Company 151, 152, 162n, 164n; 473rd Amphibian Truck Company 152, 153, 162n, 163n; 474th Amphibian Truck Company 153–54, 162n, 163n, 164n; 475th Amphibian Truck Company 162n; 476th Amphibian Truck Company 152, 153, 162n, 163n, 164n; 477th Amphibian Truck Company 151, 162n, 163n, 164n; 488th Amphibian Truck Company 162n; 490th Amphibian Truck Company 162n; 491st Amphibian Truck Company 162n; 492nd Amphibian Truck Company 162n; 493rd Aphibian Truck Company 162n; 494th Amphibian Truck Company 162n; 808th Amphibian Truck Company 162n, 163n; 809th Amphibian Truck Company 162n; 810th Amphibian Truck Company 151, 162n; 811th Amphibian Truck Company 162n; 812th Amphibian Truck Company 151–52, 162n, 163n; 813th Amphibian Truck Company 162n, 163n; 814th Amphibian Truck Company 162n, 164n; 820th Amphibian Truck Company 162n, 163n; 823rd Amphibian Truck Company 152, 162n; 824th Amphibian Truck Company 162n; 825th Amphibian Truck Company, 162n, 163n; 826th Amphibian Truck Company, 162n, 163; 828th Amphibian Truck Company 152, 162n,164n
Anderson, Private Mack B. (recipient of Silver Star) 154; *see also* Heroism
Anderson, Trezzvant W. 42, 71
Anti-aircraft artillery units: 207th Anti-Aircraft Artillery Automatic Weapons Battalion 160n, 161n; 208th Anti-Aircraft Artillery Automatic Weapons Battalion 160n, 161n; 234th Anti-Aircraft Artillery Automatic Weapons Battalion 160n, 161n; 452nd Anti-Aircraft Artillery Automatic Weapons Battalion 78–79; 477th Anti-Aircraft Artillery Automatic Weapons Battalion 160n, 161n; 933rd Anti-Aircraft Artillery Automatic Weapons Battalion 160n; 938th Anti-Aircraft Artillery Automatic Weapons Battalion 160n, 161n; 320th Anti-Aircraft Artillery Barrage Balloon Battalion 70, 79–80, 180; 450th Anti-Aircraft Artillery Battalion 93, 121, 122; 466th Anti-Aircraft Artillery Battalion 150, 160n, 161n; 484th Anti-Aircraft Artillery Battalion 154, 164n; 503rd Anti-Aircraft Artillery Battalion 148, 160n; 870th Anti-Aircraft Artillery Battalion 148, 150, 160n, 175; 897th Anti-Aircraft Artillery Battalion 121; 14th Anti-Aircraft Artillery Command 148, 149; 76th Anti-Aircraft Artillery Group 160n; 77th Anti-Aircraft Artillery Group 160n; 90th Anti-Aircraft Artillery Group 121; 76th Anti-Aircraft Artillery Gun Battalion 160n; 77th Anti-Aircraft Artillery Gun Battalion 160n; 100th Anti-Aircraft Artillery Gun Battalion 160n; 369th Anti-Aircraft Artillery Gun Battalion 160n, 161n; 741st

Anti-Aircraft Artillery Gun Battalion 160n, 161n; 742nd Anti-Aircraft Artillery Gun Battalion 160n, 161n; *see also* Coast artillery units; Field artillery units
Anzio 94, 122
AR 600-45 *see* Army Regulation 600-45
Ardennes Forest 77
Armies: 1st Army 51, 53, 61n, 65n; 3rd Army 61n, 65n, 70, 84, 176, 177; 5th Army 19, 47, 48, 49, 50, 64n, 94, 101, 102, 104, 105, 108, 111, 112, 113, 115, 122, 124, 126n, 133n, 134n, 170; 6th Army 61n, 155; 7th Army 47, 48, 54, 61n, 82, 171, 174, 176; 8th Army 67n, 147, 155; 9th Army 53, 65n, 75; 10th Army 55, 150, 155
Armored Units: 1st Armored Division 99; 7th Armored Division 53; 12th Armored Division 82, 83, 84, 91n, 170, 171; 14th Armored Division 82, 91n; 5th Armored Group 32; 17th Armored Group 87n; 56th Armored Infantry Battalion 83, 84, 170, 171; 6th Armored Infantry Regiment 49
Armstrong, Colonel J. D. 102, 103, 104-5
Army Air Corps 27, 28
Army Air Forces (AAF) 31, 32, 41, 122-23, 133n
Army Air Forces Units: 3rd Air Division 54; 10th Air Force, 154; 15th Air Force 122, 123; 4th Bomb Wing (Provisional) 54; 332nd Fighter Group 93, 122-23; 100th Fighter Squadron 122; 301st Fighter Squadron 122; 302nd Fighter Squadron 122; 99th Pursuit Squadron 32, 93, 122-23
Army Commendation Medal 59n
Army Groups: 6th Army Group, 51; 12th Army Group, 51, 53, 61n, 65n; 15th Army Group, 47
Army Regulation 600-45 38, 39, 43, 45-46, 47, 48, 51, 55, 58, 59n, 60n, 63n
Arno River 99, 100
Arnold, Thomas St. John 126n, 129n
Ashby, Charles P. 72
Assam 154
Award approval process *see* Decoration system

Baker, First Lieutenant Vernon J. (recipient of Distinguished Service Cross; Purple Heart) 97, 109, 114-18, 124, 132n, 135n, 136n, 168-70, **171**, 180; *see also* Heroism
Ballou, Major General Charles 24
*Baltimore Afro-American* 41, 118
Bastogne 77, 78, 89n
Bates, Lieutenant Colonel Paul L. 70, 73, 74, 87n
Battle of the Bulge 53, 77, 118
Beiderlinden, Brigadier General W. A. 57

Biak Island 151, 152, 163n
Blackshear, Lieutenant Colonel John P. 176
Blake, Private First Class George C. (recipient of Silver Star) 87n
Bougainville 16, 141-45, 149, 155, 157n
Bourgaltroff 75
Boyd, Brigadier General Leonard R. 157-58n
Boyd, Sergeant Oren B. (recipient of Silver Star) 94; *see also* Heroism
Bradley, General Omar N. 51, 53, 66n
Bravery *see* Heroism, individual acts of
Bremer, Captain August W. 74
British Distinguished Service Medal 70
Bronze Star: 476th Amphibian Truck Company and 164n; 452nd Antiaircraft Artillery Automatic Weapons Battalion and 79; 49th Coast Artillery Battalion and 149; definition of 65n; 317th Engineer Combat Battalion and 120; 777th Field Artillery Battalion and 78; 92nd Infantry Division and 106, 108, 110, 119, 130n, 138n; 104th Infantry Division and 82; quota system in 12th Army Group for 51; 758th Tank Battalion and 121; 761st Tank Battalion and 70, 74; 784th Tank Battalion and 75, 76; 679th Tank Destroyer Battalion and, 121
Bronze Star, individual recipients of: Harris, Technician Fifth Grade Robert W. 76; Paris, Private Maurice A. 164n; Woodson, Corporal Waverly B., Jr. 79-80, 180
Brown, Private Ben T. 82; *see also* Heroism
Brownsville affair 23, 26
Bull, Major General Harold R. 62n
Bullard, Lieutenant General Robert L. 24, 25
Buna 56
Burma *see* China-Burma-India Theater

Caledonia 141
Camp Hood 175
Campbell, Staff Sergeant William (recipient of Silver Star) 79; *see also* Heroism
Carter, Staff Sergeant Edward A., Jr. (recipient of Distinguished Service Cross) 41, 60n, 83, 84-85, 168, 170-71, **172**, 180; *see also* Heroism
Castle, Brigadier General Frederick W. 54
Castle Aghinolfi 114, 169
Casual Detachment 97
Cavalry units: 1st Cavalry Division 25; 2nd Cavalry Division 32, 35n; 92nd Cavalry Reconnaissance Troop 94; 93rd Cavalry Reconnaissance Troop 141, 142, 144, 146; 9th Cavalry Regiment 23, 35n; 10th Cavalry Regiment 23, 35n
Chapin, Second Lieutenant Neil M. 66n
Chemical Company, 24th 122

Chemical Smoke Generating Company, 161st 81
China-Burma-India Theater 139, 154–55, 156n, 164n
Choate, Staff Sergeant Clyde L. 54, 66n
Cinquale Canal 102, 113, 120
Civil War 22
Clark, Major 131n
Clark, Lieutenant General Mark W. 19, 49, 50, 64n, 101
Clay, Captain Leroy 98
*Cleveland Call and Post* 41
Climbach 75, 175, 176
Coast artillery units: 49th Coast Artillery Battalion 148–49, 160n; 76th Coast Artillery Regiment 148, 160n; 77th Coast Artillery Regiment 148, 160n; 90th Coast Artillery Regiment 121; 369th Coast Artillery Regiment, 150, 161n
Colbern, Brigadier General William H. 112, 113, 119, 174
Coleman, Second Lieutenant Kenneth W. (recipient of Silver Star) 71; *see also* Heroism
Collins, Second Lieutenant Charles R. 144
Colmar Pocket 78
Colonial militia 21–22
Combat: for African Americans not in combat units 69, 93–94, 151; history of African Americans in 15–16
Combat effectiveness, African-American 29; Army War College studies on 25–26; negative assessments of 25–26, 95–96, 99–101, 102–4, 105–6, 107–8, 111, 113, 115–17, 119, 126n, 127n, 129n, 142–43, 144; positive assessments of 82, 95, 99, 103–4, 115–17, 122, 129n, 143, 144, 145n, 148, 149, 152
Command positions, African Americans: exclusion of 24, 94; racist opinions regarding 26, 106
Communications Zone (COMZ) 80, 90n
Corps: IV 100, 113, 133n; XIV 141, 142, 156, 158n; XV 176; XXI 174
Corsica 121
Crawford, Lieutenant Colonel Joseph B. (recipient of Distinguished Service Cross) 50
Crecy, Lieutenant Warren G. H. (recipient of Silver Star) 71; *see also* Heroism
Cumby, Lieutenant Bert 98

D-Day 53, 70, 79, 151
Dabney, Captain Walter E. 111, 113, 132n; *see also* Heroism
Daniels, Jonathan 80
Daniels, Josephus 41
Davis, Brigadier General Benjamin O., Sr. 28, 98
Davis, Lieutenant General Benjamin O., Jr. 122, 123
Day, First Sergeant Norman (recipient of Purple Heart; Silver Star) 70; *see also* Heroism
Decoration system 37, 44–45, 64n, 108; *see also* Bronze Star; Distinguished Service Cross; Distinguished Unit Citation; Medal of Honor; Silver Star
Decorations boards 44–45, 48, 49, 51, 53, 55, 64n, 66n, 84, 108, 131n, 171, 174, 177; *see also* War Department Decorations Board
Devers, General Jacob L. 50, 63n
DeWitt, Sergeant Leonard C. (recipient of Distinguished Service Cross) 57
Dillon, Sergeant Alfonzia (recipient of Silver Star) 146; *see also* Heroism
Distinguished Flying Cross 122–23; 332nd Fighter Group and 122–23
Distinguished Service Cross **40**, 167; definition of 38–39; 92nd Infantry Division and 106, 108, 109, 110, 111, 113, 118, 124, 132n, 134n, 138n; 93rd Infantry Division and 147; 473rd Infantry Regiment and 130n; General MacArthur's decoration policy and 55–56; War Department Decorations Board and 44
Distinguished Service Cross, individual recipients of: Baker, First Lieutenant Vernon J. 109, 114–18, 136n, 168, 169–70; Carter, Staff Sergeant Edward A., Jr. 41, 83, 84–85, 168, 170–71, 180; Crawford, Lieutenant Colonel Joseph B. 50; DeWitt, Sergeant Leonard C. 57; Dowden, Staff Sergeant Leonard E. 147, 168, 171–72; Ericksen, Lieutenant Colonel Ray J. 49, 50; Fisher, Captain Ralph C. 49; Fox, First Lieutenant John R. 111–12, 124, 130n, 168, 172–74; Gould, Second Lieutenant Edwin F. 50; Holbrook, Captain Gilbert S. 109, 113, 134n; James, Private First Class Willy F. Jr., 83, 168, 174; Kelly, Captain John J., Jr. 49–50; Knight, Staff Sergeant Everett C. 49, 50; Moritz, Technician Fourth Grade Martin 48; Nakamura, Private First Class William K. 49, 50; Peagler, First Lieutenant Robert J. 148, 150, 162n, 168, 175; Pearson, Lieutenant Commmander Charles 56–57; Runyon, Captain John F. 109, 114–18, 136n; Smith, Captain Charles Mike 56–57; Thomas, First Lieutenant Charles L. 75–76, 168, 175–76; Thomas, Private First Class Jack N. 83, 84, 168, 176–77; Wainwright, Lieutenant General Jonathan M. 56; Walker, First Lieutenant Leland 57; Watson, Private George 139, 151, 169, 177–78; *see also* soldiers' individual listings

Distinguished Service Cross, numbers awarded: to African Americans in European Theater of Operations 70, to African Americans in Mediterranean Theater of Operations 94, to African Americans in Pacific Commands 139, to African Americans in World War II 168; percentage awarded to African Americans in World War II 91n, 168, precedents for review and elevation to Medal of Honor 19, 50, 182–83, quota system in 12th Army Group for 51, 167, 442nd Regimental Combat Team and 130n; in European Theater of Operations 51, in Mediterranean Theater of Operations 47, in Pacific Commands 54, in World War II 168

Distinguished (Presidential) Unit Citation 86n; 101st Airborne Division and 78; 969th Field Artillery Battalion and 69–70; 332nd Fighter Group and 123; 761st Tank Battalion and 42, 69–70, 73, 86n; 614th Tank Destroyer Battalion (Third Platoon, Company C) and 69–70, 75, 76; War Department Decorations Board and 44

Divisions, creation of African-American 32–33

Doss, Private First Class Desmond T. 60n

Dowden, Staff Sergeant Leonard E. (recipient of Distinguished Service Cross) 147, 155, 168, 171–72; *see also* Heroism

Doyle, First Lieutenant James M. 50, 64n

DUKWs *see* Amphibian truck companies

Eaker, Lieutenant General Ira 122
Efate 141
Eichelberger, Major General Robert L. 56
Eisenhower, General Dwight D. 19, 49, 50, 53, 54, 60n, 63n, 66n, 79, 80, 81, 82
Ellis, Technician Fifth Grade Zeno H. (recipient of Silver Star) 79; *see also* Heroism
Ellsworth, First Lieutenant Theodore R. 66n
Engineer Aviation Battalion: 810th 150; 11th 140, 150; 39th 151
Engineer Battalion: 318th 141, 142; 387th 94
Engineer Combat Battalion 317th 94, 97, 105, 111, 120, 137n
Engineer Dump Truck Company 582nd 70
Engineer General Service Regiment 96th 151
English, First Lieutenant Richard W. 74
Ericksen, Lieutenant Colonel Ray J. (recipient of Distinguished Service Cross) 49, 50
Espíritu Santo 148, 161n
European Theater of Operations (ETO) 69–70; artillery battalions in 76–80; Medal of Honor policy and practice in 51–54, 64n; number of Distinguished Service Crosses awarded to African Americans in 70; number of Silver Stars awarded to African Americans in 70, 86n, 178n; total number of Distinguished Service Crosses awarded in 51; total number of Medals of Honor awarded in 51; total number of Silver Stars awarded in 51; tank battalions in 70–75; tank-destroyer battalions in 75–76; volunteer infantry replacements in 69, 80–85

Ferguson, Lieutenant Colonel Alonzo 11, 102, 103–4, 111
Field artillery units: 171st Field Artillery Battalion 79; 333rd Field Artillery Battalion 77; 350th Field Artillery Battalion 77, 78; 578th Field Artillery Battalion 77; 593rd Field Artillery Battalion 141, 142; 594th Field Artillery Battalion 141, 146; 595th Field Artillery Battalion 141; 596th Field Artillery Battalion 141; 597th Field Artillery Battalion 94, 96, 109, 113, 119, 131n; 598th Field Artillery Battalion 94, 112, 119, 173; 599th Field Artillery Battalion 94, 119; 600th Field Artillery Battalion 94, 119, 131n; 686th Field Artillery Battalion 78; 731st Field Artillery Battalion 79; 777th Field Artillery Battalion 78; 969th Field Artillery Battalion 69, 77, 78; 999th Field Artillery Battalion 78; 333rd Field Artillery Group 77; 349th Field Artillery Group 78; 351st Field Artillery Group 78
Fish, Hamilton 27–28
Fisher, Ernest F., Jr. 95
Fisher, Captain Ralph C. (recipient of Distinguished Service Cross) 49
Foreman, Private First Class Robert L. S. (recipient of Silver Star) 77; *see also* Heroism
Fox, Mrs. Arlene
Fox, First Lieutenant John R. (recipient of Distinguished Service Cross) 111–13, 124, 130n, 132n, 133n, 134n, 168, 172–74, **173**; *see also* Heroism
*Fragment of Victory in Italy During World War II* (Goodman) 117, 126n, 135n
Friendly Islands 148

Galt, Captain William W. 50
Gardner, Colonel G. D. 60n
Garman, Private Harold A. 60n
George, Major John F. 73, 87n
Gibson, Truman 33, 42, 60n, 95, 96–97, 98

Goodman, Paul: *Fragment of Victory in Italy During World War II* 117, 126n, 135n
Gothic Line 96, 99, 110
Gould, Second Lieutenant Edwin F. (recipient of Distinguished Service Cross) 50
Griswold, Major General Oscar W. 142–43, 157n
Guadalcanal 141, 157n
Guebling 71–72
Guffey, Senator Joseph F. 43, 59n

Hackett, Captain Edward J. 66n
Hajiro, Private Barney F. 66n
Halsey, Admiral William F., Jr. 156n
Hamilton, Sergeant Joseph J. (recipient of Silver Star) 77; *see also* Heroism
Harbeson, Staff Sergeant Joe R. 48, 49
Hargrove, Hondon B. 96, 131n, 132n, 174
Harmon, Lieutenant General Millard F. 141, 142
Harris, Technician Fifth Grade Robert W. (recipient of Bronze Star) 76; *see also* Heroism
Harrison, Captain Ivan H. 74
Harrod, Dennette 106
Hendrix, Private James R. 118, 135–36n; *see also* Heroism
Heroism, individual acts of: Anderson, Private Mack B. 154; Baker, First Lieutenant Vernon J. 114–17, 136n, 169–70; Boyd, Sergeant Oren B. 94; Brown, Private Ben T. 82; Campbell, Staff Sergeant William 79; Carter, Staff Sergeant Edward A., Jr. 83, 84–85, 170–71; Coleman, Second Lieutenant Kenneth W. 71; Crecy, Lieutenant Warren G. H. 71; Dabney, Captain Walter E. 111; Day, First Sergeant Norman 70; Dillon, Sergeant Alfonzia 146; Dowden, Staff Sergeant Leonard E. 147, 171–72; Ellis, Technician Fifth Grade Zeno H. 79; Foreman, Private First Class Robert L. S. 77; Fox, First Lieutenant John R. 111–13, 172–74; Hamilton, Sergeant Joseph J. 77; Harris, Technician Fifth Grade Robert W. 76; Hendrix, Private James B. 118, 135–36n; Holloway, Technician Fifth Grade Tommie L. 153; Jackson, Private First Class Willie 79; James, Private First Class Willy F. Jr., 83–84, 174; Jefferson, Private June, Jr. 82–83; Johnson, Private Samuel 79; Lopez, Sergeant Jose M. 53; McInnis, Private Jake 110; Madison, Sergeant Harris 94; Marsh, Private Woodall 93–94; Mills, Staff Sergeant Jimmie L. 94; Nesmith, Private First Class Joseph 152; Nicholas, Private Ralph A. 152; Peagler,
First Lieutenant Robert J. 150, 162n, 175; Pierce, Private First Class Claude 83; Reynolds, Private First Class Lawrence 77; Rhodes, Staff Sergeant Fred D. 109; Rivers, Staff Sergeant Ruben 70–75; Roberts, Private Henry 109–10; Rochelle, Private First Class Herman E. 109, 113, 119; Runyon, Captain John F. 114–18, 136n; Sanchez, Technician Fifth Grade Marcus P. 152; Sermon, Private Isaac 143–44; Swindell, Private Edward I. 79; Thomas, First Lieutenant Charles L. 75–76, 175–76; Thomas, Private First Class Jack N. 83, 84, 176–77; Turley, First Sergeant Samuel J. 42, 71; Vogt, Lieutenant Robert 152; Watson, Private George 139, 177–78; Webb, Staff Sergeant Rothchild 144; Woodson, Corporal Waverly B., Jr. 79–80; Zeno, Private First Class Edgar E. 83
Herzgerode 84, 176
Holbrook, Captain Gilbert S. (recipient of Distinguished Service Cross) 109, 113, 134n
Holloway, Technician Fifth Grade Tommie L. (recipient of Silver Star) 153; *see also* Heroism
Hopson, Dr. C. F. 42
Hull, Major General J. E. 157n
Hunt, Lieutenant Colonel Hollis E. 72, 73, 87n
Hunter, Jehu C. 131n
Housing 29–30
Houston riot 23, 26

India *see* China-Burma-India Theater
Infantry units: Americal Division 141, 142, 158n; Third Marine Division 142; 7th Army Infantry Company No. 1 (Provisional) 84, 170, 180; 1st Infantry Division 61n; 2nd Infantry Division 53; 3rd Infantry Division 43, 54, 61n; 4th Infantry Division 62n; 8th (Indian) Infantry Division 101; 9th Infantry Division 83, 84, 176; 26th Infantry Division 70, 71; 27th Infantry Division 150; 31st Infantry Division 146; 36th Infantry Division 61n; 37th Infantry Division 141, 142; 41st Infantry Division 146; 71st Infantry Division 74; 77th Infantry Division 150; 88th Infantry Division 45, 102; 92nd Infantry Division 15, 16, 19, 24, 25, 29, 31, 32, 33, 43, 93, 94–121, 124, 169, 172, 174; 93rd Infantry Division 16, 24, 29, 32, 33, 34n, 43, 55, 139, 141–47, 156, 157n, 159n, 160n, 171, 181; 99th Infantry Division 82; 103rd Infantry Division 75, 76, 176; 104th Infantry Division

82, 83, 174; 148th Infantry Division (German) 106; 13th Infantry Regiment 54; 15th Infantry Regiment 50; 23rd Infantry Regiment 53; 24th Infantry Regiment 23, 31, 139, 141–44, 155-56, 181; 25th Infantry Regiment 23, 31, 141, 142, 143, 147, 157n; 26th Infantry Regiment 49; 30th Infantry Regiment 48; 39th Infantry Regiment 83; 48th Infantry Regiment 23; 49th Infantry Regiment 23; 60th Infantry Regiment 82, 83, 84, 176; 68th Infantry Regiment 50; 133rd Infantry Regiment 49; 135th Infantry Regiment 49; 179th Infantry Regiment 48; 310th Infantry Regiment 82; 313th Infantry Regiment 53; 319th Infantry Regiment 54; 337th Infantry Regiment 50; 365th Infantry Regiment 94, 95, 100, 102, 103, 104, 105, 120, 136n; 366th Infantry Regiment 31, 93, 94, 95, 101, 102, 103, 104, 106–7, 110, 111, 112, 113, 131n, 132n, 136n, 146, 172, 173, 181; 367th Infantry Regiment 31; 368th Infantry Regiment 31, 141, 146, 171; 369th Infantry Regiment 24–25, 27, 31, 141; 370th Infantry Regiment 25, 94, 97, 101, 102, 104, 105, 109, 110, 113, 114, 115, 117, 118, 119, 124, 129n, 136n, 169, 170, 180; 371st Infantry Regiment 25, 94, 95, 101, 102, 104, 105, 111, 133n, 136n; 372nd Infantry Regiment 25, 31; 411th Infantry Regiment 75, 175, 176; 413th Infantry Regiment 82, 83–84, 174; 414th Infantry Regiment 82, 83; 415th Infantry Regiment 82; 473rd Infantry Regiment 95, 104, 109, 124, 130n, 131n
Ingling, Captain Howard 54
*Integration of the Armed Forces, 1940–1965* (MacGregor) 95–96
Iwo Jima 151, 152, 153, 163n, 164n

Jackson, Andrew 22
Jackson, Private First Class Willie (recipient of Silver Star) 79; *see also* Heroism
James, Private First Class Willy F. (recipient of Distinguished Service Cross) Jr. 83–84, 168, 174; *see also* Heroism
Jeanneret, Corporal Dale W. 66n
Jefferson, Private June, Jr. 82–83; *see also* Heroism
Jenkins, Private First Class Ernest A. (recipient of Silver Star) 52
Jenkins, First Lieutenant Graham (recipient of Silver Star) 134n
Johnson, Major General Harry H. 144, 145, 147
Johnson, Private Samuel (recipient of Silver Star) 79; *see also* Heroism

Joint Board to Study Decorations (1948) 37
Jolo Island 146, 147, 171
Jordan, Jefferson, 133n

Kelly, Captain John J., Jr. (recipient of Distinguished Service Cross) 48–49
Kelly, Corporal Thomas J. 60n
Kemp, Private First Class Leroy W. 82
Kerama Island 144, 150, 175
Keyes, Lieutenant General Geoffrey 174
Knight, Staff Sergeant Everett C. (recipient of Distinguished Service Cross) 49

Landon, First Lieutenant Shirley R. 53
Lanham, Brigadier General Charles 82
Lawson, Captain J. R. 74
Lear, Lieutenant General Benjamin 66n
Ledo Road 154
Lee, Lieutenant General John C. H. 80, 81, 90n
Lee, Ulysses 95, 129n, 159n
Legion of Merit 47
Lehman, Major General Raymond G. 141, 144
Leyte 147, 151, 152, 153
Lippoldsberg 83, 174
Lopez, Sergeant Jose M. 53; *see also* Heroism
Lucas, Lieutenant Colonel Wilmer F. 162n
Luzon 147

MacArthur, General Douglas 144, 145, 146, 149, 156n, 157n, 159n, 165n, 180; controversy over Medal of Honor awarded to 56; decoration policy of 55–57
McCaffrey, Colonel William J. 105, 111, 112–13, 115, 129n
McCloy, John J. 33, 35n
MacGregor, Morris J., Jr. 16; *Integration of the Armed Forces, 1940–1965* 95–96
McHenry, Captain Irwin 74
McInnis, Private Jake (recipient of Silver Star) 109, 110, 132n, 138n; *see also* Heroism
McKenzie, Lieutenant Colonel Jack (recipient of Silver Star) 159n
MacKerson, Private B. (recipient of Silver Star) 154
McNarney, General Joseph T. 63n, 105, 129n
Madison, Sergeant Harris (recipient of Silver Star) 94; *see also* Heroism
Mariana Islands 144, 152
Marsh, Private Woodall (recipient of Silver Star) 93–94; *see also* Heroism

## Index

Marshall, General George C. 28, 32, 41, 56, 57, 60n, 146
Masching, Sergeant Edwin J. 66n
Massa 120
Mayberry, Brigadier General H. T. 82
Medal of Honor **40**, 167, 179–82; approval/disapproval process for 43–47, 48, 49, 52–53, 55–56, 58, 63n, 67n; authority to award 37–38, 44, 45, 46, 47, 55, 58; definition of 38–39; European Theater of Operations and 51–54; eyewitness testimony and 39, 48, 51–52, 55, 67n; irregularities in processing of 17, 38, 43, 45–47, 48, 49–50, 54, 55–58, 67n, 72–73, 86, 180; lack of National Guard and Reserve officers awarded 43; General MacArthur's decoration policy and 55–56; Mediterranean Theater of Operations and 47–50; number awarded in European Theater of Operations 51; number awarded in Mediterranean Theater of Operations 47; number awarded in Pacific Commands 54; number awarded in World War II 38, 179; Pacific Commands and 54–58; personal factors influencing award of 39, 41, 55–57, 58, 73, 118, 136n, 182; racism involved in award policy of 41–43, 118, 156n; *see also* Racism
Mediterranean Theater of Operations (MTO): Medal of Honor policy and practice in 47–50; 92nd Infantry Division in 93, 94–121; number of Distinguished Service Crosses awarded to African Americans in 94; number of Silver Stars awarded to African Americans in 94, 125n, 178n; number of Distinguished Service Crosses awarded in 47; number of Medals of Honor awarded in 47; number of Silver Stars awarded in 47; *see also* North African Theater of Operations (NATO)
Medunc, Private First Class Joe 145
Merritt, Private First Class Walter A. (recipient of Silver Star) 138n
Militia Act of 1792 22
Millender, Warrant Officer Robert 115
Mills, Staff Sergeant Jimmie L. (recipient of Silver Star) 94; *see also* Heroism
Milne Bay 151
Mindanao Island 146
Mitchell, Parren 97
Mock, Lieutenant Colonel Carthal F. 106–7
Mohave Desert 141
Moluccas Islands 141
Montana, Private First Class Sam 145
Monteith, Second Lieutenant Jimmie W., Jr. 53
Moore, Lieutenant Spencer C. 120

Moritz, Technician Fourth Grade Martin (recipient of Distinguished Service Cross) 48
Mormon, Staff Sergeant Conige C. 123
Morotai Island 141, 146, 159n
Mount Cauala 110
Mountain Division, 10th 105
Munemori, Private First Class Sadao 130n
Murphy, Lieutenant Colonel E. V. 115

Nakamura, Private First Class William K. (recipient of Distinguished Service Cross) 49, 50
Nakanishi, Technician Third Grade Stanley J. (recipient of Silver Star) 159n
Nalty, Bernard C. 25, 95
Nash, Phileo 80
National Association for the Advancement of Colored People (NAACP) 27, 145
Nesmith, Private First Class Joseph (recipient of Silver Star) 152; *see also* Heroism
New Caledonia 150
New Guinea 56, 144, 145, 146, 151, 177
New Hebrides Islands 141, 148, 161n
Newspapers, African-American: protesting discriminatory awards policies 41, 118; protesting lack of African Americans in combat 95
Nicholas, Private Ralph A. (recipient of Silver Star) 152
Nimitz, Admiral Chester W. 150, 156n, 157n
Normandy 76
North African Theater of Operations (NATO) 48, 49, 63n, 93
Notestein, Colonel James 102, 105, 111
Nouméa 150

Office of War Information, 80
Officers, African-American: prohibited to command white soldiers 24; racist opinions regarding 26, 73, 95, 100, 101, 102, 104, 106
Okinawa 148, 150, 151, 153, 154, 175
Okubo, Technician Fifth Grade James K. (recipient of Silver Star) 49, 50
Omaha Beach 70, 79, 180
*Omaha Star* 41, 85
Ordnance Ammunition Company, 57th 69

Pacific Commands 23, 139, 156n; amphibian truck companies in 150–54; anti-aircraft artillery units in 148–50; Medal of Honor policy and practice in 54–58; 93rd Infantry Division 141–47, 156; number of Distinguished Service Crosses awarded in 54; number of Distinguished Service Crosses awarded to African Americans in 139; number of Medals of Honor awarded in 54; number of Silver Stars awarded to African Americans in 139, 178n; number of Silver Stars awarded in 54; 24th Infantry Regiment 141–44, 155–56

Pacific Ocean Areas (POA) 156n; *see also* Pacific Commands

Paris, Private Maurice A. (recipient of Bronze Star) 152, 164n

Parrish, Technician Fourth Grade Laverne 60n

Patch, Lieutenant General Alexander M. 176

Patterson, Robert P. 37, 43, 59n, 75, 182

Patton, General George S., Jr. 48, 49, **52**, 70, 84, 176, 177

Paul, Lieutenant General Willard S. 42, 57, 71

Peagler, First Lieutenant Robert J. (recipient of Distinguished Service Cross) 148, 150, 155, 162n, 168, 175; *see also* Heroism

Pearson, Lieutenant Commander Charles (recipient of Distinguished Service Cross) 56–57

Pershing, General John J. 19, 23, 50, 182

Phelan, Lieutenant Colonel John J. 99–100, 131n

Philippine Islands 141, 145, 146, 147, 160n, 171

Pierce, Private First Class Claude 83; *see also* Heroism

Porloch Harbor 139, 177

Port Moresby 151

Presidential Unit Citation 69–70, 73; *see also* Distinguished Unit Citation

Pritchard, Lieutenant Colonel Frank S. 75

Protests: against discriminatory awards policy 41–43, 118; against lack of African Americans in combat 95; against racist treatment 23, 97

Prussman, Private First Class Ernest W. 54

Punitive Expedition 23

Punta Bianca 121

Purple Heart 59n; 827th Amphibian Truck Company and 152; 452nd Antiaircraft Artillery Automatic Weapons Battalion and 79; 777th Field Artillery Battalion and 78; 761st Tank Battalion and 70; 784th Tank Battalion and 76

Purple Heart, individual recipients of: Baker, First Lieutenant Vernon J. 169; Day, First Sergeant Norman 70


Quartermaster Regiment, 29th 139, 177

Quartermaster Truck Company, 3404th 93–94

Queen, Colonel Harold D. 111

Quota system 27, 51, 167


Racism: Army College Studies and 25–26; Medal of Honor award policy and 41–43, 118, 156n; 92nd Infantry Division and 94–121, 124, 181–82; Segregation policy and 26–29

Ramitelli 122

Randolph, A. Philip 27

Reed, Lieutenant Colonel Leon J. 80

Regimental Combat Teams: 25th 142–44, 145, 147, 156, 157n; 368th 146–47, 160n; 370th 94, 99, 100, 147; 442nd 49, 64n, 66n, 95, 104, 109, 130n

Revolutionary War 21

Reynolds, Private First Class Lawrence (recipient of Silver Star) 77; *see also* Heroism

Rhodes, Staff Sergeant Fred D. (recipient of Silver Star) 109, 132n; *see also* Heroism

Rivers, Staff Sergeant Ruben (recipient of Silver Star) 70–75, 86, 87n, 180, **183**; *see also* Heroism

Roberts, Private Henry D. (recipient of Silver Star) 109–10, 132n; *see also* Heroism

Rochelle, Private First Class Herman E. (recipient of Silver Star) 109, 113, 119, 132n; *see also* Heroism

Roosevelt, Eleanor 35n

Roosevelt, Franklin D. 28, 50, 146, 159n; concern over unmerited Medals of Honor by 41; pressure for African-American representation by 27

Rowny, Lieutenant Colonel Edward L. 97, 105

Ruhr Valley 84, 176

Runyon, Captain John F. (recipient of Distinguished Service Cross) 109, 114–18, 124, 135n, 136n, 169–70; *see also* Heroism

Ryukyu Islands 144, 148, 150, 151, 153, 154, 175


Saar River 81

Saipan 144, 151

Sakato, Private George T. 66n

Salerno 122

Sanchez, Technician Fifth Grade Marcus P. (recipient of Silver Star) 152; *see also* Heroism

Santiago, First Lieutenant Ricardo (recipient of Silver Star) 147

Searchlight Battalion, 334th 121

Searchlight Battalion, 374th 160n

Segregation policy 26–29

Selective Service Act 1940 27, 29

Serchio Valley 101, 112, 113, 173
Sermon, Private Isaac (recipient of Silver Star) 143–44; *see also* Heroism
Settle, Major Peveril O., Jr. (recipient of Silver Star) 159n
Sherman, Colonel Raymond G. 100, 101, 102, 104, 105, 115, 127n, 129n
Signal Heavy Construction Battalion, 445th 155
Siedlinghausen 83
Siegfried Line 75
Silver Star 40: definition of 38–39; quota system in 12th Army Group for 51, 167; 471st Amphibian Truck Company and 153, 163n; 473rd Amphibian Truck Company and 153, 163n; 476th Amphibian Truck Company and 153, 163n, 164n; 812th Amphibian Truck Company and 163n; 452nd Antiaircraft Artillery Automatic Weapons Battalion and 79; 317th Engineer Combat Battalion and 120, 137n; 332nd Fighter Group and 123; 92nd Infantry Division and 106, 109, 113, 119, 130n, 131n, 136n; 93rd Infantry Division and 147; 104th Infantry Division and 82; 758th Tank Battalion and 121; 761st Tank Battalion and 70, 74; 784th Tank Battalion and 75, 76; 679th Tank Destroyer Battalion and 121
Silver Star, individual recipients of: Anderson, Private Mack B. 154; Blake, Private First Class George C. 87n; Boyd, Sergeant Oren B. 94; Campbell, Staff Sergeant William 79; Coleman, Second Lieutenant Kenneth W. 71; Crecy, Lieutenant Warren G. H. 71; Day, First Sergeant Norman 70; Dillon, Sergeant Alfonzia 146; Ellis, Technician Fifth Grade Zeno H. 79, 83; Foreman, Private First Class Robert L. S. 77; Hamilton, Sergeant Joseph J. 77; Holloway, Technician Fifth Grade Tommie L. 153; Jackson, Private First Class Willie 79; Jenkins, Private First Class Ernest A. 52; Jenkins, First Lieutenant Graham 134n; Johnson, Private Samuel 79; McInnis, Private Jake 132n; McKenzie, Lieutenant Colonel Jack 159n; Mackerson, Private B. 154; Madison, Sergeant Harris 94; Marsh, Private Woodall 93–94; Merritt, Private First Class Walter A. 138n; Mills, Staff Sergeant Jimmie L. 94; Nakanishi, Technician Third Grade Stanley, J. 159n; Nesmith, Private First Class Joseph 152; Nicholas, Private Ralph A. 152; Okubo, Technician Fifth Grade James K. 49, 50; Reynolds, Private First Class Lawrence 77; Rhodes, Staff Sergeant Fred D. 132n; Rivers, Staff Sergeant Ruben 70, 75; Roberts, Private Henry D. 132n; Rochelle, Private First Class Herman E. 119, 132n; Sanchez, Technician Fifth Grade Marcus P. 152; Santiago, First Lieutenant Ricardo 147, 160n; Sermon, Private Isaac 143–44, 144, 146, 147; Settle, Major Peveril O., Jr. 159n; Swindell, Private Edward I. 79; Thompson, Captain Wesley F. 160n; Turley, First Sergeant Samuel J. 42, 71; Vogt, Lieutenant Robert 152; Walker, First Lieutenant Melvin W. 138n; Webb, Staff Sergeant Rothchild 144; *see also* soldiers' individual listings
Silver Star, number awarded: in European Theater of Operations 51; in Mediterranean Theater of Operations 47; in Pacific Commands 54; in World War II 39, 178; percentage awarded to African Americans in World War II 178n; to African Americans in European Theater of Operations 70, 86n, 178n; to African Americans in Mediterranean Theater of Operations 94, 125n, 178n; to African Americans in Pacific Commands 139
Sloan, Major General John E. 45, 62n
Smith, Captain Charles Mike (recipient of Distinguished Service Cross) 56–57
Smith, Lieutenant General Walter Bedell 53, 81
Solomon Islands 141
Sommocolonia 112, 113, 132n, 134n, 173, 174
Southwest Pacific Area 156n; *see also* Pacific Commands
Spanish-American War 23
Speyer 84, 170
Stimson, Henry L. 28, 33, 41, 56, 60n
Sulu Archipelago 146, 171
Swindell, Private Edward I. (recipient of Silver Star) 79; *see also* Heroism

Tanimoto, Sergeant Larry T. 66n
Tank battalions 32; 78th Light Tank Battalion 32; 756th Tank Battalion 75, 175; 758th Tank Battalion 32, 94–95, 102, 119, 120, 121, 131n; 761st Tank Battalion 32, 42, 69–74, 86n, 180, 181; 784th Tank Battalion 32, 70, 75
Tank destroyer battalions 31; 601st Tank Destroyer Battalion 54; 614th Tank Destroyer Battalion 69, 75–76, 175, 181; 679th Tank Destroyer Battalion 94–95, 104, 119, 120, 121, 131n; 827th Tank Destroyer Battalion 29, 75, 88n
Task Force 92, 99, 130n
Taylor, Major General Maxwell D. 78
Thayer, Captain Philip 109, 113

Thielen, Staff Sergeant Edward A. 66n
Thomas, First Lieutenant Charles L. 75–76, 168, 175–76, **177**
Thomas, Private First Class Jack N. (recipient of Distinguished Service Cross) 83, 84, 168, 176–77; *see also* Heroism
Thompson, Captain Wesley F. (recipient of Silver Star) 160n
Tinian 144
Tonga Islands 148
Tongatapu 148
Training 27, 29–32, 75, 81–82, 94, 97, 105, 117, 141, 181
Truman, Harry S 42, 56
Truscott, Lieutenant General Lucian K. 49, 50, 102, 105, 119
Turley, First Sergeant Samuel J. (recipient of Silver Star) 42, 71; *see also* Heroism
Turner, Sergeant Day G. 54

United States Joint Chiefs of Staff 156n
Utah Beach 77, 79

Valor *see* Heroism, individual acts of
Vogt, Lieutenant Robert (recipient of Silver Star) 152; *see also* Heroism
Volunteer infantry replacements 69, 80–85, 86, 91n, 174, 176

Wainwright, Lieutenant General Jonathan M. (recipient of Distinguished Service Cross) 56

Walker, First Lieutenant Leland (recipient of Distinguished Service Cross) 57
Walker, First Lieutenant Melvin W. (recipient of Silver Star) 138n
War Department Decorations Board 38, 41, 43, 44–45, 58, 60n, 62n, 108, 182
War of 1812 22
Washington, General George 21
Watson, Private George (recipient of Distinguished Service Cross) 88n, 139, 151, 155, 169, 177–78; *see also* Heroism
Webb, Staff Sergeant Rothchild (recipient of Silver Star) 144; *see also* Heroism
Weser River 83, 174
Westmoreland, Colonel William C. 176
White, Walter 27, 145, 146, 149, 159n
Wilder, Major A. D., Jr. 105
Williams, Captain David J. 72, 73, **74**, 183
Wilson, Technician Fifth Grade Alfred L. 60n
Wilson, Dale E. 127n
Wood, Brigadier General John E. 99, 101, 102, 105, 118, 124, 130n, 136n
Woodson, Corporal Waverly B., Jr. (recipient of Bronze Star) 79–80, 180; *see also* Heroism
World War I 23–25, 34n
Wyman, Major General Willard G. 74

Young, Lieutenant Colonel Charles 24

Zamboanga 146, 147
Zeno, Private First Class Edgar E. 83; *see also* Heroism

www.ingramcontent.com/pod-product-compliance
Ingram Content Group UK Ltd.
Pitfield, Milton Keynes, MK11 3LW, UK
UKHW042007140426
5217IPUK00015B/1031